Selling Tourism

Join us on the web at

hospitality-tourism.delmar.com

DEDICATION

I dedicate this book, first and foremost, to my students, past, present, and future. I also dedicate it to the vast industry that I love so much. I hope it helps you to increase the numbers of tourists that enjoy the products that you have to sell and that you are richly rewarded for your sales expertise.

Selling Tourism

H. Kenner Kay

THOMSON

DELMAR LEARNING

Australia   Canada   Mexico   Singapore   Spain   United Kingdom   United States

THOMSON

DELMAR LEARNING

Selling Tourism
H. Kenner Kay

Business Unit Executive Director:
Susan L. Simpfenderfer

Executive Editor:
Marlene McHugh Pratt

Senior Acquisitions Editor:
Joan M. Gill

Developmental Editor:
Andrea Edwards

Editorial Assistant:
Lisa Flatley

Executive Production Manager:
Wendy A. Troeger

Production Manager:
Carolyn Miller

Executive Marketing Manager:
Donna J. Lewis

Channel Manager:
Wendy Mapstone

Cover Design:
Carolyn Miller

Cover Image:
© PhotoDisc/Getty Images

Composition:
Larry O'Brien

For permission to use material from this text or product, contact us by
Tel (800) 730-2214
Fax (800) 730-2215
www.thomsonrights.com

Library of Congress Cataloging-in-Publication Data

Kay, H. Kenner.
 Selling tourism/H. Kenner Kay.
  p. cm.
 Includes bibliographical references.
 ISBN 0-8273-8648-6
 1. Tourism—Marketing. I. Title

G155.A1 K367 2002
910'.68'8—dc21 2002025714

NOTICE TO THE READER

Publisher does not warrant or guarantee any of the products described herein or perform any independent analysis in connection with any of the product information contained herein. Publisher does not assume, and expressly disclaims, any obligation to obtain and include information other than that provided to it by the manufacturer.

The reader is expressly warned to consider and adopt all safety precautions that might be indicated by the activities herein and to avoid all potential hazards. By following the instructions contained herein, the reader willingly assumes all risks in connection with such instructions.

The Publisher makes no representation or warranties of any kind, including but not limited to, the warranties of fitness for particular purpose or merchantability, nor are any such representations implied with respect to the material set forth herein, and the publisher takes no responsibility with respect to such material. The publisher shall not be liable for any special, consequential, or exemplary damages resulting, in whole or part, from the readers' use of, or reliance upon, this material.

Contents

Preface   xi
Acknowledgments   xiii

CHAPTER 1   INTRODUCTION TO THE SALES PROCESS   1

The Eight Sectors of the Tourism Industry 3
The Importance of Sales in Tourism 3
The Twelve Steps in the Sales Process 14
Step 1: Arousing Interest To Travel 15

CHAPTER 2   APPROACHING THE PROSPECT   17

Step 2: Approaching the Prospect 17
Handling More than One Customer at One Time 22

CHAPTER 3   QUALIFYING THE PROSPECT   24

Step 3: Qualifying 24
Initial Questions 25
The Game 26
Qualifying for Complex Domestic and Foreign Independent Tours 27
Identifying Special Needs and Interests 29
Client Profile 38
Travelers with Special Needs or Requests 45
Types of Prospects by Commitment 56
A Mistake to Be Avoided 58

vii

Chapter 4   PRODUCT KNOWLEDGE   60

The Importance of Product Knowledge 61
Sources of Product Knowledge 62
Coping When Product Knowledge Is Inadequate 72

Chapter 5   ANSWERING QUESTIONS, RECOMMENDING A PRODUCT OR SERVICE, AND CREATING ACCEPTANCE   74

Step 4: Answering the Client's Questions 75
Step 5: Recommending a Product or Service That Will Meet Your Client's Needs 75
Step 6: Creating Acceptance 77

Chapter 6   CLOSING THE SALE   91

Step 7: Closing the Sale 91
Ten Closing Signals 92
When Not to Close 93
Closing Techniques 94
Closing by Type of Prospect 112
Close to the Decision-Maker 112
Summary of the Closing Process 113

Chapter 7   SELLING TECHNIQUES USING THE TELEPHONE   114

Incoming Calls 115
Using One's Voice and Language Skills Effectively 120
Outgoing Calls 122
Word Spelling 127
Summary 130

Chapter 8   OVERCOMING OBJECTIONS   132

Step 8: Overcoming Objections 132
Step 9: Closing Again 146
Summary 146

CHAPTER 9   SELLING-UP   147

Step 10: Selling-Up 147
Twelve More Opportunities for Selling-Up 158
Fifteen Selling Points That Will Help a Client to Accept a
    Higher-Priced Tourism Product 159

CHAPTER 10   CUSTOMER SERVICE   161

Step 11: Providing Customer Service 162
You Have to Tell Your Client 162
Preparing the Customer's Package 176
Ethics in Selling Tourism 178
Novelties or Favors 186

CHAPTER 11   FOLLOW-UP PROCEDURES   188

Step 12: Follow-Up Procedures 188

CHAPTER 12   THE MOST IMPORTANT SALE YOU MAKE
MAY BE YOUR FIRST!   196

The Most Important Sale You Make May Be Your First! 197
Searching for a Prospective Employer 197
Using Closing Techniques to Close the Deal (Get the Job) 199

Appendix   205
Glossary   207
Bibliography   215
Index   217

Preface

*S*elling Tourism is designed for students of tourism, travel, and hospitality programs. It is also useful for people working in the tourism industry. Most companies and organizations in the tourism industry could make use of *Selling Tourism* as a training guide for new employees who are involved in sales as well as a reference book for your present staff.

Many people tend to speak of the tourism industry as if it were a single entity. In fact, it is a multifaceted group of industries. To make it easier to understand, the dozens of tourism industries have been organized into eight sectors:

- **Accommodations**
- **Food and Beverage**
- **Adventure and Recreation**
- **Tourism Services**
- **Attractions**
- **Transportation**
- **Travel Trade**
- **Events and Conferences**

Figure 1-3 lists 72 subsectors, which only serves as an example. One could probably produce a list of well over a hundred subsectors. But one thing they all have in common is that they serve a visitor's needs while he or she is away from home.

All of the sales texts that I have ever seen for the "tourism industry" tend to focus on one or two sectors of the industry rather than the entire eight sectors. In *Selling Tourism*, I present a more balanced approach to tourism, applying selling principles to all eight sectors of the tourism industry. Selling in some sectors and subsectors of the tourism industry is relatively simple compared to selling complex tours, independent tours, or long intermodal travel plans. For example, most people in a lineup for tickets to an attraction or special event have already made up their mind to buy, and the job of the salesperson is largely to take the order and fill it.

But even in these positions there come times when the employee in the ticket booth has to become an expert salesperson. This would certainly be true when a customer wants to make arrangements for a group, or when a customer has a problem fitting the event into his or her schedule, or when a customer has any other problem preventing him or her from making a buying decision.

Because more sales skills are required for "big sales" like major tours, independent tours, and long intermodal transportation itineraries, more time and space are applied here to these items. But tips on maximizing the number of "small sales" are also provided. Small operators can learn from airlines, large tour operators, and hotel chains how they handle specific problems in selling their products.

The sales process is presented in 12 steps with the principles applied to various sectors of the industry. A positive attitude toward selling combined with problem solving is emphasized as the key to more sales.

Each chapter begins with a list of learning objectives. This is followed by a list of key terms. These key terms are explained in the text material and are summarized in the glossary at the end of the book. Discussion questions help you review the chapter highlights.

The material in the text is organized around the 12 steps of the sales process. That list of steps is presented at the end of Chapter 1. The various steps are discussed in sequence throughout the chapters, culminating in a thorough discussion of the greatest sale you will ever make (Chapter 12).

Acknowledgments

I would like to acknowledge the dedicated assistance and encouragement provided by Lillian M. Beauvais, which enabled me to complete this extremely time-consuming task. I would also like to acknowledge John Dalton, an outstanding public speaker on "Selling," who gave me the inspiration to learn all I could about selling, especially as it pertains to the tourism industry.

The author and Delmar Learning also wish to thank the following reviewers for their time and content expertise:

Debra Barnick
Lakeland Community College

Nancy Chappie
Travel University International

Sherry A. Hine
Mid-Florida Tech

Beth O'Donnell
Edmonds Community College

Introduction to the Sales Process

OBJECTIVES

After studying this chapter, you should be able to:

- Identify the eight sectors of the tourism industry
- List examples of each sector of the tourism industry
- Explain the importance of sales for each of the eight sectors of the tourism industry
- List the twelve steps in the sales process
- Describe various ways in which a tourist's interest is aroused to explore and experience a tourist destination

KEY TERMS

tourism industry	occupancy rate	prepaid air tickets
bottom line	cost price squeeze	markup
the sale	load factor	break-even
qualify	commissions	unqualified prospects
amenities	override commissions	prospect
guest mix	domestic	
referrals	transborder	

1

We often speak of the **tourism industry** as if it was one industry. However, the tourism industry is an umbrella term for many industries, which collectively provide the products and services desired by people while they are away from home. They vary from attractions such as human made wonders like the world's tallest tepee in Medicine Hat, Alberta, Canada (see Figure 1-1), to nature's wonders such as the zebras and elephants of South Africa (see Figure 1-2).

FIGURE 1-1

Saamis Tepee, Medicine Hat, Alberta. *(Photo by Dr. Gerry Prince)*

FIGURE 1-2
Nature's wonders.
(© PhotoDisc/Getty
Images)

THE EIGHT SECTORS OF THE TOURISM INDUSTRY

For the purpose of analysis and discussion, the industries that make up the tourism industry have been grouped into eight sectors (see Figure 1-3).

THE IMPORTANCE OF SALES IN TOURISM

One thing that all eight sectors and the branches within each sector have in common is that their **bottom line** relies on sales! Without the tourists and business travelers and the money they spend for products and services while they are away from home, no branch of the tourism industry could survive. It is impossible to remain viable by simply handing out free information. Even state, provincial, and national tourist boards that seem to be giving out free information are governed by budgets that are based upon the amount of new business that their promotions are going to generate.

It is the job of everyone working in a tourist information office to convert inquiries into sales. In many cases the person providing the tourist with the information is not the one who collects the money for the sale. Counselors in a government-sponsored tourist information office may have guided a visitor to attend a special event, or see an

THE EIGHT SECTORS OF THE TOURISM INDUSTRY

ACCOMMODATIONS
Resorts & Lodges
Cabins & Bungalows
Fishing & Hunting Camps
Campgrounds
Summer Camps
Recreation Camps
Country Inns
Bed & Breakfast Locations
Tourist Homes
Hostels
Time-share Facilities

TOURISM SERVICES
Government Tourism Departments
Information Centers
Research Services
Advertising Agencies
Marketing Companies
Trade Press
Professional Associations
Tourism Consultants & Educators
Tourism Suppliers
Retail Operations
Auto Clubs
Duty-free Shops

FOOD & BEVERAGE
Restaurants & Dining Rooms
Coffee Shops
Fast-food Outlets
Pubs, Lounges & Nightclubs
Cabarets
Club Facilities
Institutions
Catering Operations
Specialty (e.g., Medieval Feast)

ADVENTURE & RECREATION
Adventure Tourism
Fishing Facilities
Golf Facilities
Hunting Facilities
Marine Facilities
Parks
Ski Resorts
Tennis Facilities
Ecotourism

ATTRACTIONS
Amusement Parks
Cultural Tourism
Galleries
Heritage & Historical Sites
Industrial Tourism
Interpretive Centers
Museums
Native Tourism
Parks & Gardens
Recreational Parks

TRANSPORTATION
Air Carriers
Automobile Rentals
Cruise Lines
Gas Stations
Motor Coaches
Railways
Recreational Vehicles
Taxis
Sight-seeing Helicopters and Planes

TRAVEL TRADE
Tour Guides
Tour Operators
Tour Wholesalers
Travel Agencies
Local Sight-seeing

EVENTS & CONFERENCES
Conferences
Conventions
Exhibitions
Fairs
Festivals
Special Events
Trade Shows

FIGURE 1-3

The eight sectors of the tourism industry.
(Courtesy of the Pacific Rim Institute of Tourism)

attraction, or book a particular accommodation facility. Yet the payment may actually be received at the location at which the service will be received or at a travel agency. But the counselor at the government-sponsored tourist information office has actually made **the sale** if he or she has been successful in getting the tourist to make a buying decision. Every effort to convert the inquiry into action should be made.

Some tourist information offices actually provide reservation services for tourists. In these offices, counselors should qualify the prospects and close the sale as if they were a consultant in a travel agency.

In other tourist information offices supported by members of the tourism industry, counselors are not allowed to recommend one property over another. However, just providing the tourist with a long list of all suppliers does not provide the service the tourist is seeking.

Counselors should **qualify** prospects by asking questions to limit the list to a few or even two suppliers and then let the prospect choose from a very short list. For example, if the tourist were looking for accommodations, questions regarding location, quality, price, **amenities**, preference between chains or unique properties, and **guest mix** would limit the choices to a reasonable number from which the prospect could make an informed choice. Guest mix is a term to describe the type of people (based on demographics like age, family status, income level, occupation, etc.) who usually stay at a hotel or other accommodation facility. Once the customer has made a decision, the counselor should offer to call the reservations number for the tourist.

Often, the people actually providing the services are not directly involved in closing the sale, yet they are still crucial to the sales process. Their service must meet or exceed the expectations created by the salesperson. Their service will largely determine whether their customer will become a repeat customer. It is important that he or she thanks the customer for the business and asks for repeat business and **referrals**.

For most of the branches of the tourism tree, the relationship between sales and success are obvious. In the Accommodations sector a healthy **occupancy rate** is required or the organization will soon be out of business.

The Adventure and Recreation sector is growing rapidly but requires excellent salespeople because these experiences are usually relatively expensive. Salespeople have to convince their prospects that their products are of exceptional quality and that they provide the opportunity for a unique experience.

For example, Wilderness Odysseys Seal River Canoe/Raft 12-Day Tour costs $3,638.00. But check the quality. What does the $3,638.00 really cover? This Wilderness Odyssey has a maximum of

14 guests per trip, all meals while on the river, state-of-the-art safety provisions, experienced guide, archaeologist, local naturalists, and First Nations native partners. You cannot expect this type of personalized service for the cost of a bus tour. But it takes an expert salesperson to convince a prospect of the value of such a unique tour. (See Figure 1-4.)

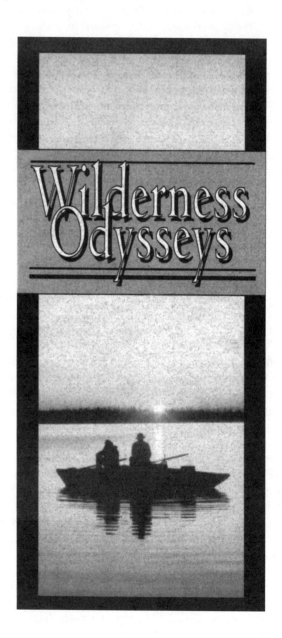

FIGURE 1-4

Wilderness Odysseys
tour brochure.
*(Courtesy of Wilderness
Odysseys, Ltd.)*

Special Events and Conferences will cease to exist unless sales justify them. Conferences are not only expected to be successful financially for the organizing body, but those who attend expect that ideas learned at the conference will increase their sales. New technology is usually introduced at conferences, providing new ways of achieving profitability.

The importance of sales within the Food and Beverage sector is obvious. How many times have you seen a food and beverage operation close its doors because of insufficient sales? Have you ever been disappointed to find that a really good restaurant with very fine food has gone out of business? This usually happens because the owner was an excellent chef but did not have the sales and marketing skills to make it a success. Or, perhaps the owner had the sales skills but did not have the teaching skills to effectively train the staff to sell.

Within the Transportation sector, not only are sales important to maintain services, but they are becoming more crucial every year because of the **cost price squeeze**. For example, each year the cost of operations increases, but the airlines cannot increase their prices proportionately or the public will perceive the service to be too expensive and stop using it. In order to maintain relatively stable prices, the carriers must sell a greater and greater percentage of their seats to remain viable. (See Figure 1-5.) The percentage of seats sold is known as the **load factor**.

FIGURE 1-5

Airline costs are soaring. (© PhotoDisc/Getty Images)

Travel agencies make their income from **commissions** on sales. Without sales there can be no business, no agency, and no job. A travel counselor must sell a high volume just to pay the expenses of providing him or her a place to work. Over and beyond this, a travel counselor must sell many high-yield products in order to make a reasonable income. Not only does the total commission increase with more sales, but also the rate of commission increases as plateaus are reached to earn **override commissions**. Override commissions can be simply defined as a greater rate of commission for selling more. (See Figure 1-6.)

Remuneration of Sales Personnel

In any sales position, your income is directly related to the total amount of your sales.

Salespeople can be remunerated in three ways:

   1. salary

   2. commission

   3. a combination of salary plus commission

In addition to pay, travel consultants often receive industry benefits. Many tourism operators realize that most travel consultants working in agencies are extremely motivated by the opportunity for free or reduced price travel. These travel experiences cost the principal a lot less than their value to the travel consultant. Tour operators and other tourism suppliers know very well that travel consultants who have firsthand knowledge with their products will be much more effective in selling these products.

Salary

If you are in a sales position in which you are paid a salary, your sales production must justify your salary, and ultimately your job. If not, you can expect your salary, or more likely, your job to be cut.

On the other hand, if your sales are excellent, you should be able to effectively demonstrate to your employer that you deserve an increase in salary. This usually does not happen automatically. You have to be able to prove that you produce more sales than other salespeople do and/or that you are producing considerably more sales than you have in previous years. To have that proof, you must keep accurate records to substantiate your claims.

The advantage of a salary is evident. You will have a steady income each pay period in spite of fluctuating market conditions. Many beginning salespeople without established sales records prefer a salary because of the apparent security it provides. It makes it easier to budget and temporarily removes the pressure to sell.

Carnival
2000 Commission Program

Commission Levels

Agencies that do not belong to a consortium, or belong to a consortium that Carnival does not have an agreement with, fall under our Individual Override Program. Commission is determined by the number of guests **sailed** by the agency in a calendar year compared to the targets listed below. The targets are per agency location.

Commission[1]	*Annual Sailed Guests*[2]
10%	0 – 14
11%	15 – 24
12%	25 – 49
13%	50 – 74
14%	75 – 99
15%	100 – 349
16%	350 +

The targets for earning increased commission are even lower than those listed above for agencies that belong to one of the many consortiums with which Carnival has an agreement, making it even easier to earn higher commission! Check with the consortium for details.

[1] Any commission level earned above 10% applies exclusively to the cruise fare portion of individual and group bookings. Pre/Post option packages, the Cruise Vacation Protection Plan[SM], FlyAweigh® Airfare Supplements and cruise-only transfers are commissionable at 10%. Port charges, all taxes/fees, bookings calculated at net rates and any components not specifically noted above are non-comissionable. The commission level targets noted above are valid during calendar year 2000. Carnival reserves the right to change at any time, without notice, commission levels, the items that qualify for override commission and the items that are commissionable. Port charges include: taxes/fees assessed by governmental and other agencies; costs incident to entering/leaving ports such as pilotage; and costs incurred while in port such as stevedoring, waste removal and payroll for port-related functions.

[2] **How Sailed Guest Productivity is Determined**

Productivity is calculated on a calendar year basis in seven-day equivalents. Guests sailing on 1–5 day cruises count ½, guests on 6–9 day cruises count as one, guests on 10–12 day cruises count 1½ and guests on 13 day or longer cruises count as two. All guests occupying a cabin count as productivity, with the exception of free group guests (tour conductors), reduced agent fares, and ship charters. Guests are considered "sailed" once their cruise is completed.

Earning Increased Commission

Agencies are eligible for an increase in commission once they have sailed enough guests in a single calendar year to exceed any of the targets above. The agency must then advise Carnival by calling 800-327-7276 in order for their commission to be increased. Once increased, the new commission will apply to bookings made from the date Carnival is notified forward.

FIGURE 1-6

2000 Commission Program. *(Courtesy of Carnival Cruise Lines)*

Employers will not take the risk of paying high or even moderately high salaries for unproven salespeople. Therefore, salaries in sales careers in the tourism industry tend to be less than the commissions earned by top salespeople. Remember that if your sales do not justify your job, your job will not be justified. Look for new employment!

Commission

With this system, the volume of sales he or she produces strictly governs the salesperson's income. A percentage of each sale is the salesperson's reward. For travel agencies, override, or a greater rate of commission, is earned for selling more of a particular company's products or services. Override commissions can make the difference between a profitable travel agency and one that goes bankrupt. On a sale that provides 10 percent commission, at least 8 percent is necessary to pay the overhead or costs of running the business. This means that the profit is just 2 percent maximum. An override of only 1 percent increases the profit on the sale from 2 to 3 percent, an increase of 50 percent in profit. An increase in commission to 12 percent would raise the profit for the agency from 2 to 4 percent, an increase in profitability of 100 percent.

Referring to Carnival Cruise Lines 2000 Commission Program shown in Figure 1-6, if an agency sold 100 passengers on a Carnival cruise in one year, it would receive 700 percent more profit per passenger than if they had sold only 14 passengers.

In today's market, an agency has to sell a lot of high-yield products. Management studies commission levels and prepares a list of preferred suppliers so that higher levels of commission can be earned. Large agencies and particularly chains can reach higher levels of override commissions. Many small agencies have joined together in consortiums so that they can achieve commission levels similar to the large operators.

Selling air tickets used to be most travel agencies' number one or number two moneymaker. More and more, airlines are encouraging passengers to book online on the Internet.

Most airlines have eliminated commissions completely. Travel agencies strongly promote those that still pay reasonable commissions or consolidators (those who buy large blocks of space that the airlines consider to be excess capacity) that provide net fares which leave room for a profit margin.

In order to avoid losing money on selling air tickets, most agencies now add a service charge when selling an air ticket. The amount of service charge can vary from one agency to another but is usually anywhere from $15.00 to $35.00 for a **domestic** or **transborder** ticket and from $25.00 to $70.00 for an international ticket. There are many variables in determining the amount of service charge agencies add to air tickets. Two of the main variables are the total amount of business a customer is doing with the agency and the cost of doing business in a particular community. For example, most agencies in a large city like New York would add on a larger service charge because their overhead including salaries and rent are much more than in a small town. Many travel agencies are charging service charges for changes, refunds, cancellations, and **prepaid air tickets**. This is in addition to any charges levied by the airlines for these services.

The service charge added to an air ticket has encouraged some customers to make their own reservations and purchase their tickets on the Internet. However, many customers appreciate the service of a good travel consultant. A passenger is not able to compare the prices of all the alternatives easily, and often the advice of a good travel consultant will save the client much more money than the cost of the service charge. Also, many customers do not mind paying a relatively small service charge to have a professional make all their travel reservations with a single telephone call or visit to the office.

Rather than deal with thousands of travel agencies, most airlines prefer to deal with consolidators. Because of the large volume of seats purchased by the consolidators they are given very good prices. The consolidators then sell these seats through travel agencies at net prices, and the travel agent adds on a **markup**, the same as retailers of merchandise would do.

Also many travel agencies are promoting charter airlines rather than scheduled carriers because the charter carriers pay much better rates of commission. Many agencies have changed their focus to specialize in selling items that are more profitable than selling airline tickets. Some agencies specialize in selling cruises. Others specialize in selling tours.

In any sales position, a salesperson can expect to receive more income if he or she can bring more income to the company. In some companies, the percentage of commission income rises as certain plateaus of sales are achieved. Sometimes these plateaus will be based on total sales. Other times, the plateaus may be based on sales of certain products of preferred suppliers.

Most beginning salespeople are really nervous about being paid strictly by commission. "What will happen if I don't make enough commission to cover my expenses?" Perhaps you should be prepared for this for the "learning period" (your first few months). But even if you were on salary and this situation persisted past the "learning period," your job will have been terminated.

Salespeople on commission earn what they are worth according to the sales they have made. All good salespeople would much rather be paid commission than salary. If they are really good, they will earn much more than the average salesperson on salary.

However, living on straight commission is not without problems. Income will vary greatly from month to month, and season to season. Income will vary with the economic times and trends. So, it is essential that commission salespeople develop great discipline in budgeting to spread their income over the slack periods.

But remember, the best salespeople will still sell and earn more in tough times than mediocre salespeople. Also during periods of economic downturn, the people on salary with the lowest sales records can expect to be the first to be laid-off or fired. Before taking on a sales position, determine what marketing efforts the company will expend to drive business to the salesperson.

A Combination of Salary Plus Commission

People working on this system are usually paid a basic low salary, supplemented by a rather low rate of commission. This provides a salesperson some measure of security and allows a good salesperson to raise his or her total income to an acceptable level.

Some salespeople start working for salary plus commission. Others request to change to salary plus commission after building a degree of confidence in their sales ability. Alternatively, employers may convince an employee who has demonstrated a potential for increased sales to change from straight salary to a combination of salary plus commission to motivate him or her to increase sales.

The advantage of working for a combination of salary plus commission is obvious. You would have a certain salary with which you could budget your regular expenses. You would also have the opportunity to earn more if times are good, or if you are a superior salesperson. The point still remains. If you are a really good salesperson, you will make more on straight commission!

Tour operators and tour wholesalers must sell most of their seats just to reach the **break-even** point. Additional seats sold yield a modest profit. However, those last seats sold are almost pure profit.

Most government-sponsored attractions must increase sales to cover their operating costs. More and more, government services are expected to be self-supporting and not to be a drain on the tax base. If a government-sponsored attraction is offered free of charge, it is operated so that money can be earned on other goods and services that the tourist will require while being drawn to the attraction.

Privately run attractions are always profit driven. Disneyland and Walt Disney World are often used as the model for success. Disney operations spend a great amount of time and training to develop a very efficient sales staff.

To many people who have not been involved in sales, the image of the door-to-door salesperson comes to mind. One pictures the salesperson fighting to get a foot in the door so that he or she can deliver a hard-sell pitch to an audience of mostly **unqualified prospects**. (See Figure 1-7.)

Selling tourism is different! It is fun! It is the true measure of success in the business we love! The product we are selling is one that brings joy to others. The door-to-door salesperson is banging on doors of many people who are not the least bit interested in the product being promoted. The large majority of people we approach in the tourism industry really want what we have to sell and just need

FIGURE 1-7

A salesperson trying to get a foot in the door.

FIGURE 1-8

A happy customer receiving a ticket from an agent.

some help to make the tourism experience possible for them. (See Figure 1-8.)

Talking about the importance of sales, your most important sale might be your first. The **prospect** is a potential employer. The product is your services. The conclusion of a successful sales presentation is that you get the job. See Chapter 12 for details on how to close this deal.

THE TWELVE STEPS IN THE SALES PROCESS

1. Arousing interest to travel
2. Approaching the prospect
3. Qualifying
4. Answering questions
5. Recommending a product or service
6. Providing enough information to create acceptance
7. Closing the sale
8. Overcoming objections
9. Closing again
10. Selling-up
11. Providing customer service
12. Following-up

STEP 1: AROUSING INTEREST TO TRAVEL

For most people, traveling to a tourist destination has an intrinsic curiosity. Little is required to arouse the interest of potential clients to take a trip. Many things in our society motivate people to explore and experience a tourist destination. Movies, television, books, magazines, newspapers, and the Internet do the tourism industry a great favor in arousing the interest of the traveling public at no expense to the tourism industry.

Even more influential are the personal descriptions of trips taken by family members, friends, neighbors, and coworkers. There is more trust in personal contacts than there is in advertising or publicity. Word-of-mouth publicity is the single most effective source of new customers for the tourism industry.

Which type of product the traveler seeks and which company or organization he or she will approach for further information are largely the result of effective marketing. A compelling photo such as Collette Tours' photo of penguins in a brochure or advertising can move a prospect to make a booking for a particular tour. (See Figure 1-9.) As a result of the interest created by word-of-mouth publicity plus the marketing efforts of the tourism industry, the most difficult step in the sales process has been accomplished by the time a potential customer approaches you either in person or by telephone. Interest has already been aroused. The company has probably spent a substantial amount on marketing to arouse the interest of prospects. When prospects respond by telephone, come in to the office, or by any other means, management expects travel consultants to convert as many of these inquiries as possible into sales.

FIGURE 1-9

Unique attractions like penguins in Antarctica. (*Courtesy of Collette Tours*)

Discussion Questions

1. What are the eight sectors of the tourism industry?

2. Describe examples of types of businesses or organizations in each of the sectors of the tourism industry.

3. Explain the importance of sales for each of the eight sectors of the tourism industry.

4. List the 12 steps of the sales process in order.

5. Describe various ways in which a tourist's interests are aroused before they telephone or come to your place of business

Approaching the Prospect

OBJECTIVES

After studying this chapter, you should be able to:

● Greet prospects in a courteous, friendly, and enthusiastic manner

● Identify seven approaches used by salespeople when greeting prospects

● Describe the advantages and disadvantages of each of the seven approaches to prospects

● Serve two or more customers at one time

KEY TERMS

traditional approach

modern approach

greet the customer by name

introduction approach

assumed sold approach

merchandise approach

qualified prospect

icebreaker approach

qualifying questions

loose ends

STEP 2: APPROACHING THE PROSPECT

When prospects first arrive at your office, it is essential that you acknowledge their arrival. Greet them in a timely, friendly, courteous, and enthusiastic manner. It is important that you project an image of pride in yourself and your company or organization. It is amazing how the Walt Disney Company has instilled these values in their staff and how McDonald's has done the same thing in the fast-food business. When a prospect enters your office, stop what you are doing, stand up, and approach him or her with a warm smile and direct eye contact. (See Figure 2-1.)

FIGURE 2-1

Meeting a customer
with a warm smile.
(© PhotoDisc/Getty
Images)

Your smile can convey a number of significant messages to the
customer:

- I am glad to see you.
- I enjoy my job.
- I am easy to talk to.
- I am confident in my abilities.
- I am a helpful person.
- I am relaxed with you and you can be relaxed with me.

Conversely, if you force your smile or do not smile at all, a totally
different set of messages is sent:

- I am insincere.
- I cannot be trusted.
- I am in a bad mood.
- You are bothering me.

FIGURE 2-2
Eye contact.
(© PhotoDisc/Getty Images)

To be successful, you must truly enjoy working with people and you need to be able to show this enjoyment to each customer with whom you deal. Think of each new sales encounter as a positive new adventure. It can really be exciting, and that excitement will show itself to each new customer.

> *Eye contact is another do-or-die area of first impressions. Direct eye contact with your customer in conjunction with your smile can do a great deal to put the person at ease. Eye contact demonstrates an interest in that person. It shows that you are not distracted and will give your fullest attention to the person's needs.*[1] (See Figure 2-2.)

Seven Approaches Used by Salespeople

There are seven commonly used approaches used by salespeople. The first one is rarely successful. The other six can be effective in specific situations.

1. The Traditional Approach
2. The Modern Approach
3. Greeting the Prospect by Name Approach
4. The Introduction Approach
5. The Assumed Sold Approach
6. The Merchandise Approach
7. The Icebreaker Approach

There is no single correct greeting for every initial contact with a prospect.

The Traditional Approach

The **traditional approach** to greeting a customer has been to ask, "May I help you?" The traditional response has been, "No, I am just looking." The customer does not even break stride or establish eye contact with the salesperson. The chances of closing a sale with this approach are negligible. In a sales situation, asking a question that can be answered with a yes or no is a deadly sin, because if the answer is no, the sales presentation is finished.

The Modern Approach

Most companies today encourage their sales staff to start a conversation with a potential customer by saying, "How may I help you?" This **modern approach** presents a positive approach to the customer and is much more likely to result in a response that will lead toward closing the sale.

Greeting the Prospect by Name

If you can **greet the customer by name**, do so. For example, "Good morning, Mrs. Anderson" or "Good afternoon, Stephano." Whether to use the client's first name or family name depends upon your relationship with him or her and your previous encounters with the customer. When in doubt, use the family name with the appropriate title. For example: Mr., Mrs., Miss, Ms, Master, Father, Sister, Reverend, Doctor, Sir, Captain, and the like. If you are not absolutely sure of the name, never take the chance of using the wrong name!

People from countries outside of North America are usually much more formal than Americans or Canadians. Address people from other countries formally unless you are invited to address them by their first name.

The Introduction Approach

The **introduction approach** is more personal and appropriate for a major sale than the "How may I help you?" approach. Examples of when the introduction approach would be appropriate would include selling a cruise, an adventure tour, or a fishing, hunting, golf, or tennis vacation.

With a stranger, a good approach is to greet him or her and to introduce yourself. For example, "Good afternoon, my name is Kenner Kay." The natural reaction would be for the prospect to introduce himself or herself. If the prospect does not provide an introduction, a simple, "And your name is . . . ?" will certainly encourage the client to reveal his or her name. Use the prospect's name as soon as possible to let the client know you were listening and to imbed the name in your memory. And use it often. If you have a chance to write it down, do so. The writing process helps you to remember the name and also allows you to refer back to it.

Whether to use your first name only or your full name depends upon the situation. Within the tourism industry, we usually communicate on a first name basis. With a new prospect, using your full name will leave it open for the client to complete the introduction as he or she prefers. If the client provides a full name, you should address him or her by the family name with the appropriate title until invited to use the first name.

The Assumed Sold Approach

The **assumed sold approach** is a derivative of the assumed sold closing technique as described in Chapter 6. In some sectors of the tourism industry, speed and efficiency are the primary concerns of both the salesperson and the customer. The salesperson takes the stance that the prospect is going to buy and begins to process the order. In effect, the salesperson is using a sales technique as a greeting and bypasses steps 2–6 of the sales process. For example, in a line for tickets to a tourist attraction or special event, the salesperson assumes that the prospect is going to buy and begins to process the order with a question like "How many tickets do you require?" or "Which sightseeing excursion would you like to take?"

The Merchandise Approach

The **merchandise approach** can be used effectively if the salesperson observes that the customer is focusing on a particular piece of merchandise. The salesperson will use a compliment about the item as an opener. For example, "That soapstone carving was created here in Barrow by a world famous artist." Or, "Can you imagine yourself sailing on that beautiful ship?" This technique can be effective by a skillful salesperson with a **qualified prospect**.

The Icebreaker Approach

Using the **icebreaker approach**, the salesperson concentrates on establishing a rapport with the prospect before an attempt to sell anything. Some clever icebreaker or question about a major event is used to start a conversation. Once the conversation has been established, the salesperson gradually tries to move the topic toward the item he or she is selling. This can be effective but certainly is not appropriate for the customer who is in a hurry. There is always the chance that the icebreaker may fall flat and actually turn away the customer. Although most people would love to talk about the Super Bowl, a question or comment about it might completely turn off someone who hates football.

HANDLING MORE THAN ONE CUSTOMER AT ONE TIME

If you are on the telephone when the client arrives, you should explain the situation to the person on the other end of the line and ask permission to put him or her on hold for a minute. Wait for an answer. Do not just assume that the caller does not mind being put on hold. If the caller cannot wait for a minute, ask for permission to call back at a specified time. Ask the newly arrived customer, "How may I help you?" Explain how long you will be busy with the first customer on the telephone and determine whether the new client is willing to wait or whether an appointment to return will be preferable. If possible, find a brochure on the topic that interests the prospect, then return to your phone call in no more than one minute.

If you are busy with another customer in the office, excuse yourself for a minute to acknowledge the new prospect. As with the interrupted phone call, find out briefly how you may help the new client. Explain how long you will be and ask if the new client is willing to wait. If the new prospect cannot wait, schedule an appointment that is convenient for the customer.

Many teenagers are very casual on a first date regarding making arrangements for a future encounter. Often they say something like, "I'll see you around" or "I'll see you." In reality, such vague statements rarely result in another date. As people mature, they often learn a few good **qualifying questions** that would benefit any salesperson: When (what date)? What time? Where?

If one's dating partner specifies a day, time, and place for the next date, the chances of it happening are increased immensely. In business, the same principle applies. **Loose ends** often mean you will never see the prospect again. Loose ends usually result in losing contact with the prospect and the loss of an opportunity to close a sale. Whenever you are talking to a client about a future meeting, agree on a date, a definite time, and a specific place. The chances are very good that the client will be there.

If something comes up to prevent the appointment, the client will feel obligated to call to reschedule the appointment. On the other hand, if you don't pin down the date, time, and place, the prospect will probably become part of your sales history. Change that to . . . your ~~sales~~ *history!*

If it is possible to find something to read regarding the client's request, it will make the time go faster for the waiting client and it may save you time by answering some of the prospect's questions. In any case, you should not keep the first customer waiting at your desk for more than one minute.

In the tourism business, it is not unusual to have more than one customer at a time. To serve more than one customer at a time in a timely, courteous, efficient, and confident manner is very difficult for a new employee. Through role-playing situations with no time restrictions at first and then gradually reducing the time limits to less than 60 seconds, one can gain the skills to handle these situations as normal procedure.

Note

1. Gerald P. Jung, *A Practical Guide to Selling Travel* (Englewood Cliffs, NJ: Regents/Prentice Hall, 1993): 5.

Discussion Questions

1. What is the modern approach? What advantages does the modern approach have over the traditional approach?

2. What advantages does greeting the prospect by name have over all other approaches?

3. What are the advantages of the introduction approach?

4. List five different examples of situations in the tourism industry in which you could effectively use the assumed sold approach.

5. List one precise example in the tourism industry in which you could use the merchandise approach for actually selling merchandise.

6. Describe how you could adapt the merchandise approach to selling a tourism experience rather than merchandise.

7. Describe how you would handle a situation in which you were serving a customer at your desk and the telephone rings with a prospect requesting information.

8. Describe how you would handle a situation in which you were serving a customer on the telephone and another customer entered your office.

CHAPTER **3**

Qualifying the Prospect

OBJECTIVES

After studying this chapter, you should be able to:

- Qualify prospects to determine their wants and needs

- Develop an accurate client profile

- Determine the level of quality preferred by the customer for transportation and accommodations

- Determine the prospect's level of commitment to the tourism experience

KEY TERMS

closing	proof of identity	needs
sell-up	continuum	wants
proof of citizenship	client profile	Inuit

STEP 3: QUALIFYING

Qualifying is the process of determining a client's needs to see whether you have a product or service to satisfy those needs.

People who call on your organization either in person or by telephone are prospects. They may or may not become customers. We hope they will become customers. More than in almost any other industry, most tourism industry prospects are qualified prospects. A qualified prospect is a person who could benefit from your product or service. Why else would they go to or telephone a tourism organization if they did not have an interest in traveling to or experiencing a tourist destination?

If the prospect is a qualified prospect, he or she should become a customer if the salesperson does his or her job correctly. If someone approaches an organization for tourist information because he or she really wants to visit a tourist destination and the salesperson is unable to make the necessary arrangements (that is, reservations, bookings, or sale), time has been wasted, not only by the salesperson but the prospect as well.

INITIAL QUESTIONS

The salesperson qualifies the prospect as quickly as possible to determine the needs of the customer and whether the salesperson has a product or products that will satisfy those needs. You always need answers to four initial questions before you can make any travel recommendation:

1. *Where* would you like to travel?

2. *When* would you like to go?

3. *How long* would you like to stay?

4. *How many* people will be traveling?

Answers to three additional questions help refine the recommendation in most situations:

- Ages (where applicable)—"Is there anyone in your party eligible for children's, youth, or senior citizen's discounts?"

- Mode of transportation (If there is a choice)—For example, "Would you prefer to travel from Washington to Boston by Amtrak or by air?" or "Do you wish to travel from Vancouver to Victoria by ferry and motor coach or by air?"

- Class of service (if there is a choice)—"Do you prefer first class or . . . ?" Do not assume that every prospect wants the least expensive ticket. For as many as 15 percent of customers, convenience and comfort are of primary importance!

After you have answers to these four to seven questions, you need three pieces of additional information to make a booking, reservation, or sale by any other term:

1. Names (family name, first name, initial, and title [e.g., Mr., Mrs., Miss, Ms])

2. Contact (phone number of the customer who made the booking with you), preferably a residential and business number

3. Most carriers also request a phone contact number at the destination as well.

With this basic information, you can often go directly to making a reservation, which is indeed **closing** the sale. If transportation is included in the tourist's arrangements, close the deal on the transportation first. If the client makes a commitment to book the transportation, he or she is going! You now have the opportunity to **sell-up** and to create time for yourself to look up further information regarding other details requested. Make an appointment to get back to the client either by telephone or an office appointment to take care of the other details.

Note: Regulations for international and transborder travel (travel between Canada and the USA) have recently become much more stringent. Most international travelers to the USA require a passport. The family name, plus the first name in full, and middle initial as listed on one's passport are required on the ticket. For transborder passengers from Canada who were born in Canada, either a passport or birth certificate is required. If the passenger is using a passport, it is important that the name on the ticket be the same as on the passport. If the passenger is using a birth certificate as **proof of citizenship**, then it is important that the name on the ticket match the name on the birth certificate. Also, if a Canadian citizen is using a birth certificate as proof of citizenship, then he or she needs **proof of identity** as well. Proof of identity would be a government issued picture identification with a signature. Also an international passenger must register a telephone contact of whom to contact, with the U.S. Immigration Service before embarking on an airplane, ship, or any other mode of transportation in case of emergency.

Because of the heightened security measures in effect since the events of September 11, 2001, it is necessary to check-in at an airport much earlier than previously required. If a passenger has baggage to be checked, it is now necessary to check-in at least 90 minutes before departure for a domestic flight and two hours prior to departure for an international flight. If a passenger has only carry-on baggage, check-in must be at least 60 minutes prior to departure for domestic flights.

Carry-on baggage is limited to one piece with measurements of length plus width plus height totaling 45 inches or less. In addition to this, a passenger may carry on one personal item such as a briefcase, purse, laptop computer, or small backpack.

Passengers must have proof of travel on the same day in the form of a boarding pass, paper ticket, or airline or travel agency-generated printed confirmation for E-ticket travel.

THE GAME

Many prospects enter your office without any idea of actually making a booking on their mind. They come in with the idea that they need some information. To receive the information they require, they ask questions.

To move these casual inquiries toward a booking, the salesperson must qualify the prospect. The salesperson obtains the qualifying information he or she needs by asking questions. It often becomes a game, the salesperson versus the prospect.

John Dalton conceptualized the game that salespeople and prospects play in a form similar to a board game (see Figure 3-1). He simply called it *The Game.* There are two players, the salesperson and the prospect. Each "Q" represents a question. The players progress toward their goals by asking questions. The one who is first to obtain all the answers he or she needs wins *The Game.*

If the salesperson obtains all the answers he or she needs first, the salesperson makes the sale. If the prospect obtains all the information he or she requires before the salesperson qualifies, the prospect wins. Whether it is verbalized or not, the prospect will say to himself or herself, "Thank you. I have all the information I need. Good bye!" The prospect does not need the salesperson any more. He or she knows everything needed to make his or her own booking. If the salesperson makes a cardinal error, he or she goes directly to **the box**. You cannot get out of **the box**. You lose! You lose the game, and you have lost the sale! Two pieces of advice for the salesperson to stay out of the box:

1. Never, ever, ask a question that can be answered by a "yes" or "no." If the answer is "no," you are in **the box**. You can't get out. You lose!

2. Never answer two questions without asking one. If you do, you will end up in **the box** and the prospect will win!

QUALIFYING FOR COMPLEX DOMESTIC AND FOREIGN INDEPENDENT TOURS

For more complicated tourist arrangements like domestic independent tours or foreign independent tours, much more information is required. When the average person thinks of a tour, one usually imagines an escorted tour, like a group tour by bus, train, or ship, with a tour escort. Or one might think of an inclusive tour charter that includes a charter flight, transfers between the airport and the accommodations, plus the accommodations, and perhaps some other local services or meals, and the services of a destination representative of the tour operator.

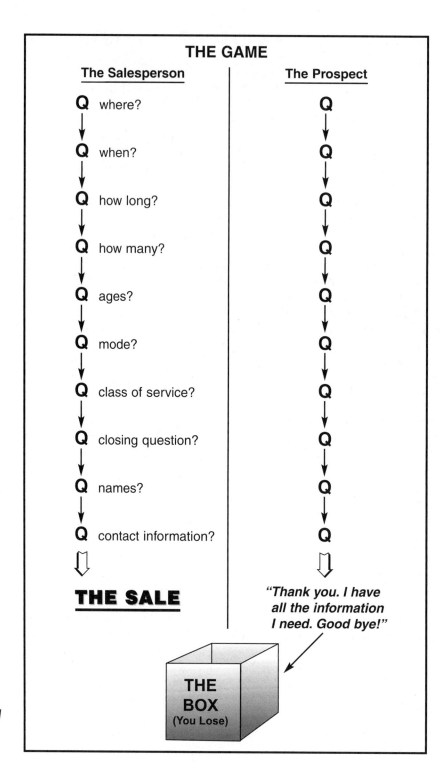

FIGURE 3-1

"The Game." *(Adapted from a concept developed by John Dalton)*

However, many people prefer independent tours planned to meet their own specific needs. The differences between an independent tour and independent travel are:

- For independent travel, the traveler makes all or most of his or her own reservations and often does much of this at the location or while he or she is traveling.

- For independent tours, the customer contacts a travel consultant, usually an employee of a travel agency, with a request to plan a tour, custom-made for the customer. The independent tour will be preplanned and usually prepaid. It will include transportation, accommodations, and all or some of the sightseeing. If the tour is within the area comprising the United States of America and Canada, it is considered a domestic independent tour. If the tour is outside of the United States of America or Canada, it is considered a foreign independent tour.

For most travelers seeking a travel package, the travel consultant has to find one or two packages that most closely meet the customer's needs. But, for clients requiring independent tours, there are many more variables. The travel consultant must determine the needs of the customer for each element that will be included in the tour. This requires a lot of research to select all the client's preferences.

Independent tours are more expensive for the customer than package tours and can be very profitable to the travel agency. But, they are very time-consuming and require a lot of expertise. Always require a nonrefundable deposit before preparing such an itinerary. This deposit will be applied to the total cost of the trip if the client does travel.

IDENTIFYING SPECIAL NEEDS AND INTERESTS

Identifying special needs and interests will help you to arrive at a suitable recommendation that will satisfy the client. Most tourists are multimotivated. There are a number of continuums on which you have to evaluate your client. I use the term **continuum** because there can be a wide range of difference between customers and they may be anywhere between the extremes.

Purpose of Travel

There are four parameters to be scrutinized regarding a client's purpose of travel.

Business, Pleasure, or Both?

Is the purpose of travel for business or pleasure or some combination of business and pleasure? The needs and preferences may differ significantly. If an employee has vacation time available, most companies and organizations do not mind the employee taking vacation time before or after a business trip. The advantages for the employee are significant. The cost of the transportation has been paid for as part of the business trip resulting in a very inexpensive vacation.

Circle a number between 1 and 7 in Figure 3-2 to indicate where you feel this customer should be placed on this continuum. Add comments to clarify the situation or to show the differences in this request from the general profile.

To Be Alone or to Meet People?

Does the client wish to be alone or to meet people? At one end of this continuum, people desire to be completely on their own, without any interaction with staff or other tourists except for service needs, which they hope will be satisfied as efficiently as possible. Another client may have a need to be surrounded by many other people constantly. Most people would want something between these two extremes.

One's placement on this continuum may vary from time to time, depending upon one's marital status, social standing, and social needs. Circle a number between 1 and 7 in Figure 3-3 that best represents your client's need to be alone or to meet people. Add comments, which will help you make appropriate recommendations for this customer.

Relaxation or Excitement?

Some clients desire to be active every waking hour of the day and night. Some wish for a wide variety of activities. Others prefer to be immersed in a single activity. And some cherish inactivity.

PURPOSE OF TRAVEL:
Business, Pleasure, or Both?

BUSINESS		BUSINESS and PLEASURE			PLEASURE	
1	2	3	4	5	6	7

Comments: _____

_____

_____

FIGURE 3-2

Business, pleasure, or both?

PURPOSE OF TRAVEL:
To Be Alone or to Meet People?

TO BE ALONE   TO MEET PEOPLE

1   2   3   4   5   6   7

Comments: _____

_____

_____

FIGURE 3-3
To be alone or to meet people?

One factor that affects people with regards to their placement on this continuum is the intensity of stimulation in their daily lives. Some people are extremely stressed in their daily lives and particularly in their jobs. On a vacation, their primary goal is to escape from this stress.

On the other hand, many feel that their daily lives are boring, so they strive for enough excitement on a holiday to carry them through to their next holiday. Of course, the majority of the public is spread out along a continuum between these two extremes. One's placement on this continuum would vary with his or her current stimulation level. Circle a number between 1 and 7 in Figure 3-4 to indicate where you feel this customer should be placed on this continuum. Add comments to clarify which activities the customer seeks or how he or she desires to savor inactivity.

PURPOSE OF TRAVEL:
Relaxation or Excitement?

RELAXATION   SOME OF EACH   EXCITEMENT

1   2   3   4   5   6   7

Comments: _____

_____

_____

FIGURE 3-4
Relaxation or Excitement?

```
┌─────────────────────────────────────────────────────┐
│             PURPOSE OF TRAVEL:                        │
│          To Stay Put or to See the World?             │
│                                                       │
│  TO GET AWAY FROM EVERYTHING        TO SEE THE WORLD  │
│                                                       │
│  1       2       3       4       5       6       7    │
│                                                       │
│  Comments: _____  │
│  _____│
│  _____│
└─────────────────────────────────────────────────────┘
```

FIGURE 3-5

To stay put or to see the world?

To Stay Put or to See the World?

The fourth variable in one's purpose of travel is the client's desire to stay put or see the world. Initially, this continuum seems much like the relaxation-excitement continuum. In some ways it is, but the difference is that the relaxation-excitement continuum addresses the activity level desired on a holiday. The stay put-see the world continuum addresses whether the client would like to remain in one place or prefer to travel continuously. People who prefer to stay put may vary from those who wish very little activity to those who wish to explore a single destination in great depth.

On the other hand, learning largely motivates those who desire to see the world. Indicate in Figure 3-5 where you feel your customer should be placed on this continuum. Add comments to clarify the situation, or to show the differences in his or her request on this particular occasion.

Quality of Accommodations

Do not ask how much they would like to spend! They probably do not know how much accommodations will cost at the tourist destination.

Do not ask an open-ended question regarding a client's request for quality in accommodations or tour. They will probably not know what is available and will not know the terminology regarding quality. Terminology like star ratings and terms like deluxe, first class, and tourist class vary so much from one location to another that it can be completely confusing to the public. The customer will probably respond with a vague answer like "Not too expensive."

Customers who reply, "Not too expensive," may really be looking for a bargain price on a very good tour or hotel—at special or off-season rates; or they may be looking for the lowest priced budget item that you can find. In these two cases, the needs of the customers are very different. The best way to pin the prospect down regarding quality desired is to offer a choice. "When you are in Washington, would you prefer best available or moderately priced accommodations?" Not only listen, but also closely observe body language to evaluate the reaction.

Only if you discern that they might be uncomfortable with either of these choices, offer them the budget option. If they choose best available, that is exactly what they want and they will not expect a low price. If they choose moderate, they fully understand that the price will be in the middle range and also understand that they cannot expect top quality. If they do instruct you to book a budget property, they must understand that the property is one of the least expensive available and that they cannot expect anything more than basic accommodations.

Any shortcomings of a property should be made clear before a final decision is made. More complaints are received regarding accommodations than all other travel arrangements combined. It is very important to get this part of the qualifying process right! Pin the client down regarding the quality he or she expects.

There is seldom a misunderstanding regarding the terms budget or moderate. But sometimes the best available might be inappropriate. In a small town not located on the well-beaten tourist circuit, the best available hotel or motel might be the only one you would recommend. In a very large city or world famous resort, very good accommodations might be available at the top end of your client's means, but the best available might be so expensive that only the rich and famous could afford them. In such cases, don't hesitate to substitute a very good or even a good hotel instead of the best available.

When you are qualifying a client regarding his or her preference for quality in accommodations, you want to keep it simple. Offer only two choices at a time. "Would you prefer best available or moderate accommodations when you are in Lake Tahoe?" However, as you get to know your client better, you can fine-tune his or her preferences on the continuum by adding comments.

On this continuum (see Figure 3-6), number 1 would truly represent the best available; 2 would represent very good accommodations, but not the most expensive. Numbers 3, 4, and 5 would represent the moderate range with 3 representing the top end of moderate, but in the client's mind, not too expensive. Number 4 would represent the mid-range of moderate, and number 5 would represent accommodations with the normal amenities expected for a moderate property but at the low end of the price range for moderate properties. This could be because it might be an older property or might not be as well located as other properties.

```
┌─────────────────────────────────────────────────────────────┐
│                  QUALITY OF ACCOMMODATIONS                    │
│                                                               │
│   BEST AVAILABLE              MODERATE              BUDGET     │
│                                                               │
│   1        2        3        4        5        6        7     │
│                                                               │
│   Comments: _____│
│                                                               │
│   _____│
│                                                               │
│   _____│
└─────────────────────────────────────────────────────────────┘
```

FIGURE 3-6

Quality of accommodations

Number 6 would indicate that the client wants inexpensive accommodations but clean and comfortable, considering the price. Number 7 would indicate that the client seeks the lowest price available and will probably endure some discomfort or inconvenience to obtain this price.

Comments might include preference for certain chains of hotels or motels, or a preference for small or independent properties or ones that are unique to the destination. They may also include requests for certain amenities like a swimming pool, fitness center, shopping center adjacent, or baby sitting service.

Quality of Tours

As with accommodations, do not ask a customer how much he or she would like to spend! Most customers do not know how much it will cost to travel to a particular tourist destination. People are reluctant to tell a salesperson the most they are prepared to pay because they feel that the salesperson will try to sell them the most expensive package within their means, whether they need it or not.

Determine the prospect's needs based on quality of accommodations, what is included, and conversely what is not included. It is easy to sell a less expensive package, but will the customer be satisfied, and will you receive repeat business and referrals?

How Secure Is Your Client?

How secure your client is will probably influence his or her choice for guided or independent travel services and whether he or she wants to travel with a group or would prefer individual travel arrangements. It will also be an important factor in selecting a safe destination.

There are five parameters to be scrutinized regarding a client's concern for security.

Physical Safety

The first parameter of security is concern for physical safety. How well established an air carrier is and their safety record may be primary considerations for some clients. The apparent safety of a destination would be another. Violence of any kind, but particularly violence against tourists, such as the indiscriminate gunning down of a busload of tourists in Egypt in 1997 will surely deter many tourists from visiting Egypt for years to come.

The events of September 11, 2001 have greatly impacted client concerns about physical safety. Counselors should advise travelers regarding the relative safety of destinations. Many clients will be very cautious regarding which carrier to choose and some are reluctant to fly. Rail travel has increased in popularity since September 11, and many people are vacationing closer to home.

I had a client—Ted—who was fascinated by the native cultures of Colombia. I booked Ted on an independent tour, tailored to his specific interests. On the airplane enroute to Colombia, a fellow passenger told Ted that there was a college for pickpockets in Bogotá. Ted spoke to the purser (passenger service supervisor) on board and made a reservation for a return flight on the same aircraft.

He never left the airport. After his return, I asked Ted if anyone made an attempt to pickpocket him. "No." I asked him if he saw any attempt to pickpocket anyone else. "No." But his fear for his physical security denied him any opportunity to enjoy a trip that he had anticipated for years. Of course I was wrong! There were so many positive vibrations about his opportunity to research the native cultures of Colombia, I never thought to probe his concern for physical security.

Often, the salesperson can determine how secure the customer is through the client's body language and from his or her conversation. But, sometimes it is important to ask direct questions to determine his or her comfort level before recommending a tourism product.

Other tourists may actually seek out such a destination to see what it is really like and to study the causes of the problems. Circle a number from 1 to 7 in Figure 3-7 to indicate where you feel this customer should be placed on this continuum. Add comments regarding the client's specific concerns.

Travel Experience

The second parameter regarding security refers to travel experience. This can vary from the client who travels every week as part of his or her job, to the client who has never traveled before. (See Figure 3-8.) Comments may be important here because a client may be very experienced with domestic travel but a first time traveler to an international destination. Or, another traveler may be experienced traveling

FIGURE 3-7

Concern for physical
safety

```
┌─────────────────────────────────────────────────────────┐
│              HOW SECURE IS YOUR CLIENT?                   │
│                 Concern for Physical Safety               │
│                                                           │
│   INSECURE                                        SECURE  │
│                                                           │
│   1        2        3        4        5        6        7 │
│                                                           │
│   Comments: _____│
│                                                           │
│   _____│
│                                                           │
│   _____│
└─────────────────────────────────────────────────────────┘
```

FIGURE 3-8

Travel experience

```
┌─────────────────────────────────────────────────────────┐
│              HOW SECURE IS YOUR CLIENT?                   │
│                    Travel Experience                      │
│                                                           │
│   FIRST TIME TRAVELER        LIMITED        EXPERIENCED   │
│                                                           │
│   1        2        3        4        5        6        7 │
│                                                           │
│   Comments: _____│
│                                                           │
│   _____│
│                                                           │
│   _____│
└─────────────────────────────────────────────────────────┘
```

in English-speaking countries and other countries where English is well understood, but may be truly insecure traveling to a country in which hardly anyone speaks English.

Something Familiar or Something Different?

The third parameter regarding security addresses the desire of a client for something familiar or something really different. Cultural differences may be the primary reason for traveling for one client, but for another that would be a constant source of tension. Ask travel and tourism students to close their eyes and visualize the best place they have ever visited. Then ask them to visualize the place that they have not visited but would most like to visit if they had a chance. Finally, ask them which one they would choose if they had only one choice, their most memorable destination or the most desired location that they have not visited. Travel and tourism students select the most

```
HOW SECURE IS YOUR CLIENT?
Something Familiar or Something Different?

FAMILIAR              SOMEWHAT DIFFERENT   REALLY DIFFERENT

1        2        3        4        5        6        7

Comments: _____

_____

_____
```

FIGURE 3-9

Something familiar or something different?

desired location that they have not visited by a large majority. However, pose the same question to the general population, and you will find an almost equal split between those who desire something familiar and those who prefer something different.

Circle the number between 1 and 7 in Figure 3-9 that best represents the client's appetite for something familiar or something different. Add comments regarding tourism experiences that the client desires and any experiences the client wishes to avoid.

Foreign Language

The fourth parameter regarding security concerns language. How comfortable is the customer in a place where his or her language is not well understood? (See Figure 3-10.)

```
HOW SECURE IS YOUR CLIENT?
Foreign Language

VERY UNCOMFORTABLE                NO PROBLEM AT ALL

1        2        3        4        5        6        7

Comments: _____

_____

_____
```

FIGURE 3-10

Foreign language

```
┌─────────────────────────────────────────────────────────────┐
│                  HOW SECURE IS YOUR CLIENT?                    │
│            Comfort with a Different Segment of Society         │
│                                                                │
│   VERY UNCOMFORTABLE                      NO PROBLEM AT ALL     │
│                                                                │
│   1        2        3        4        5        6        7      │
│                                                                │
│   Comments: _____ │
│                                                                │
│   _____ │
│                                                                │
│   _____ │
└─────────────────────────────────────────────────────────────┘
```

FIGURE 3-11

Comfort with a different segment of society

Comfort with a Different Segment of Society

The fifth parameter concerns how comfortable people from one segment of society will be when immersed in a completely different segment of society. (See Figure 3-11.) City people may not feel comfortable in a wilderness setting, and rural people may be apprehensive in a large city environment. Upper-class people may feel very uncomfortable with lower-class people. Likewise, lower-class people may feel just as uncomfortable with upper-class people. In today's society it is quite possible that lower-class people might be able to afford the same holiday as upper-class people. If you discern a possible problem with the type of travel chosen and a particular client, discuss it frankly. Perhaps suggest an alternative destination or make some recommendations on how to cope. Sometimes this might be as simple as what to wear. Be sure to recommend accommodations with an appropriate guest mix for your clients.

CLIENT PROFILE

A **client profile** provides the salesperson with the information necessary to make reservations for a client precisely and efficiently. Good listening skills are required to complete an accurate client profile. (See Figure 3-12.) Information obtained on each booking should be added to the profile as well as feedback from follow-up calls. Client profiles make it easier for the salesperson to meet the client's **needs** more accurately. Also, the most significant function of the client profile is that it makes it unnecessary to ask for all the same information again for a repeat customer.

Cognizance of the prospect's nonverbal messages, including body language, will be combined with the answers to questions and the client profile to make a recommendation that will satisfy the client's **wants** and needs. Once the salesperson has the client's profile, he or she can make individual travel arrangements tailored to the customer's needs and wants. *(continues on page 44)*

CLIENT PROFILE

Family Name: _____   First Name: _____

Prefers to be called: _____   (Birth Date: _____)

Anniversary: _____

Passport: Country: _____ Expiration Date: _____

Passenger Type: Senior: ___   Adult: ___   Youth/Student: ___   Child: ___

Family Members:

    Spouse: _____   (Birth Date: _____)

    Child: M / F   (Birth Date: _____)

    Child: M / F   (Birth Date: _____)

    Infant: M / F   (Birth Date: _____)

Phone: Home: _____   Business: _____

    Prefers to be called: at home ___   at work ___

    Between: _____ A.M./P.M. and _____ A.M./P.M.

    Best days to be called: _____

FAX: Home: _____   Business: _____

E-MAIL: _____

Home Address

Apt/Suite: _____   Street Address: _____

City/Municipality: _____   State/Prov. _____

ZIP/Postal Code: _____

Business Address

Apt/Suite: _____   Street Address: _____

City/Municipality: _____   State/Prov. _____

ZIP/Postal Code: _____

(continued)

FIGURE 3-12   Client profile.

CLIENT PROFILE *(continued)*

WHERE HAS HE/SHE TRAVELED BEFORE?

Destination	Package/Supplier	Accommodations	When
_____	_____	_____	_____
_____	_____	_____	_____
_____	_____	_____	_____

Which Mode of Transportation Is Preferred?

Air: _____   Ship: _____   Rail: _____   Motorcoach: _____   Car: _____

Comments: _____

_____

_____

Which Class of Service Is Preferred?

AIR: First Class: _____   Business Class: _____   Coach/Economy: _____   Budget: _____

CRUISE: Outside: _____   Inside: _____   Best Available: _____   Moderate: _____   Budget: _____

RAIL: Club/First Class: _____   Coach: _____   Sleeping Car Preference: _____

CAR: Full Size: _____   Mid-Size: _____   Compact: _____   Sub-Compact: _____

Special Type or Request: _____

SPECIAL INTERESTS

_____

_____

_____

SPECIAL NEEDS

_____

_____

_____

(continued)

FIGURE 3-12   *(continued)*

CLIENT PROFILE (continued)

PURPOSE OF TRAVEL:

Business, Pleasure, or Both?

BUSINESS   BUSINESS and PLEASURE   PLEASURE

1   2   3   4   5   6   7

Comments: _____

_____

_____

To Be Alone or to Meet People?

TO BE ALONE   TO MEET PEOPLE

1   2   3   4   5   6   7

Comments: _____

_____

_____

Relaxation or Excitement?

RELAXATION   SOME OF EACH   EXCITEMENT

1   2   3   4   5   6   7

Comments: _____

_____

_____

To Stay Put or to See the World?

TO GET AWAY FROM EVERYTHING   TO SEE THE WORLD

1   2   3   4   5   6   7

Comments: _____

_____

_____

(continued)

FIGURE 3-12   *(continued)*

CLIENT PROFILE *(continued)*

PURPOSE OF TRAVEL: *(concluded)*

To Avoid the Opposite Sex or to Seek the Opposite Sex?

AVOID THE OPPOSITE SEX   SEEK THE OPPOSITE SEX

1	2	3	4	5	6	7

Comments: _____

_____

_____

QUALITY OF ACCOMMODATIONS

BEST AVAILABLE   MODERATE   BUDGET

1	2	3	4	5	6	7

Comments: _____

_____

_____

HOW SECURE IS YOUR CLIENT?

Concern for Physical Safety

INSECURE   SECURE

1	2	3	4	5	6	7

Comments: _____

_____

_____

Travel Experience

FIRST TIME TRAVELER   LIMITED   EXPERIENCED

1	2	3	4	5	6	7

Comments: _____

_____

_____

(continued)

FIGURE 3-12   *(continued)*

CLIENT PROFILE *(concluded)*

HOW SECURE IS YOUR CLIENT? *(concluded)*

Something Familiar or Something Different?

FAMILIAR		SOMEWHAT DIFFERENT			REALLY DIFFERENT	
1	2	3	4	5	6	7

Comments: _____

_____

_____

Foreign Language

VERY UNCOMFORTABLE					NO PROBLEM AT ALL	
1	2	3	4	5	6	7

Comments: _____

_____

_____

Comfort with a Different Segment of Society

VERY UNCOMFORTABLE					NO PROBLEM AT ALL	
1	2	3	4	5	6	7

Comments: _____

_____

_____

Preferred Form of Payment: Credit Card: _____ Check: _____ Cash: _____ Invoice: _____

Credit Card: Type of Card: _____ Company: _____

Card Number: _____ Expiration Date: _____

Name (as it appears on the card): _____

FIGURE 3-12   *(concluded)*

Depending on the specific nature of the company or organization with which you are working, some of the information on the usual client profile may not be required. Other information may be required for your specific situation. I suggest that you start with the Client Profile provided in Figure 3-12 and modify it to meet your unique needs using a personal computer. Also, if client profiles are kept on a personal computer, it will be easy to add or change the information included. Birth dates and anniversary dates are included because it is good public relations to send a card on these occasions.

Different Information for Specific Sectors

Examples of different information that may be required for specific sectors of the tourism industry could include the following items.

1. Accommodations sector
   - Preference for a smoking or nonsmoking room
   - Preference of location of the room

2. Food and Beverage sector
   - Favorite table
   - Special occasions like birthdays or anniversaries
   - Preference for a smoking or nonsmoking table

3. Adventure and Recreation sector
   - Does the client have his or her own equipment?
   - If not, what are his or her preferences of equipment?

4. Attractions sector
   - Time of year he or she likes to visit
   - If affiliated with a group, information regarding the group

5. Transportation sector
   - Class of service preferred
   - Preference for an aisle or window seat
   - Preferred carriers
   - Frequent flier program memberships
   - Preferred travel dates
   - Group affiliation
   - Information about the group

6. Events and Conferences sector
   - Information about groups including:
     — "Raison d'être" (reason for being)
     — Important contacts
     — Dates for change in leadership

7. Tourism Services sector
   - The requirements here would vary so much that each organization would have to discuss the type of information it would require on a client profile form and develop one tailored to its own needs.

8. Travel Trade sector
   - The client profile illustrated in Figure 3-12 should be effective for most travel agencies but could always be modified for special needs.
   - Tour operators, tour wholesalers, and local sight-seeing companies would want to modify the basic client profile to reflect the specific products they offer.

TRAVELERS WITH SPECIAL NEEDS OR REQUESTS

It is always wise to ask a client if he or she has any special need or request. However, five categories of clients usually have special needs:

- People traveling with young children
- People making arrangements for unaccompanied minors
- People with special dietary needs
- Business travelers
- Physically or mentally challenged travelers

Traveling with Young Children

People traveling with young children, particularly infants, often need assistance in airports, rail stations, and cruise ports. The carriers are pleased to provide assistance. You should request appropriate assistance when making reservations. Also, advise your client that the carriers provide preboarding for travelers with infants and small children. Advise them to listen for preboarding announcements.

Unaccompanied Minors

Check with the airline or other carrier before making reservations for unaccompanied minors. The rules can vary from one airline to another. Children's fares are usually not applicable. The adult fare will be paid plus an escort fee for each flight segment. In the USA, this is normally $30.00 to $60.00 for a round trip. Most U.S. based carriers will accept unaccompanied minors between the ages of 5 and 11.

United Airlines will accept unaccompanied minors between the ages of 5 and 7 only on nonstop flights. Children 8 to 11 are allowed to fly on connecting flights. Unaccompanied children must pay the adult fare plus a $60.00 escort fee for each direction.

Delta will accept children from 5 to 11 years for nonstop, direct, or connecting service. The adult fare must be paid plus a $40.00 escort fee for direct service or $75.00 for connecting service in each direction.

Air Canada will accept unaccompanied minors between 5 and 7 years of age for direct service only. Unaccompanied children between 8 and 11 will be accepted for connecting flights. Unaccompanied children will be charged the adult fare plus a service charge of $40.00 one way, or $80.00 return (in Canadian funds). Japan Airlines will accept unaccompanied minors from 3 months to 11 years of age with no fee for escort service, but the ticket must be paid at the adult fare.

The rules and charges vary greatly from one carrier to another and are subject to change at any time. Therefore, it is essential to check with the carrier at the time of the booking.

Airlines always require full details regarding who is bringing the child to the airport and who is receiving the child at the destination. This information would have to be written and signed by the parent or guardian. Details required would include the name, address, and phone number of the person taking the child to the airport and their relationship to the child. Similar information would be required for the person receiving the child at the destination.

Both the person dropping the child off at the airport and the person receiving the child at the destination would be required to have proof of identity, including a photograph and signature. Many airlines require two pieces of identification. Daytime flights are preferred for unaccompanied children, and most airlines will not book them for the last flight at night. If the flight were to be delayed, they would not want an unaccompanied minor to be stranded in an airport overnight.

For rail travel, Amtrak and Via Rail Canada regulations are similar. They will carry unaccompanied minors between the ages of 8 and 11 on direct service only. Travel is only allowed on trains traveling during daylight hours. The parent or guardian must take the child to the station and introduce him or her to the ticket agent. Forms have to be completed by the parent or guardian. A letter is required stating who will be picking up the child, including address, phone number, and relationship. Via Rail Canada also charges an escort fee, which is presently $10.00.

Special Dietary Needs

Most major airlines have a wide variety of special meals available for passengers with special needs. Special meals are prepared for passengers with special dietary requirements and also for different religious specifications. Usually, special meals have to be ordered at least 24 hours in advance, but normally you would do it at the time of booking. Examples of special meals offered by most major airlines include:

Asian vegetarian	low cholesterol
bland (for ulcer problems)	low fat
diabetic	low salt
fruit platter	Muslim
gluten (meat and vegetable diet)	nonlactic
Hindu	oriental
kosher	vegetarian
low calorie	vegetarian lacto-ovo

Business Travelers

Some businesses insist that all employees travel at the lowest fare possible. However, many businesses allow their employees or at least their executives to travel first class, where available, or business class on other routes. Always ask business travelers which class they would prefer—first/business class or coach.

When it comes to accommodations, there are two primary considerations for most business travelers:

1. A hotel that is conveniently located, close to where he or she will be conducting business.

2. A hotel that has the amenities required by the business traveler. There are two types of amenities that business travelers require:

    a. Amenities within rooms—for example, voice mail, a working desk, and a computer hook-up. Sometimes businesspeople require space for meetings or for entertaining clients. Some hotels have special floors reserved for women business travelers.

b. Amenities available in a business center within the hotel. Many of the top commercial hotels have an amazing array of facilities available for business travelers, including:

- private work space
- telephone and modem access
- hand-free headsets
- conference call capability
- facsimile machine
- photocopier
- private phone booths with comfortable seating and desk space
- local and international newspapers
- business magazines
- computers with Internet access
- a scanner
- laminating machine
- private boardroom

Most businesspeople travel to the same cities frequently and have a favorite hotel in each city. Ask if he or she has a favorite hotel at the destination and make a note in the file so that you do not have to ask the same question again. If the business traveler is not familiar with the destination, ask which of the amenities listed will be required. Research the various possibilities and recommend one or two suitable properties. Once the business traveler has chosen a particular hotel, keep it on file. Subject to follow-up after his or her return, use it next time to avoid going through the same selection process again.

Travelers with Physical or Mental Disabilities

For travel counselors who are servicing travelers with physical or mental disabilities, I highly recommend *The Disabled Traveller—A Guide for Travel Counsellors*, by Cinnie Noble (Toronto: Canadian Institute of Travel Counsellors of Ontario, 1991). Cinnie Noble has also written a useful guide for your clients who are disabled or elderly: *Handi-Travel: A Resourcebook for Disabled and Elderly Travellers*, available from The Director of Operations, Easter Seals March of Dimes National Council, 90 Eglington Avenue East, Suite 511, Toronto, Ontario M4P2Y3; telephone: 416-932-8382.

A travel consultant requires much more detail when qualifying a client with disabilities as compared to the average traveler. (See

Figure 3-13.) Some questions pertain to most disabilities. Others are specific to certain conditions.

"Thinking that disabled and unable are synonymous will interfere with any servicing of people with disabilities as well as the development of this specialized market and their right to integration into the mainstream of travel."[1] "Keep in mind that disabled people are people first."[2] "The handicap is usually one-dimensional and in every other way, most disabled people are the same as others. To make travel arrangements, detailed knowledge of disabilities is not usually necessary, though information about functional limitations is often required, e.g., the person can (or cannot) walk."[3]

Before making reservations, it is necessary to know your client's special needs. Advise your client to contact you well in advance because travel arrangements for people with disabilities are more complicated than for others. Airlines and other carriers often have limits to the number of passengers with disabilities that they will carry. The number of hotels and other facilities that can accommodate guests with disabilities are limited, and those that do usually have only a few rooms that are designed to accommodate people with disabilities.

Travel consultants not used to serving travelers with disabilities may be nervous about asking personal questions about a client's disability. But direct questions result in direct answers. "Most people want to share information about their disabilities so that appropriate arrangements are made . . ."[4]

WHO IS "INCAPACITATED"?

A passenger is defined by airlines as "incapacitated", "handicapped" or "disabled" when his or her physical condition or medical disorder, including mental illness, requires the airline to supply individual attention which is not normally extended to other passengers, such as on enplaning or deplaning, during the flight, in an emergency evacuation, or during ground handling at airports.

This definition covers those who are medically ill or temporarily disabled persons, both ambulatory or non-ambulatory, and those whose conditions are considered as variable and who, therefore, require medical clearance prior to each air journey. It also refers to the more common cases of permanently disabled persons whose physical or mental conditions are stable.

Note the captain (pilot) retains the authority to refuse the transportation of *any* passenger whose condition would jeopardize his or her own well-being or that of the other passengers.

FIGURE 3-13

The Disabled Traveller... Who is "Incapacitated?" (Courtesy Canadian Institute of Travel Counsellors of Ontario)

Four terms used to describe people with disabilities are important: ambulatory, self-reliant, nonambulatory, and non–self-reliant. (See Figure 3-14.)

Classifications for Special Services

A list of classifications for special services is provided in Figure 3-15.

FIGURE 3-14

The Disabled Traveller... Definitions pertaining to airline travel. *(Courtesy Canadian Institute of Travel Counsellors of Ontario)*

DEFINITIONS PERTAINING TO AIRLINE TRAVEL

Ambulatory • A person considered as ambulatory is able to walk, board the aircraft unassisted, (even if slowly), with aids such as a cane or crutches, and is able to move about in the aircraft cabin unassisted. In many cases, ambulatory passengers require a wheelchair for the distance to and from the aircraft, i.e., across the ramp, finger dock or mobile lounge. Unless a serious medical condition exists, ambulatory passengers are usually considered self-reliant.

Self-Reliant • The disabled passenger who is independent, self-sufficient and capable of taking care of all his or her physical needs in flight, is considered self-reliant. This passenger requires no special or unusual attention beyond that afforded to the general public, except that assistance in boarding and deplaning may be required.

Non-Ambulatory • A person who is non-ambulatory is someone who is unable to move about within the aircraft unassisted. This person cannot ascend or descend steps but is able to make his or her way to and from the cabin seat. He or she requires a wheelchair to and from the aircraft or mobile lounge and must be carried up and down steps. He or she is considered self-reliant unless a serious medical condition exists.

Non-Self-Reliant • The disabled passenger who is incapable of self-care during the flight and who depends upon another person to look after personal physical needs, is considered non-self-reliant. Thus, the non-self-reliant person requires a *personal attendant*.

A **personal qualified attendant** is any person who is technically competent or otherwise capable of assisting the disabled passenger to an exit in the event of an emergency and attending to his or her personal needs during the flight.

Note: *Determination of self-reliance:* Some airlines will accept the disabled passenger's statement of self-reliance with the knowledge that a disabled person is well aware of his or her limitations and acts accordingly. Other airlines, however, request medical confirmation.

CLASSIFICATIONS

Disabilities, in terms of each individual's physical capabilities and requirements for special services, have been classified into three major categories in the U.S.A. A fourth category has been added in Canada. When making an airline booking, you will be required to determine into which category your client fits.

WCHR • This usually includes persons who are ambulatory as defined [in Figure 3-14]; that is, someone who can walk, board the aircraft unassisted, even if slowly, with walking aids, and is able to move about in the aircraft cabin unassisted. Wheelchair assistance may be required for long distances. Blind, deaf and developmentally disabled persons are usually included in this category. Unless a serious medical condition exists, ambulatory passengers are usually considered self-reliant.

WCHS • This classification includes those who are considered non-ambulatory as defined above. The person cannot ascend or descend steps but is able to make his or her way to and from the cabin seat. These passengers require a wheelchair to and from the aircraft and must be carried up and down stairs. They are considered self-reliant unless a serious medical condition exists.

WCHC • A passenger who is unable to walk from the aircraft door to the seat or toilet, who is immobile and requires a wheelchair to and from the aircraft or mobile lounge, who must be carried up and down steps and to and from the cabin seat, and who cannot take care of his or her physical needs in flight, is considered non-self-reliant and requires a personal attendant. See definition of non-reliant persons and personal attendant [in Figure 3-14]. This designation does not usually apply to vision- and hearing-impaired persons unless newly impaired and not able to manage on their own. The designation does not typically apply to senior citizens who are capable of self-care during the flights.

It is important to note a fourth classification, WCHP, in Canada.

WCHP • This passenger is immobile but self-reliant, requires a wheelchair to and from the aircraft or mobile lounge, and must be carried up and down steps to and from the cabin seat. This passenger is rehabilitated, self-reliant and capable of taking care of all physical needs in flight. He or she will have taken precautions to avoid the necessity of using the aircraft washrooms and requires no special attention, except boarding or deplaning assistance, beyond that afforded to the general public. This passenger may travel without a personal attendant in accordance with approved numerical restrictions.

Note: This category can only be used when dealing with Canadian carriers. When using other than a Canadian carrier, and the client can be classified according to the category WCHP above, refer to the passenger as "self-reliant" when making the booking. Other airlines have varying policies regarding the carriage of persons classified in this way.

FIGURE 3-15

The Disabled Traveller...
Classifications.
*(Courtesy Canadian
Institute of Travel
Counsellors of Ontario)*

A special client profile form for travelers with disabilities, like the one prepared by Cinnie Noble as shown in Figure 3-16, will help you obtain the information you need when making reservations. It will also make it unnecessary to ask the same questions again for future bookings.

The seat request information regarding smoking or nonsmoking is redundant for most carriers, because most of them do not allow smoking. It is very important to keep the information on the client profile form on file. You will not have to take your time or your client's time to obtain the same information for his or her next trip.

It might be a good point during your follow-up call to say, "Mrs. Petersen, I appreciate your feedback. This information plus the information you gave me before your departure will make it easy for me to serve you more efficiently on your next trip."

When making reservations, be sure to advise the reservationist of your client's disability and any special requests required. For any travelers with disabilities, try to book nonstop transportation, if possible. If not, try to book direct service, which may have intermediate stops but no change of aircraft or vehicle. If connections are necessary, make sure that you allow extra time to move from one aircraft or vehicle to another, considering the disability. Travelers who require assistance are the last to deplane and will be preboarded on the connecting flight.

Air reservations are usually made with the first carrier for domestic or transborder travel. For international trips, reservations should be made with the transatlantic or transpacific carrier. Make sure that other carriers used on your client's itinerary are informed regarding your client's special needs. This will normally be done by the carrier with whom you have made the reservations, but check to make sure that they do this.

Special Requirements for Clients with Mobility Impairments

"Management of the bowels and bladder is a subject that may require consideration when discussing travel for persons who use wheelchairs."[5] Principal considerations are the duration of the trip and the type of assistance required.

When counseling persons who use wheelchairs, sit down so that you can communicate at eye level. Airlines and other carriers will require information about the passenger's wheelchair. Is it manual or motorized? If motorized, which type of batteries are used? "Nonmotorized wheelchairs are usually carried free of charge. Motorized wheelchairs are not always accepted."[6]

If the passenger cannot move about the aircraft without assistance, request a boarding chair, sometimes referred to as a Wellington chair, at the time of the booking. Passengers can be seated in a front

(continues on page 55)

CLIENT PROFILE FORM

Name: _____

Address: _____

City: _____ Province: _____ Code: _____

Phone Number: Area Code (   ) _____

Citizenship _____ Passport No. _____

The following information is required to plan a trip which will best meet the individual travel needs. The information is confidential and will be used only as a guideline in planning your trip.

1. What is the name of your disability? [Check appropriate box(es)]

Multiple Sclerosis	❑	Paraplegia	❑
Arthritis	❑	Quadriplegia	❑
Cerebral Palsy	❑	Stroke	❑
Spina Bifida	❑	Parkinson's Disease	❑
Other (please name)			

2. What type of aid(s), if any, do you require and that you will take on your trip?

Cane(s)	❑	Wheelchair	❑
Crutches	❑	No Assistance	❑
Braces	❑	Other (please explain) _____	

3. If you use a wheelchair, are you able to:
   Stand without assistance?   No ❑   Yes ❑

   If yes, are you able to:
   Walk without assistance?   No ❑   Yes ❑

   If yes, are you able to:
   Climb steps without assistance?   No ❑   Yes ❑

   Are you able to:
   Transfer from one seat to
   another without assistance?   No ❑   Yes ❑

   Are you able to:
   Propel your wheelchair on
   level ground unassisted?   No ❑   Yes ❑

   Is the wheelchair you will be traveling with:

   Manual? ❑ Width _____

   Electric? ❑ Width _____

   (Measure widths from outside tire rims. Width is needed when arranging accommodation.)

   If the wheelchair you will be travelling with is electric, what types of batteries will you use?

   Non-spillable
   dry cell/gel cel   ❑
   Acid packed   ❑   *(continued)*

FIGURE 3-16

The Disabled Traveller... Client profile form. (Courtesy of Canadian Institute of Travel Counsellors of Ontario)

CLIENT PROFILE FORM
(concluded)

4. Will you be taking along any required equipment such as a respirator or oxygen?

   No ❏   Yes ❏

   If yes, please explain _____

5. Are you on a special diet?   No ❏   Yes ❏

   Name: _____

6. Please describe limitations of your specific disability relevant to travelling, e.g., lack of balance, inability to walk. _____

   _____

7. What type of assistance will you require while travelling? (e.g., assistance to airplane seat, wheelchair accommodation.) _____

   _____

8. Are you currently undergoing medical treatment?

   No ❏   Yes ❏

   If yes, please explain _____

   (In some cases there are medical reasons why persons undergoing medical treatment are not encouraged to fly. When in doubt prospective passengers are advised to contact their physician.)

9. Will you be travelling:
   Alone?   ❏
   With a companion?   ❏
   With a companion who can provide
   any necessary assistance?   ❏

10. If you have travelled before, what problems, if any, have you encountered in relation to your physical limitations? _____

    _____

    _____

    _____

11. Seat request:
    Near washroom   ❏   Not necessary   ❏
    Smoking   ❏   Non-smoking   ❏
    Other (please explain) _____

Optional:
   Weight _____ lbs. (Note: Response may be required by some airlines for persons who do not walk and have to be lifted.)

In cases where travel consultants are coordinating group travel and are using the form for a profile of tour members, additional and optional questions are:

Hobbies, interests _____

Occupation _____

Date of Birth _____

FIGURE 3-16

(concluded)

row on a Boeing 747, DC 10, or L-1011, making it unnecessary to transfer to a boarding chair. Inform the reservationist that your client will require a wheelchair and assistance with baggage at the destination.

"Some airlines ask for a medical note stating eligibility to travel; some accept non-walking wheelchair users only when accompanied; some accept the person who is required to travel with the person with the disability to travel at 50% of the airfare; while others require disabled people to complete forms about their degree of mobility."[7]

Special Considerations When Counseling a Client Who Is Visually Impaired

"Blind or visually-impaired people do not live in a tragic world of unending darkness. Many do, in fact see in varying degrees and make good use of the vision that remains. If you are not sure how much a person sees, ask. . . . Speak to a blind person in a normal tone of voice. Do not speak to or question the blind person through another person. Speak directly to him or her, using his or her name. . . . It is most helpful to provide travel information for your clients who are vision-impaired, by tape."[8]

For those who can see but cannot read normal size print, prepare the details of the trip in large, bold print. Another possibility is to print out the details so that another person can translate them into Braille. In some cases, the blind client may want you to describe the trip itinerary while he or she writes the information in Braille. When doing this, get a feel for pacing so that you know when to pause and when to proceed.

Passengers with vision impairments are eligible for preboarding. Advise the reservationist, at the time of booking, that your client would like assistance and preboarding. Advise your client that he or she will be given assistance with deplaning after the other passengers have departed. For persons with dog guides, window seats are recommended so that other passengers do not have to step over the dog. Instruct your clients to advise airline personnel about their vision impairment, so that the staff and crew will be ready to provide appropriate services.

If you are booking a cruise for a client with a visual impairment, always check with the line whether a guide dog will be accepted, and if so, whether there will be a fee.

Special Considerations When Counseling a Client Who Has a Hearing Impairment

"Do not refer to a hearing-impaired person as a deaf-mute or deaf and dumb. A person with a hearing-impairment is acceptable terminology."[9] "Deafness has often been referred to as *The Invisible Handicap* since it is often difficult to recognize persons who have impaired hearing."[10] Provide detailed written directions, including maps and diagrams.

Make sure that you communicate face to face with clients who have hearing impairments. Determine if he or she can hear better from one ear or the other. If so, speak to that ear. Reduce unwanted interference. Close the window, turn off the radio or background music, and make sure that your meeting place is free of other outside sound. "Try to speak expressively, using facial expressions and gestures. Maintain eye contact when you are communicating."[11]

Speak directly to your client, even if he or she has an interpreter present. Try using any sign language you know. If the client does not understand, he or she will let you know. But he or she will appreciate that you are trying. Recently, dogs have been trained to assist people with hearing impairments in similar ways that dog guides have been assisting people with visual impairments for years. If your client is traveling with a guide dog, make sure that each airline or other carrier is informed and make sure that there are no restrictions.

Advise passengers to carry a statement that the dog is a hearing-ear dog guide and to carry a certificate of health for the dog. An escort is usually required if a person is both visually and hearing impaired.

When booking hotels for clients with hearing impairments, be sure that this status is recorded in the reservation data in order to alert fire departments or other emergency crews in the event of an emergency.

TYPES OF PROSPECTS BY COMMITMENT

There are three types of prospects according to their commitment:

1. *Prospects committed to a specific type of tourism experience.* These prospects are already sold. The job of the counselor is to be a good listener and to fill the order with exactly what the client wants as efficiently as possible.

2. *Prospects committed to a nonspecific tourism experience.* These prospects are qualified prospects because they really want to visit a tourism destination but have an unclear idea of the exact type of tourism arrangements they would like. These people require the counseling skills of a good salesperson. Good questioning techniques mixed with small portions of recommendations are required to help these clients clarify exactly what they want included. A competent counselor should be able to successfully book such a sale.

3. *The uncommitted prospect.* These prospects may have a very vague idea of where they want to go and of what they want to do once they arrive at the tourist destination. They prob-

ably have some vague concept of the costs involved and may not be sure whether they would like to spend their disposable income on a tourist destination or some other alternative. These prospects are the most challenging. They may be a complete waste of time. On the other hand, they could become valuable new customers requiring highly personalized counseling skills of a good salesperson.

Some uncertain but likely prospects may not voice their bewilderment and need for information for a variety of psychological reasons. Some are hesitant about stating their wishes to a stranger. Others are suspicious of what you are going to tell them. They may feel that you are going to try to sell them something more expensive than they want. It could be that they have an unclear idea of the role of the tourism counselor and whether the service rendered will cost them anything. Others are afraid of being embarrassed if they cannot afford the tourist experience they have in mind.

The first step with uncommitted prospects is to set them at ease and make them feel comfortable to ask questions. The second and a very important step is to qualify the prospect to determine whether he or she is a realistic prospect. If the prospect is going to travel to a tourist destination, he or she must have two things:

1. the time to travel

2. the money to travel (either now or in the form of credit)

To determine whether the prospect has the time to travel, simply ask questions about when he or she would like to travel. If the prospect cannot give you dates, mention that the price varies dependent on the season and you do not want to misquote the price. Suggest a season first. If there is no objection, suggest a month. "Would you be traveling in July?" If not, the prospect will correct you. Once you have a month, then suggest a particular date or a choice of two dates. If the date is not a possibility, the prospect will correct you.

If this line of questioning is unsuccessful, it is possible that someone else is responsible for selecting the vacation dates. This could be the employer or spouse. Ask when he or she will know the dates. Make arrangements either to telephone him or her or preferably for an office visit once they know. Make arrangements for a definite date and time for a follow-up appointment.

Heighten his or her interest by emphasizing the points that he or she has brought up and assign homework to do—some research or reading about the tourist destination. This should be attraction oriented rather than product centered. For example, if they have expressed an interest in traveling to Churchill, Manitoba (polar bear capital of the world), you could suggest that they do some reading about the polar bears, the **Inuit** culture, and the flora and fauna of the region. You could give them information available from the Canadian Tourism Commission and Travel Manitoba. You could give them a list of books available at the library or local bookstores.

If you have a videotape on the destination, you might lend it to the prospect. This might pique his or her interest to enable an easy booking. It will also save you time because many of their questions will be answered by viewing the video. *Suggestion:* Require a refundable deposit on the tape to ensure that the customer returns it to you. It also provides you with another opportunity to close the deal.

There are two principal methods to determine whether prospects have the financial means to travel to a tourist destination. One is to ask them if they have established a budget for their trip. If they have, and it is realistic, proceed towards closing the sale. If they have not, try the other approach, which is to give them a "high average" estimate, watching very closely for their reaction.

Three reactions are possible. One reaction is approval or acceptance. In this case, proceed towards closing and look for the opportunity to sell-up.

The second possible reaction is a neutral response. This usually indicates that the cost is not prohibitive and that you should concentrate your sales approach on other features—quality, value for money paid, inclusive features, and a comparative analysis of how much it would cost to do the trip on their own.

The third possible reaction is one of rejection or disapproval. Try to determine the strength and nature of the disapproval. Use the techniques for overcoming objections discussed in Chapter 8.

A MISTAKE TO BE AVOIDED

Once I spent more than 28 hours, over a three-week period, working out the details of a complex foreign independent tour to Europe for a delightful couple. Delightful couple or not, the short version is that they never did go. I was infuriated that I had spent 28 hours of work for nothing. I vowed that I would never do that again.

I pondered what to do if a similar situation occurred in the future. I thought, "What would an airline or a large tour company do about such a situation?" I knew the answer. They would have required a nonrefundable deposit. If you are a small operator in the tourism industry, study what the large operators and carriers do regarding certain situations and learn from their experience.

Notes

1. Cinnie Noble, C.M., LL.B, *The Disabled Traveller: A Guide for Travel Counsellors* (Toronto: Canadian Institute of Travel Counsellors of Ontario, 1991), 7.

2. Ibid., p. 8.

3. Ibid., p. 3.

4. Ibid., p. 9.

5. Ibid., p. 6.

6. Ibid., p. 99.

7. Ibid., p. 47.

8. Ibid., p. 16.

9. Ibid., p. 22.

10. Ibid., p. 18.

11. Ibid., p. 21.

Discussion Questions

1. List four initial questions you would always have to ask in qualifying a prospect who is interested in making travel arrangements. What are three additional qualifying questions that need to be asked in most situations?

2. In addition to the answers to the seven qualifying questions, what are the two other pieces of information that you need to make a reservation?

3. Describe how *The Game*, devised by John Dalton, works.

4. Describe how you would determine the quality of accommodations desired by a prospect.

5. Describe three types of prospects by commitment.

4

Product Knowledge

OBJECTIVES

After studying this chapter, you should be able to:

- Explain the importance of product knowledge to establishing credibility with a prospect, that you are a professional, and that you know your product or service well

- Explain the importance of product knowledge to answering a client's questions

- Explain the importance of product knowledge to matching your knowledge of the product with your knowledge of the customer, gained from effective qualifying, to recommend a product or service that will successfully meet the client's needs

- Discuss, in detail, various ways of obtaining product knowledge

KEY TERMS

confidential tariff	profit margin	computer reservations
net tariff	principal	system (CRS)
net rates	office copy	blind search
overhead	desk copy	

After greeting and qualifying the prospect, the next three steps in the sales process are answering the prospect's questions, recommending a product or service, and creating acceptance for your recommendation. To be successful in these three stages of the sales process, it is essential that your product knowledge is competent.

Before going on to the next three steps of the sales process, we discuss the importance of product knowledge and various ways of obtaining it.

THE IMPORTANCE OF PRODUCT KNOWLEDGE

The importance of product knowledge cannot be overemphasized. I remember it well, dividing sales students into groups of three to practice selling the products of a major tour company using their extensive brochure including more than 25 tours, each with a number of options and choices of hotels. In each group, one member was to be the salesperson, one the customer, and the third an observer with a checklist to evaluate the various steps of the sales process.

All of the students became enthusiastically involved in the activity except one group, which included the two top students in the class. They did not seem to be involved in the role-playing exercise. After about 15 minutes, I approached this group to inquire why they were not participating in the sales exercise.

They told me that they could not effectively sell the product until they thoroughly understood every detail about the product they were going to sell. So they were studying the brochure to acquire the knowledge to effectively sell the tours.

They were absolutely right! When I observed the other groups more closely, I found many of the salespeople frantically fumbling through the brochure for the answers to their customer's questions. Many were giving wrong answers or just could not find the answers to their client's questions.

Even though I had given the students three days to study the brochure, it was inadequate for the number of tours involved. Also, they needed to know, more specifically, which kinds of questions customers would ask and the types of information they would require to make a buying decision.

For a new salesperson with a company or organization, there is seldom time during the first few frantic weeks to learn all of the product knowledge during normal working hours. Even though you are not paid overtime, take the brochures and other literature and do homework until you feel really comfortable with your product knowledge.

If you are working for a company that has only its own products or services to sell, it should not take too long to become comfortable with your product knowledge. If you sell a large number of products produced by others, as a travel agent does, the learning process never ceases.

More brochures come into a travel agency than the sales staff can reasonably handle. Management will make decisions regarding which companies will be preferred suppliers, which brochures from other suppliers will be kept for clients with specific requests, or when preferred suppliers are sold out. Most other brochures will be discarded.

Whenever a new brochure comes into the office, and management decides it is going to be promoted, employees must make time to study it for new products, changes in existing products, and changes in prices. Changes in the rules regarding deposits, payment of balances, penalties for cancellations or changes in dates must also be noted. If liabilities can be covered by insurance, the salesperson must be fully informed regarding premiums, coverage, and exclusions.

Have you ever gone into a store to ask questions about a product before making a buying decision and found that the salesperson knew less about the product than you did? What was your reaction? More important, did you buy the product at that location?

Product knowledge is crucial! Formal courses of study can rarely provide all the product knowledge you need to sell effectively. Products keep changing frequently, so you must constantly update yourself.

SOURCES OF PRODUCT KNOWLEDGE

Brochures

Most tourism products and services are described in text and pictures in a brochure for prospective clients. Some brochures include a tariff (prices accompanied by regulations applying to various rates). These regulations will usually include restrictions regarding dates that specific fares can be used, and penalties for cancellation or changes. Sometimes the tariffs are not included in the brochure but are printed on a separate sheet that can be inserted into the brochure. The advantage of this approach for the company is that the brochure does not have to be reprinted every time the prices change.

Other times the company produces a **confidential tariff** for the use of the salesperson only, and not the customer. It is for the use of the salesperson only for one of two reasons. First, it might be complex and only understood by a trained professional. Second, it might be a **net tariff** to which a markup must be added to cover the seller's costs plus an allowance for profit.

In the tourism industry, selling prices were fixed traditionally and all customers paid the same price, regardless of where they purchased the product. Today, more and more companies are using **net rates**. These are the rates the seller pays to the supplier. The seller must add a markup to cover **overhead** (company costs) plus a **profit margin**. With net tariffs, the customer does not get to see what the seller has to pay the **principal** (the company providing the goods or service).

The salesperson must thoroughly study the brochure and tariff as soon as it comes into the office. If time is not available during office hours, it will be necessary to take it home to study it closely. Highlight or underline key selling points. Do the same for important regulations or restrictions regarding special prices. Compare the new brochure and tariff with the previous one to note changes. These could include price changes, new products, new destinations, or the use of different hotels or other accommodations. Discard the old brochures as soon as they are out of date. If you have not received the new one, order it. Retain one **office copy** or **desk copy** until the new ones arrive.

For the new salesperson, it is highly unlikely that you will have enough time in the office to study all the brochures you need to sell. Divide the product into reasonable numbers and take some home each evening to study. It would be wise to start with the products you are expected to sell most frequently.

Customers

Customers are your best source of product knowledge. In most cases, their information is right up-to-date, and of course, it is from the customer's point of view. The follow-up stage of the sales process should always be used to fill in the gaps of your product knowledge. Any time you think of a question you would like answered by a customer returning from a destination that you want to learn about, write it down so that you will not forget to ask it. Careful notes should be taken of customer's comments and filed with your destination sales kit.

In some cases, you may call extremely good customers who have been to a destination recently to obtain background information. It is advised that you do this for customers who are very close to you and considered friends as well as customers. Always ask if they mind your inquiry.

Sometimes tourism companies do not sell directly to the tourist but only through travel agents. In this case, they should make a deliberate effort to obtain feedback from the travel agents. If they are also the providers of the service, they should obtain customer feedback while the customer is using their services.

Global Distribution Systems

For travel agents, airline employees, and others working in the transportation sector, the most valuable source of product knowledge is the **computer reservations system (CRS)**. Recently, the terminology is changing to GDS, standing for Global Distribution System. Virtually everything available in printed form can be retrieved from the GDS.

Not limited to the airline schedules and tariffs, it has a plethora of tourism information including:

- general information on destinations
- documentation necessary for travel to and from foreign countries
- health measures required and recommended for international travel
- surface transportation including automobile rentals and rail.
- climate
- maps of major cities, countries, and regions

Airlines have also concluded contracts with cruise lines, hotels and other accommodation suppliers, automobile rental companies, and tour operators, which are also hosted in their global distribution systems. Some tourism companies may have their own computerized reservation system, but it probably would not contain as much information as those of the large airlines.

The four leaders in central reservations systems are Galileo, Sabre, Amadeus, and Worldspan. To inquire about being online with these systems, contact:

Within the USA	**Within Canada**
Galileo International	Galileo Canada Distribution
9700 West Higgins Road	Systems Inc.
Rosemont, IL 60018	330 Front Street West
Phone: 847-518-4000	Toronto, ON M5V 3B7
Web site: <http://www.galileo.com>	Phone: 800-655-7115
Sabre	Sabre
4255 Amon Carter Blvd.	5001 Yonge Street
Mail Drop 4203	Suite 1504
Fort Worth, TX 76155	North York, ON M2N 6P6
Phone: 817-963-8373	Phone: 416-218-5445
Web site: <http://www.sabre.com>	
Worldspan	Worldspan
300 Galleria Parkway NW	5925 Airport Road, Suite 400
Atlanta, GA 30339	Mississaga, ON L4V 1W1
Phone: 770-563-7400	Phone: 877-953-7726
Fax: 770-563-7004	Fax: 905-676-0776
E-mail: info@worldspan.com	
Web site: <http://www.worldspan.com>	

Amadeus Global Travel Distribution
9250 N.W. 36th St.
Miami, FL 33178
Phone: (305)499-6000
Web site: <http://www.amadeus.net>

If your company or organization does not have access to a comprehensive reservation system but you do regular business with either a travel agency, airline, or other online company, they will provide you with the information from the global distribution system. However, it would be unfair to continually request information from their GDS unless you provide them with a substantial amount of business.

Trade Reference Manuals

Major sectors of the tourism business have trade reference manuals for the use of colleagues in the industry. If you need the information they contain on a frequent basis, you should purchase them. If you require information from them infrequently, you may be able to obtain the information from a colleague who uses them regularly.

Trade manuals use consistent formats and terminology, which make them easy to comprehend by professionals in the industry.

Airline References

The *Official Airline Guide*

Usually referred to in the industry as the *OAG*, the *Official Airline Guide* is the most complete schedule of flights. The *OAG* is published in two principal volumes. The North American Edition is published every two weeks. It provides schedules for flights within and between the USA and Canada, including Hawaii and Alaska. It also includes flights to and from the USA and Canada, the Caribbean islands, Mexico, Bahamas, and Bermuda.

Flights between all other destinations are published monthly in the WorldWide Edition of the *OAG*. There is also a Pocket Flight Guide edition, which is primarily used by frequent fliers. The Pocket Flight Guide comes in four volumes: the North American Edition, the Europe/Africa/Middle East Edition, the Pacific/Asia Edition, and the Latin American/Caribbean Edition.

Both the North American Edition and the WorldWide Editions of the *OAG* are available on diskettes and CD-ROM, and they can be installed on a network file server, which should be useful to teaching and training institutions. To order the *OAG*, contact:

Official Airline Guide
P.O. Box 56742 (for the North American Edition)
P.O. Box 57519 (for the WorldWide Edition)
Boulder, CO 80321-1703
Phone: 800-323-3537
Fax: 630-574-6565 or 630-574-6568

For most tourism companies, it is useful to obtain system time-tables from the airlines that serve their regions. Airline sales representatives can provide the information required for special fares to be used with packages and groups.

Passenger Air Tariff

Passenger Air Tariff is the principal source for international air tariffs, rules, and routings. It is a joint publication of IATA (The International Air Transport Association) and SITA. To order *Passenger Air Tariff*, contact:

Passenger Air Tariff
Clock Tower Road
Isleworth, Middlesex
United Kingdom
TW7 6DT
Phone: 44-181-232-3640
Fax: 44-181-232-3538

Cruise References

The CLIA Cruise Manual

The *CLIA Cruise Manual* is an excellent reference book for information on members of the Cruise Lines International Association (CLIA). CLIA is a trade association of almost all cruise lines in the world. This annual publication includes port maps, deck plans of ships, sample menus, and activity programs. If you wish to purchase this publication, contact:

CLIA Cruise Manual
Cruise Lines International Association
500 Fifth Avenue – Suite 1407
New York, NY 10110
Phone: 212-921-0066
Fax: 212-921-0549
Web site: <http://www.cruising.org>

The *OAG Cruise and Ferry Guide*

The *OAG Cruise and Ferry Guide* lists cruises by departure dates and types of cruises, including ocean cruises, river cruises, yacht and schooner cruises, cargo ships that also carry passengers, and ferries. To order the *OAG Cruise and Ferry Guide,* contact:

> *OAG Cruise and Ferry Guide*
> 2000 Clearwater Drive
> Oak Brook, IL 60523
> Phone: 800-323-3537, extension 6406
> Fax: 630-574-6568
> You may order online at: <http://www.oag.com>

The *Official Steamship Guide*

The *Official Steamship Guide* lists cruises by geographic region and sailing dates. It also has a separate section for point-to-point sailings. To order this publication, contact:

> *Official Steamship Guide*
> 911 Crosspark Drive
> Suite D-247
> Knoxville, TN 37923
> Phone: 800-783-4903 or 423-531-0392

The *Official Cruise Guide*

The *Official Cruise Guide* provides a background of cruise lines and portrays a description of the ships, including schedules, deck plans, and maps of the ports of call. To order this publication, contact:

> *Official Cruise Guide*
> c/o Cahners Travel Group
> P. O. Box 10709
> Riverton, NJ 08076
> Phone: 800-360-0015
> Fax: 856-786-8203

Ford's *International Cruise Guide*

In addition to normal cruises, *Ford's Guide* lists freighters, which also carry passengers. Contact:

> Ford's Freighter Travel
> 19448 Londelius Street
> North Ridge, CA 91324
> Phone: 818-701-7414

Thomas Cook European Timetable

Thomas Cook European Timetable is usually considered to be a railroad reference, but it also lists shipping services in the English Channel, the North Sea, the Baltic, and the Mediterranean. Ferry services and their links to train services are also listed. It is issued monthly. It can be ordered from:

> Forsyth Travel Library, Inc.
> 44 South Broadway, 11th Floor
> White Plains, NY 10601
> Phone: 800-367-7984
> Fax: 914-681-7251
> Web site: <http://www.forsyth.com>

Star Service, The Critical Guide to Hotels and Cruise Ships

The *Star Service, The Critical Guide to Hotels and Cruise Ships* is listed later under "Hotel and Accommodation References," but it also includes useful evaluations of cruise ships. To order the *Star Service*, contact:

> *Star Service, The Critical Guide to Hotels and Cruise Ships*
> c/o Northstar Travel Media
> 101 West 6th Street, Suite 350
> Austin, TX 78701
> Phone: 201-902-1784
> Fax: 201-902-1916
> Web site: <http://www.starserviceonline.com>

Cruise Travel

For current news in the cruise industry, refer to *Cruise Travel*, a magazine that is published six times a year. To order a subscription, contact:

> *Cruise Travel* Magazine
> Subscriptions Office
> 990 Grove Street
> Evanston, IL 60201
> Phone: 847-491-6440
> Web site: <http://www.cruisetravelmag.com>

Rail References

Thomas Cook European Timetable and Thomas Cook Overseas Timetable

Thomas Cook European Timetable contains timetables and general information for rail services within Europe and Russia (including both the European and Asiatic regions). It is published monthly.

Thomas Cook Overseas Timetable contains timetables and general information for rail services in other parts of the world including the USA and Canada.

To order these publications, contact:

Forsyth Travel Library, Inc.
44 South Broadway, 11th Floor
White Plains, NY 10601
Phone: 800-367-7984
Fax: 914-681-7251
Web site: <http://www.forsyth.com>

Motor Coach Reference

Russell's Official National Motor Coach Guide

Russell's Official National Motor Coach Guide is the standard reference guide for the USA and Canada. It can be ordered from:

Russell's Guides, Inc.
P.O. Box 278
Cedar Rapids, IA 52406
Phone: 319-364-6138
Fax: 319-365-8728
Web site: <http://www.russellsprinting.com>

Information for International Travelers

The Travel Information Manual

Often referred to as "the *TIM,*" the *Travel Information Manual* is owned by a consortium of 14 international airlines and managed by IATA Netherlands Data Publishing. For people working in either outgoing or incoming international tourism, this book can be one of the most useful sources of information regarding regulations and procedures for passports, visas, health regulations, customs, and currency restrictions. Purchase of outdated copies is possible at special prices for training purposes. To order a subscription, contact:

Travel Information Manual (TIM)
Subscriptions Dept.
P.O. Box 49
1170 AA Badhoevedorp
The Netherlands, Europe
Phone: 31-(0)20-403-7923
Fax: 31-(0)20-403-7978
E-mail: lentinga@iata.org

Hotel and Accommodations References

There are many hotel and accommodations references available. Most companies and organizations within the tourism industry would need more than one.

Official Hotel Guide

The *Official Hotel Guide (OHG)* is probably the most useful reference guide. It contains detailed descriptions of more than 30,000 hotels and resorts in about 200 countries and territories. To order the *Official Hotel Guide*, contact:

> *Official Hotel Guide*
> c/o Northstar Travel Media
> 101 West 6th Street, Suite 350
> Austin, TX 78701
> Phone: 201-902-1784
> Fax: 201-902-1916
> Web site: <http://www.starserviceonline.com>

Hotel and Travel Index

Hotel and Travel Index is the most extensive publication in the industry. It lists over 45,000 hotels and resorts in about 200 countries, but it does not include as much detail as the *Official Hotel Guide*.

To order the *Hotel and Travel Index*, contact:

> *Hotel and Travel Index*
> c/o Northstar Travel Media
> 101 West 6th Street, Suite 350
> Austin, TX 78701
> Phone: 201-902-1784
> Fax: 201-902-1916
> Web site: <http://www.starserviceonline.com>

OAG Travel Planners

OAG Travel Planners include reservation phone numbers, major airport diagrams, and city center maps. It comes in three editions:

The *Business Travel Planner for North America* includes the USA, Canada, Mexico, and the Caribbean; the *European Edition*; and the *Pacific Asia Edition*.

To order these publications, contact:

> *Official Airline Guides*
> P.O. Box 55665 (for the North American Edition)
> P.O. Box 58108 (for the European Edition)

P.O. Box 58272 (for the Pacific Asia Edition)
Boulder, CO 80321-1703
Phone: 800-323-3537
Fax: 630-574-6565

Star Service

Star Service describes approximately 10,000 properties throughout the world, which is considerably fewer than either the *Official Hotel Guide* or the *Hotel and Travel Index*, but it provides more detailed evaluations of each property. The *Star Service* also includes evaluations of ships. To order the *Star Service*, contact:

Star Service, The Critical Guide to Hotels and Cruise Ships
c/o Northstar Travel Media
101 West 6th Street, Suite 350
Austin, TX 78701
Phone: 201-902-1784
Fax: 201-902-1916
Web site: <http://www.starserviceonline.com>

Caribbean Gold Book

The *Caribbean Gold Book* has listings of accommodations in the Caribbean countries plus the Bahamas, Turks and Caicos Islands, and Bermuda. To order a copy, contact:

Caribbean Gold Book
Caribbean Publishing Co.
2655 Lejune Road
Suite 910
Coral Gables, FL 33134
Phone: 305-443-5900
Fax: 305-569-0431
Web site: <http://www.caribbeantravel.com>

Tour References

Official Tour Directory

To obtain the *Official Tour Directory*, contact:

Official Tour Directory
Thomas Publishing Company Inc.
Five Penn Plaza
New York, NY 10001
Phone: 212-629-2175

Master-Key

Master-Key is a confidential tariff produced by the World Association of Travel Agencies. It contains national tourist information, tariffs for various tour services, meeting and assistance, transfers, hotel listings, and details of WATA membership and procedures. *Master-Key* was published for over 30 years in book form and is now available on the Internet. To order the *Master-Key*, contact:

World Association of Travel Agencies
14 Rue Ferrier
1202 Geneva, Switzerland, Europe
Phone: 022-731-47-60
Fax: 022-732-81-61
E-mail: wata@wata.net
Web site: <http://www.wata.net>

COPING WHEN PRODUCT KNOWLEDGE IS INADEQUATE

If a customer asks a question for which you do not have an answer, there are two golden rules:

Rule 1: Never try to fake it. If you fabricate an answer, you are bound to be caught sooner or later, and you will lose all credibility with the "former prospect."

Rule 2: Do not be embarrassed. Nobody knows the answers to every question that a prospect can ask. Acknowledge that you do not have the answer at hand, but exude an air of confidence that you will obtain the information requested. Be sure to give yourself enough time to obtain the information allowing for unexpected problems.

The time it will take to determine the answer to your client's question will depend upon whether the answer will be found within your office or from an outside resource. Another important factor is whether you know where the answer can be found or if you will have to embark on a **blind search**.

A blind search is when you are searching for information for a customer and you do not know where to start your search. Start with your coworkers in your office. If they do not know, ask your supervisors. If they do not have the answers, contact your friends and colleagues in other companies or industry organizations.

Regardless of the situation, you can have confidence in one thing. You do not work in a vacuum. There are many resources available to find the answer to your query. These resources can be classified into three categories: library resources, people resources, and the Internet.

Library resources would include all the trade references described previously plus books and articles about the destination. People resources would include coworkers in your office, your supervisors, tourist boards, the principals, friends and colleagues working for other companies within the industry, and especially customers who are knowledgeable about the destination.

With diligence, you can find the answer to any question a client may pose. If you promise to find out some information for a customer, make sure that you do so. Also make sure that you get the information to the customer within the time frame that you have specified.

If the search becomes more complicated than you first expected and you do not have the search completed by your stipulated time, contact the customer. Inform him or her of the problems you have encountered, provide information that you have received to date, and give your best estimate of when you will have the remainder of the information requested. Failure to get back to customers with requested information is one of the pre-eminent complaints of consumers in the tourism market.

Discussion Questions

1. Why do you think product knowledge is essential to establishing credibility with a prospect?

2. Explain how effective qualifying can enable you to match what you know about your customer with what you know about your product or service to make a recommendation that will meet your client's needs.

3. What can we learn from our customers?

4. In which publication can you find a wide variety of tours to different destinations and special events? If you were a local tour operator, why would it be important for your tours to be listed in this publication?

5. What are the two golden rules when you do not know the answers to a client's question?

6. If you do not have the answer to a client's question, what are the three principal types of sources for answers?

CHAPTER 5

Answering Questions, Recommending a Product or Service, and Creating Acceptance

OBJECTIVES

After studying this chapter, you should be able to:

- Explain why it is important for you to complete the qualifying process before answering all of the prospect's questions

- Explain why it is important not to give too much information at this point in the sales process

- Offer products or services that will satisfy the prospect's needs and wants

- Offer conclusive proof that your proposal will satisfy the prospect's needs and wants

- Use the reservations computer, brochure, or tariff to demonstrate the economic value of your recommendation

KEY TERMS

all-inclusive	favor	economic value
frequent flyer program	testimonial	cost comparison
novelty	benefits	

STEP 4: ANSWERING THE CLIENT'S QUESTIONS

Most prospects approach a tourism office just for "some information." They usually do not have it on their minds that they are going to buy something. Early in the dialogue, the client will usually ask a number of questions. You may be able to answer some of these questions during the qualifying process, but you should never answer two questions without asking one.

If the customer obtains all the information he or she requires before you complete the qualifying process, chances are you will never have a chance to close the sale. Explain to the prospects that you can't provide accurate information before you know more precisely where and when they want to travel. This will provide you with the opportunity to obtain all the information that you need to make a recommendation and to proceed toward a booking. In other words, complete the qualifying process before answering all your client's questions. Once you have a clear idea of the prospect's travel requirements, you are in a position to answer his or her questions accurately. However, do not get engulfed in minute details at this point because you might be wasting your time giving too much information and confusing the client.

- You might be providing a lot of information about a package or destination that might not even be available.
- The detailed information you could be giving might not be correct for the travel arrangements that the customer eventually books.

Answer the essential questions at this stage, but save the details until both you and the customer know for sure that he or she is going to the tourist destination that you have been discussing. Details that the customer will need if he or she is really going to the tourist destination should be discussed later.

STEP 5: RECOMMENDING A PRODUCT OR SERVICE THAT WILL MEET YOUR CLIENT'S NEEDS

To offer products or services that satisfy the prospects needs and wants, you must be a good listener. Offer products that satisfy the prospect's needs and wants. Use the prospect's own statements to show that your proposal meets his or her needs.

Your recommendation should match the client's wants and needs as determined in the qualifying process. The "where," "when," "how long," and "how many" should be straightforward.

If you feel confident that you know exactly which product or service will meet your client's needs, recommend it! If you are not quite sure which one will best meet your customer's needs, give him or her a choice of two. (See Figure 5-1.) Never offer more than two products at a time because it may confuse people. If there are multiple choices, one will usually have to go home to read more about the choices, and think about it instead of making a buying decision.

A prospect went to a travel agency recently, to see whether it would be possible to make a booking for a deluxe (best available) **all-inclusive** vacation in Jamaica for the next Saturday. He was given three brochures and a list of 20 different properties. It was the following Wednesday before he was able to read and digest all this material. He never did go. If he were presented with a clear option between two choices that met his expectations (needs), he would probably have decided on the spot.

Business Travel

If the purpose of travel is business, you should choose accommodations according to the following criteria:

1. A location that is convenient to where the business will be conducted.

FIGURE 5-1

A choice of two.

2. A property that has a business center with the facilities that a businessperson requires, including on-line computer hook-ups, Internet access, facsimile services, e-mail, photocopy service, and secretarial services.

3. If the client is a member of a **frequent flier program**, he or she may prefer a hotel that will offer points towards future travel.

STEP 6: CREATING ACCEPTANCE

Offer conclusive proof by clearly demonstrating that the benefits of your recommendation will satisfy your client's desires to visit the tourist destination that you are discussing. Pictures are more credible than words. They can clearly demonstrate the splendor of the scenery and attractions. (See Figure 5-2, for example.) Pictures can show how much fun people are having while attending a special event or participating in an activity. Pictures can also show how spectacular a sporting event can be.

Testimonials are particularly useful and should be used much more in the tourism business. They are direct statements from the customer's point of view. They provide credibility for the product or service that you are recommending. If a customer compliments either your recommendations or your service, thank him or her sincerely.

FIGURE 5-2
Lake Louise, Banff National Park, Alberta, Canada.

Ask if you may have permission to use the statement as an endorsement. You can take the statement down verbatim or even better persuade the customer to write it down in his or her own handwriting.

Twillingate Island Boat Tours uses the following testimonial by travel writer Percy Rowe of the *Toronto Sun* in their brochure. "Not only is Twillingate noted for its numerous icebergs, it boasts one of Canada's most beautiful coastlines. Chase the pavement to the end, I was told, and you will come to Twillingate. It may as well have been chase the rainbow, because on this summer day Twillingate was a fairy-mix of land and sea."

One technique that is particularly useful is asking clients if they would mind sending you a postcard from the destination. If you ask, they will usually send one. If you do not ask, you will be lucky to receive a postcard from 1 out of 50 to 100 clients. A positive response is enhanced if you make your request at the time of presenting the client with a **novelty** or **favor** like a bottle of champagne or some other gift when you give them their tickets. The postcard not only gives you a picture to add to your sales file for the destination, but it also gives you a **testimonial**. It is wise to ask your client's permission to use the postcard as a testimonial. (See Figure 5-3.)

Usually the client will comment only about the best features of the tourist destination that he or she is visiting. If the customer complains about something that was not up to expectations, it provides you with a head start at resolving the problem before he or she returns.

The experiences of others can be used even if you do not have permission to use direct statements as testimonials. But be sure not to attribute the statement to a particular client. For example, "I have had many clients who have stated that Universal Studios is the most fascinating attraction in California." If you could add specific statements by particular individuals, this would be even more effective.

Personal Experience

Personal experience, if used appropriately, can help you to establish credibility. It can be used to establish that you are very knowledgeable about the destination. Tour companies and destinations go to considerable expense and effort to educate travel agents about their products and destinations because they know from experience that travel agents will sell at least three times as much of a product with which they are thoroughly familiar.

Details on how problems can be avoided or best dealt with at a destination also help establish credibility with your personal experience. For example, a travel agent was in Hong Kong recently and she learned that it cost a $12.00 service charge to cash one traveler's

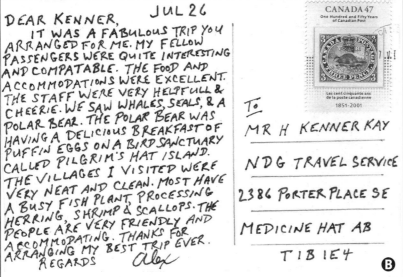

FIGURE 5-3

Ask clients to send you a postcard. (A) Front of postcard (Iceberg Alley); (B) Back of postcard (testimonial).

cheque. The interest for a cash advance on a credit card was much less. Her advice for her clients would be to deposit a positive balance in a credit card account and take out cash advances as you need them and pay no interest or service charge. This advice from her personal experience would certainly give a client confidence in the salesperson's knowledge.

Other examples could include special restaurants, nightclubs, attractions, and activities not included in brochures. A personal description of the Goldener Adler Hotel and Restaurant in Innsbruck would certainly heighten a client's desire to visit Austria. The Goldener Adler means Golden Eagle in English. Founded in 1390, it is "known far and wide in other countries as the travelling quarters of princely blood and noble spirits. . . . Many a crowned head has slept peacefully there. In February 1573 Archduke Ferdinand II organized in Innsbruck a shooting match open to all comers, and to this tourney countless great ones were invited. Duke Albert V of Bavaria and his son came with a train of 416 people and 580 horses."[1] Goethe, Germany's most famous author, was a frequent guest of the Goldener Adler. The Goethe-Stube (Goethe-Room Restaurant and Bar) is named after this notable guest. The most visible change in the last 610 years is that they have converted the stable into another bar and restaurant. At the Goldener Adler you can enjoy live zither music with your gastronomic Tirolean delights. Your personal description, supplemented by quotations, testimonials, postcards, and personal photographs would be irresistible.

Similarly, a personal description of the Lido nightclub show, arguably the best in the world, in Paris, would certainly help close a sale for a trip to France.

A travel counselor used her personal experiences at Parque Laguna de Chankanaab and Playa San Francisco to help close a number of sales to Cozumel, Mexico. Parque Laguna de Chankanaab is connected with Chankanaab Bay by a subterranean channel. "The lagoon, sheltered bay, and offshore Yukab Reef all provide sanctuary for a fascinating diversity of marine life, including coral, sponges, crustaceans, turtles, moray eels, and tropical fish. A sunken boat, a religious statue, and encrusted anchors and cannons in the bay are popular with divers and snorkelers."[2]

To this description add your personal experience of beautiful fish eating out of your hand and the hundreds of colorful fish swimming within 12 to 18 inches from you—just enough to give you and them personal space. Your personal experience combined with the quotation should convince any diver or scuba diver that this is the place to go. Of course, personal photos, postcards, and testimonials will enhance your ability to close this sale.

In the qualifying process, you determined whether the client preferred to be alone or to meet people. If you are not sure what to recommend on this continuum, you could contact a colleague who has been to the destination, another customer who has been there recently, the tourist board, or a knowledgeable person from a tour company servicing the destination.

Also in the qualifying process you ascertained where the customer fit on the relaxation or excitement continuum. If you are not sure what to recommend regarding this continuum, follow the same advice just given. Contact a colleague, knowledgeable customer, tourist board, or contacts at tour companies.

Recommending Accommodations

Keep a file for each destination, including unique accommodations and others to be recommended for various reasons. Be sure to have at least one recommendation in the best available, moderate, and budget categories plus a recommended airport location. Include photos, testimonials, and notes regarding why you would recommend it. This will be your preferred supplier list. When selecting your preferred suppliers, there are a number of considerations:

- amount of commission
- timely and efficient payment of commissions
- client satisfaction with the property
- location
- value for money paid
- unique qualities found only at this location

Quality of Tours

As with accommodations, keep a file of recommended tours to each destination. Include those that would be of interest to people with special interests. As with accommodations, include photos, testimonials, postcards, and notes why you would recommend it. Obtain copies of the hotel brochures for properties used in tours. Hotel brochures contain a lot more information and photographs of properties than tour brochures and can often aid in closing a sale or convincing a customer to upgrade.

Concern for Safety

Keep a file of safety statistics and articles about the safety records of your company and your suppliers. As members of the tourism industry, we know that commercial airline travel is the safest way to travel. But, if there is an air disaster anywhere, it is front-page news around the world. It can seriously affect business, particularly for the carrier involved, even if the airline's lifetime safety record has been exemplary. Obviously, terrorist attacks around the world have impacted public consciousness. Similarly, tourists being stranded in a foreign country by a bankrupt tour company or people losing their money because of an insolvent tour company gain instant notoriety. Tourists react with a hesitancy to book a packaged tour.

Tour companies that are members of the United States Tour Operators Association (USTOA) are required to post a $1,000,000 bond to protect consumers. (See Figure 5-4.) Use this to assure your customers that their money is safe. Why would you recommend any

FIGURE 5-4

$1 million USTOA consumer protection. *(Courtesy of the United States Tour Operators Association)*

$1 Million Consumer Protection

The Standard For Confident Travel

O*ver the years, you have no doubt experienced memorable and pleasurable vacations, as a result of purchasing tours or vacation packages. The vast majority of companies operating tours and packages are financially stable. However, in recent years, bankruptcies involving a small number of tour operators have caused concern among the traveling public.*

Recognizing the need to provide travelers with a solid financial safety net that protects their investment in a vacation package, the United States Tour Operators Association has implemented a $1 Million Consumer Protection Plan. A part of USTOA's Financial Security Program, this plan has been carefully designed to protect the consumer, and demonstrates the commitment of each of our Active Member companies to financial integrity and stability.

Robert E. Whitley
President, USTOA

About USTOA

The United States Tour Operators Association (USTOA), founded in 1972, is a professional organization representing the tour operator industry. USTOA's Active Members, whose tours encompass the entire globe, are among the world's leading tour operators. To become an Active Member of USTOA, a tour operator is required to have a total of 18 references from a variety of industry sources and financial institutions, and must meet specific minimums in terms of tour passengers and/or dollar volume. The company must also be in business at least three years under the same management in the U.S., carry a minimum of $1,000,000 professional liability insurance, and participate in USTOA's $1 Million Consumer Protection Plan.

So, when you see the USTOA logo with the emblem identifying the $1 Million Consumer Protection Plan, you can be confident that it represents a financially stable company and a standard by which to measure the security of your travel investment.

company that was not a member of the USTOA unless it could prove that it had equivalent consumer protection?

In Canada, the provinces of British Columbia, Ontario, and Québec have licensing laws, which require bonding. In other provinces and territories, it is important to determine whether your client's funds are protected when you forward them to a tour operator. If your supplier is bonded, use this to assure your clients that their funds are safe.

 A prime goal of USTOA is to help protect you, the consumer, against loss arising from bankruptcy or insolvency of an Active Member tour operator. USTOA's $1 Million Consumer Protection Plan was designed to ensure the financial strength and stability of each Active Member company, and demonstrates a firm commitment to protecting consumers.

The $1 Million Consumer Protection Plan requires each USTOA Active Member company to post $1 million in security, in the form of a bond, letter of credit or certificate of deposit. The security, to be held by USTOA, is solely for use in reimbursing customers for tour payments or deposits lost in the event of:

- A USTOA Active Member bankruptcy;
- A USTOA Active Member insolvency;
- Failure of a USTOA Active Member company to refund consumer deposits or payments within 120 days following the cancellation of a tour(s) or vacation package(s), or the material failure to complete performance of a tour(s) or vacation package(s).

How Does The $1 Million Plan Work?

Q: What is covered?
A: The plan protects consumers from loss of deposits and payments for tours or vacation packages in the event of a USTOA Active Member bankruptcy or insolvency, or the material failure to complete performance of tour(s) or vacation package(s).

Q: When can I file a claim?
A: A claim can be filed when a tour operator declares bankruptcy or is insolvent, or 120 days following the failure of a tour operator to refund a payment or deposit after a material failure to complete performance of a tour(s) or vacation package(s). The plan covers tours or vacation packages purchased up to seven days following official notification to USTOA of an Active Member's bankruptcy or insolvency.

Q: What are the rights of credit card companies under the plan?
A: Credit card companies that have honored chargeback claims from consumers who would have been eligible to file claims under the Plan will be entitled to reimbursements from the Plan for the chargeback.

Q: If I decide to cancel, does the $1 Million Consumer Protection Plan cover me?
A: No. Individual trip cancellation insurance is available, and may be obtained through your travel agent or tour operator.

Q: What if I've already paid for a tour or vacation package in advance, and the tour operator goes bankrupt before the scheduled departure date?
A: You are covered within the limits of the coverage as long as your payment or deposit was made within seven days following notification to USTOA of the bankruptcy or insolvency.

Q: Is there an extra charge for this coverage?
A: No. Each time you travel with a USTOA Active Member company, your deposits and payments for tours and vacation packages are automatically protected up to the limits of the coverage at no extra charge.

Q: How is a claim made?
A: Claim forms can be obtained from USTOA's office at 342 Madison Avenue, Suite 1522, New York, NY 10173, or by calling the association at (212) 599-6599, or e-mail: ustoa@aol.com.

Q: Is there a deadline for filing claims?
A: Yes. Claims must be filed no later than ninety (90) days after the bankruptcy, insolvency or failure to refund on account of nonperformance, as the case may be.

Q: Who will reimburse me?
A: Reimbursements will be made through USTOA.

Your Travel Agent

USTOA's Active Member companies offer a wide array of tours and vacation packages, all sold through travel agents. An experienced, professional travel agent can help you select the tour or vacation package that's best suited to your requirements, and that will give you the best value for your travel dollar.

Further information on USTOA and its Active Members can be obtained by writing to:
UNITED STATES TOUR OPERATORS ASSOCIATION
342 Madison Avenue, Suite 1522, New York, NY 10173
(212) 599-6599 • Fax: (212) 599-6744
E-mail: ustoa@aol.com • Web site: www.ustoa.com

FIGURE 5-4
(concluded)

Something Familiar or Something Different

Testimonials will be most influential for either end of this continuum. Photographs would also be invaluable.

Compare the two products offered under the following headings: Inclusions and exclusions of each.

Point out the advantages and disadvantages of each, emphasizing the **benefits**. Don't say, "You get what you pay for!" It is derogatory and makes the customer feel foolish. Instead, take the positive approach, pointing out the benefits, including the value of the higher priced item. If a form like the Comparative Analysis For Tours, Figure 5-5, was prepared as a template on computer software, the sections for Features, Sight-seeing Tours, Itinerary/Accommodations, and Comments would expand for the number included for any particular tour.

After studying a number of tours of the California Coast, I decided that I would recommend two in the best available category. The two that I decided I would sell were Collette Tours, *"California Coast,"* and Globus Tours, *"California Coast Vacation."* How did I decide on these two tours to recommend in the best available category for this destination? Both were high-quality tours in the best available category based on their inclusions and accommodations. Both tours covered more or less the same territory in the same time frame.

As with most tours, they promote their tours by the number of days on the tour. But for cost comparison, it is better to calculate the cost per diem by dividing the total price by the number of nights, because the cost of accommodations is usually the most significant factor in costing a tour. Also, the last day of a tour usually does not include anything except possibly breakfast and probably transfers. Therefore, it is more meaningful to compare the number of nights than the number of days, particularly when you are comparing prices.

Although these two tours are very similar there are some significant differences, which I clarified in the Comments section. (See Figure 5-6.) The Globus tour is $90.00 more than the Collette tour, which I would express as $11.25 per night or 5 percent to de-emphasize the price difference. Also if you were trying to sell the Globus tour you could stress that it includes three more meals, three boat cruises, and excellent hotels making it good value for ". . . only $11.25 more." On the other hand, if you were trying to close the sale with the Collette tour, you would emphasize that it is $90.00 less expensive and includes Yosemite National Park and Capistrano. Also, for Hollywood fans, Mann's Chinese Theatre and the Stars Walk of Fame would probably be decisive features for the Collette package.

Your insertions into the Comments section would summarize the points that will probably decide which tour the customer will choose.

COMPARATIVE ANALYSIS FOR TOURS

DESTINATION: _____   QUALITY: _____

Co. _____ _____   Co. _____ _____

No. of nights: _____   _____

FEATURES:

_____   _____

_____   _____

MEALS INCLUDED:

    BREAKFASTS _____   _____

    LUNCHES _____   _____

    DINNERS _____   _____

SIGHT-SEEING TOURS:

_____   _____

_____   _____

ITINERARY/ACCOMMODATIONS:

_____   _____

_____   _____

_____   _____

_____   _____

COST/PERSON FOR (DATE): _____

$ _____ $ _____

COST/DIEM: $ _____ $ _____

COMMENTS: _____   _____

_____   _____

_____   _____

_____   _____

_____   _____

FIGURE 5-5   Comparative Analysis For Tours form.

COMPARATIVE ANALYSIS FOR TOURS

DESTINATION: California Coast   QUALITY: Best Available

Co. 1. Collette's California Coast Tour   Co. 2. Globus's California Vacation Tour

No. of nights: 8   8

FEATURES:

Yosemite National Park	Cruise of San Francisco Bay
Mann's Chinese Theatre, LAX	Steam Train — Redwood Country
"Stars Walk of Fame," LAX	Cruise to Catalina Island
Mission San Juan Capistrano	Cruise of San Diego Bay

MEALS INCLUDED:

BREAKFASTS	5	8
LUNCHES	0	1
DINNERS	6	5

SIGHT-SEEING TOURS:

San Francisco	San Francisco
Yosemite National Park	Santa Barbara
Mann's Chinese Theatre, LAX	San Diego
Stars Walk of Fame, LAX	Hearst Castle
17 Mile Drive	17 Mile Drive
Big Sur	Big Sur
San Diego Zoo	

ITINERARY/ACCOMMODATIONS:

San Francisco	San Francisco
Galleria Park/Sir Francis Drake	The Westin St. Francis
Yosemite National Park	
Yosemite Lodges/Tenaya Lodge	
Monterey	Monterey
Casa Munras	Monterey Hyatt Regency
Solvang	Solvang
Danish Country Inn/	Rancho Santa Barbara
Royal Scandinavian Inn	

(continued)

FIGURE 5-6   Comparative analysis of two California Coast tours.

COMPARATIVE ANALYSIS FOR TOURS
(concluded)

ITINERARY/ACCOMMODATIONS *(concluded)*:

Los Angeles	Long Beach
Westin Bonaventure	Renaissance Hotel

Anaheim	
West Coast Hotel	

San Diego	San Diego
US Grant Hotel	Travelodge Harbor Island

COST/PERSON FOR (DATE): JULY 17

$1,719.00	$1,809.00

COST/DIEM: $214.88 $226.13

COMMENTS:
* Yosemite National Park	$90.00 more/$11.25 per day
San Diego Zoo	(approximately 5%)
Capistrano	more meals
Mann's Chinese Theatre	* 3 boat cruises
Stars Walk of Fame	Santa Barbara
	* excellent hotels

* Indicates key feature

FIGURE 5-6   *(concluded)*

Use the reservations computer, brochure, or tariff to demonstrate the **economic value** of your recommendation by showing the cost of your recommendation compared with other possibilities. For anyone who thinks that an airfare quotation is expensive, show them the difference between the promotional fare quoted and the "regular coach or economy fare." Usually, this will convince them that your offer is a good deal. Convince them that if they wait, they may have to pay the higher fare.

For example, if a prospect was discussing travel from New York to Seattle on February 5 (Figure 5-7) returning on February 19, and today is December 30, the line number 1 fare could be used. This fare is $240.00 plus taxes, round trip. The booking must be made at least 21 days prior to travel. The passenger must be staying over a minimum of one Saturday and a maximum of 30 days. Travel must be on a Tuesday or Wednesday. If the passenger waits until January 23, this

```
*$DNYCSEA05FEB^UA                                      *SHORT $D*
**   SEE RULE FOR COMPLETE INFORMATION ON VUSA FARES **
UA         NYC-SEA DEPART 05FEB
                                      (TAXES/FEES NOT INCLUDED)
          USD    FARE         MIN/  XL  TVL DATES    TKT DATES
      CX  FARE   BASIS    AP  MAX   FE  FIRST/LAST   FIRST/LAST
    1 UA  240.00R WOE21NQX 21^ SU/30 ^^    -/-          -/-
    2 UA  277.22R WE21NX   21^ SU/30 ^^    -/-          -/-
    3 UA  314.42R WE14NX   14^ SU/30 ^^    -/-          -/-
    4-UA  349.78R WE14NMSZ 14^ SU/-- ^^ 01SEP/28FEBC    -/-
    5-UA  368.38R WE14NMBZ 14^ SU/-- ^^ 01SEP/28FEBC    -/-
    6 UA  370.24R VE21NX   21^ SU/30 ^^    -/-          -/-
    7 UA  463.26R VE14NX   14" SU/30 ^^    -/-          -/-
    8 UA  241.86  SDGWAJFK --  --/-- --    -/31MARC     -/-
    9 UA  241.86  SDGWALGA --  --/-- --    -/31MARC     -/-
   10 UA  556.28R QE14NX   14^ SU/30 ^^    -/-          -/-
   11 UA  292.00  HCLVUSA  --  --/-- ^^    -/31MARC     -/-
   12 UA  309.00  HCHVUSA  --  --/-- ^^    -/31MARC     -/-
   13 UA  643.72R HOE21NQ  21^ SU/30 ^^    -/-          -/-
   14 UA  340.00  HLVUSA   --  --/-- ^^    -/31MARC     -/-
   15 UA  701.40R HE21NQ   21^ SU/30 ^^    -/-          -/-
   16 UA  360.00  HHVUSA   --  --/-- ^^    -/31MARC     -/-
   17 UA  837.22R MOE14NQ  14^ SU/30 ^^    -/-          -/-
   18 UA  894.88R ME14NQ   14^ SU/30 ^^    -/-          -/-
   19 UA  894.88R ME0MLNQ   ^  SU/30 ^^    -/-          -/-
   20 UA  682.00  BCHVUSA  --  --/-- --    -/31MARC     -/-
   21 UA  702.33  MM       --  --/-- --    -/-          -/-
   22 UA  755.00  BVUSA    --  --/-- --    -/31MARC     -/-
   23 UA 1026.05  BA3      03  --/-- --    -/-          -/-
   24XUA 1081.86  MTSTR    --  --/-- --    -/-          -/-
   25XUA 1109.77  MTGUA    --  --/-- --    -/-          -/-
   26 UA 1109.77  BUA      --  --/-- --    -/-          -/-
   27 UA 1202.79  YUA      --  --/-- --    -/-          -/-
   28 UA 1437.21  Y        --  --/-- --    -/-          -/-
```

FIGURE 5-7

Apollo printout of fares from New York to Seattle for February 5. (*From Apollo Global Distribution System*)

fare would definitely not be available and the customer might have to pay the fare on line 23, $1,026.05 one way or $2,052.10 round trip plus taxes.

The point that most clients do not realize is that not all seats on an aircraft are available at any special promotional fare. As few as 20 seats may be sold at the special "seat sale" price. When these are sold, the passenger must move to a higher fare that could even be the full coach fare, which in this example is listed on line number 28, which is $1,437.21 one way or $2,874.42 round trip plus taxes, more than the promotional fare listed on line number 1. This is almost 1,200% of the special promotional fare. Therefore, the salesperson should always emphasize shortage of space at the promotional fare to help the customer make a buying decision now! Interestingly, I called

United Airlines later the same afternoon as I received the quotation of $240.00 and it was no longer available. If my client had not decided to buy two hours earlier, it would have cost a lot more and perhaps it would now be unaffordable.

Cost Comparison

When trying to convince a prospect that the price of a relatively expensive tour package or Fly-Cruise is a good value for money paid, use a **cost comparison** between the cost of the package and if they did it on their own. (See Figure 5-8.)

A cruise to five international ports of call in five different countries plus the port of embarkation was approximately the same as a one-week stay in one destination. If you added the extra airfare to the five ports of call included on the tour plus the additional transfers, the Fly-Cruise Package would save at least $304.00 over independent travel. Also the cruise ship does most of its traveling at night while you are sleeping. On the other hand, the air flights would be during your prime vacation time. Another factor to consider, if you enjoy wine with a meal or a drink while you are watching entertainment, drinks are about half the price on a ship as they are on land. (In Chapter 6, Figure 6-5, suggestions show how this information can be used to close a sale.)

COST OF SEVEN-DAY CRUISE COMPARED WITH INDEPENDENT TRAVEL

Item	7-Day Cruise	Item	7-Day Independent Tour
Outside Cabin Cat HH	$2,273.00	Share Double or Twin	$1,241.10
Transfers in San Juan	24.00	Transfers Round Trip	20.35
Government Fees and Taxes	45.07	Entertainment	140.00
Air Add-on SEA-SJU	579.00	Airfare SEA-SJU	1,063.50
Taxes and Other Charges		Taxes and Other Charges	38.45
Port Charges	25.00		
Total	$2,946.07	Total for 1 Destination Only	$2,503.40
		Additional Airfare for the Same Itinerary as the Cruise	624.65
		Extra Transfers	122.10
Total for the Air-Sea Package	$2,946.07	Total for Air-Land Tour	$3,250.15

FIGURE 5-8   Air-sea package versus independent travel.

Notes

1. Dr. A. Dreyer, *A Historically Famous Tyrolese Inn* (Osterrechische Alpenpost, no. 5, 1912).

2. *Mexico Travel Book* (Heathrow, FL: AAA Publishing, 2000), 358.

Discussion Questions

1. Why is it important for you to complete the qualifying process before answering all of the prospect's questions?

2. Why is it important to not give too much information before the sale is closed?

3. List five examples of conclusive proof that you could use to convince a prospect to accept a tourism experience that will satisfy his or her needs or wants.

4. Explain how you could use the reservations computer, brochure, or tariff to demonstrate the economic value of your recommendation.

Closing the Sale

OBJECTIVES

After studying this chapter, you should be able to:

● Define the term *closing*

● Define the term *trial close*

● Phrase trial close questions that will confirm the effectiveness of the sales presentation to the present moment, and to move it forward toward closing

● Listen for and be able to identify closing signals

● Describe seven situations when it is not a good time to close

● Describe and use 10 closing techniques

KEY TERMS

trial close	Closing to Resistance Close	option
closing techniques		Assumed Sold Close
Choice Close	Shortage Close	dominant people
I Would Recommend Close	Special Deal Close	dependent people
Summary Close	Option Close	detached people
Minor Points Close	time-limited	decision-maker
T-Account Close	option date	

STEP 7: CLOSING THE SALE

Closing is the process of asking a prospect a question that solicits an answer that gives the sales person consent to complete the sale.

"*Closing* is the climax of a sales presentation. Closing a sale is exciting. Only by closing does a salesperson determine whether all that went into the presentation worked. . . . Closing is a matter of leading prospects to the point of decision."[1]

A **trial close** is a question asked during the early stages of a sales presentation to determine how effective you have been up to that point. Often the trial close is based on a statement that the prospect has made and is asked to confirm that you have understood what he or she has been saying. It also re-enforces a positive sales point you have made.

A very positive reaction to a trial close may indicate that the customer is ready to make a buying decision already. Even if you have barely started to describe the benefits and sales features of an item or service, stop, and close now! A series of positive answers to trial closes will definitely lead to an opportunity to close the deal.

TEN CLOSING SIGNALS

A closing signal is any indication, verbal or nonverbal, indicating that a prospect is ready to make a buying decision.

Look for closing signals and attempt to close whenever you perceive one. *When* you do it can be as important as *how* you do it! Timing is crucial!

1. As mentioned previously, a very positive reaction to a trial close provides you with an opportunity to close the deal earlier than you could have imagined. Close!

2. A lag in the conversation indicates that all the important questions have been answered. Close!

3. Questions about details indicate that the prospect has decided to buy. Close!

4. If the client agrees with your sales points, it indicates that your recommendation is a good one. Close! If you are not sure whether the client concurs with your sales point, ask.

5. If the client asks which one you would recommend, it indicates that he or she is ready to buy but needs a little help in deciding which choice of products or service is better for him or her. So, be helpul! Recommend and state why you recommend the choice you have suggested, then close!

6. If a prospect asks a question about the form of payment, or amount of deposit required, or when payment is due, the prospect has made up his or her mind. Close and collect the payment.

7. Any time the client indicates that he or she understands the value or advantages of your offer, the opportunity is there for you to close!

8. Any compliment regarding the product, service, company, or you personally may signal a closing opportunity. Close!

9. Once an objection has been successfully overcome, close!

10. Nonverbal closing signals like a change in posture, voice, or facial expression can indicate a change in attitude and may be a closing signal. A shift forward in a sitting position may indicate heightened interest. A shift backward in sitting position could indicate relaxation and a decrease in resistance to closing. A smile or affirmative nod may indicate the customer is ready to buy. If a prospect uncrosses his or her arms and the hands are opened, the body language is indicating a more receptive frame of mind. Watch nonverbal signals to help you know when to close!

WHEN NOT TO CLOSE

Sometimes there are signs that indicate that it is not a good time to attempt to close. Seven examples of situations that indicate that it is not the right occasion to close include:

1. when a client fails to respond with a positive response to a trial close

2. immediately after a significant interruption has interfered with the buying mood

3. when you feel that your sales presentation was inadequate or hurried

4. when the client has insufficient information on a complex or technical subject

5. when the prospect has made an objection and the objection has not been countered

6. when the client has asked for more information and the information requested has not been given

7. when the prospect seems hostile or defensive

Have a Clear Idea of What You Have to Sell

For each destination or product that you have for sale, you should have a clear picture in your mind of the choices and quality level of those products, tours, or services that you would recommend. Sell those that meet the clients' wants and needs.

CLOSING TECHNIQUES

Closing techniques are strategies used to bring a customer to a buying decision. The best closing technique to be used depends upon the type of goods or service being sold, the type of customer, the situation, and of course, whether you are comfortable with it. However, you should become skillful with at least a number of closing techniques so that you can adjust to different types of customers and different situations.

Note: If transportation is included in the tourist's arrangements, close the deal on the transportation arrangements first! If the client makes a commitment to book the transportation, he or she is going! You now have the opportunity to sell-up (see Chapter 9) and to create time for yourself to look up further information regarding other details requested. Make an appointment to get back to the client either by telephone or an office appointment to take care of the other details.

There are 10 fundamental closing techniques. The advantage of using descriptive names for each closing technique is that it makes it easier to remember each of the closing techniques, and if one can remember the descriptive name, it will probably provide insight to the details of how to use the closing technique. At the end of the description of each of the 10 closing techniques, there are two examples of how to use each technique.

Using the Ten Closing Techniques

Using the information from Figure 6-1, a Comparative Analysis of Collette's California Coast Tour and Globus's California Vacation, you will see how each of the ten closing techniques can be used. After each example using the California Coast tours, there will be an example of the closing technique using a different sector or subsector of the tourism industry.

The Choice Close

The **Choice Close** is a favorite of many salespeople because it leads a prospect to a buying decision without heavy pressure. The salesperson simply asks a question to determine which of two choices the client prefers. If the client responds positively to either choice, consider the sale closed.

Never offer more than two choices. Too many choices may confuse people, and often they will respond by saying, "I'll have to go home and think about that." And never ask a question to which the

COMPARATIVE ANALYSIS FOR TOURS

DESTINATION: California Coast   QUALITY: Best Available

Co. 1. Collette's California Coast Tour   Co. 2. Globus's California Vacation Tour

No. of nights: 8   8

FEATURES:
   Yosemite National Park   Cruise of San Fransico Bay
   Mann's Chinese Theatre, LAX   Steam Train—Redwood Country
   "Stars Walk of Fame," LAX   Cruise to Catalina Island
   Mission San Juan Capistrano   Cruise of San Diego Bay

MEALS INCLUDED:

   BREAKFASTS   5   8

   LUNCHES   0   1

   DINNERS   6   5

SIGHT-SEEING TOURS:
   San Francisco   San Francisco
   Yosemite National Park   Santa Barbara
   Mann's Chinese Theatre, LAX   San Diego
   Stars Walk of Fame, LAX   Hearst Castle
   17 Mile Drive   17 Mile Drive
   Big Sur   Big Sur
   San Diego Zoo

ITINERARY/ACCOMMODATIONS:
   San Francisco   San Francisco
      Galleria Park/Sir Francis Drake   The Westin St. Francis

   Yosemite National Park
      Yosemite Lodges/Tenaya Lodge

   Monterey   Monterey
      Casa Munras   Monterey Hyatt Regency

   Solvang   Solvang
      Danish Country Inn/   Rancho Santa Barbara
      Royal Scandinavian Inn

(continued)

FIGURE 6-1 Comparative analysis of Collette's California Coast Tour and Globus's California Vacation.

COMPARATIVE ANALYSIS FOR TOURS
(concluded)

ITINERARY/ACCOMMODATIONS *(concluded)*:

Los Angeles	Long Beach
Westin Bonaventure	Renaissance Hotel
Anaheim	
West Coast Hotel	
San Diego	San Diego
US Grant Hotel	Travelodge Harbor Island

COST/PERSON FOR (DATE): JULY 17

$1,719.00 $1,809.00

COST/DIEM: $214.88 $226.13

COMMENTS: The Globus Tour costs $90.00 more/$11.25 per diem or approximately 5% more.
* Yosemite National Park
   San Diego Zoo   more meals
   Capistrano   * 3 boat cruises
   Mann's Chinese Theatre   Santa Barbara
   Stars Walk of Fame   * excellent hotels

* Indicates key feature

FIGURE 6-1   *(concluded)*

client can answer yes or no. Always make it a choice between two alternatives that you can sell.

Situation 1

Mr. and Mrs. Rodgers have been discussing Collette Tours California Coast Tour and Globus Tours California Vacation with you. You discern that either tour would meet the customers' needs and you cannot perceive a distinct advantage for either one. This is an ideal situation to use the Choice Close.

Close: "Mr. and Mrs. Rodgers, both of these tours seem to meet your requests. Which one looks more attractive to you?"

Summary: If the customers express any preference, you have closed the deal. Proceed to book it by either entering the necessary data in the computer or calling the tour operator on the telephone.

New York All Day	Statue of Liberty/Ellis Island Plus Upper and Lower Manhattan
Boat ride to the Statue of Liberty	Boat ride to the Statue of Liberty
Tour of Upper and Lower Manhattan	Tour of Upper and Lower Manhattan
Observation Deck of the Empire State Bldg.	Columbia University
23 miles of touring	20 miles of touring
9½ hours	7 to 8 hours

FIGURE 6-2

Comparison of the "New York All Day" tour and the "Statue of Liberty, Ellis Island, Plus Upper and Lower Manhattan" tour.

Situation 2

You are working for Gray Line of New York City. Mr. Larry Doherty inquires about an all day tour of New York City. You have described two tours to Mr. Doherty (see Figure 6-2). Mr. Doherty seems to be pleased with both tours offered. To him the significant difference is that the New York All Day tour includes a spectacular view from one of New York's skyscrapers, which he has always wanted to see, and the other tour includes Columbia University, from where his mother graduated.

Close: "Well Mr. Doherty, both tours seem to be of interest to you. The only problem is that you would like to see both the view from the Empire State Building and Columbia University. I suggest that you choose the tour that you prefer and take in the other attraction on your own. Which of these two tours would you prefer?"

Summary: The suggestion that Mr. Doherty could see one of the attractions on his own can help clear his mind regarding which tour he would prefer. When he indicates that he would prefer, for example, the New York All Day tour, close the deal and issue the ticket.

The I Would Recommend Close

The **I Would Recommend Close** is the perfect response for the customer who asks which choice you would recommend. These customers have more or less made up their minds to buy and just need a little help to decide which one. So, help them! Recommend one and say why you recommend it. And then, ask for the sale.

Situation 1

Mr. and Mrs. Lehman have been discussing Collette Tours California Coast Tour and Globus Tours California Vacation with you. They seem to be having a difficult time deciding between the two tours, so you help them. Mrs. Lehman has been doing most of the talking, so you present your close to her.

Close: "Both are quality tours, Mrs. Lehman, but the Collette tour may be better for you. You mentioned that you are looking forward to seeing the mountains of California, and the Collette tour includes Yosemite National Park. You also mentioned that you were looking forward to seeing Hollywood, and the Collette tour includes both Mann's Chinese Theatre and 'Stars Walk of Fame.' Would you like me to check whether there is any space available?"

Summary: Go straight to the reservations computer or telephone, determine whether space is available, and book it. It is very unlikely that Mr. and Mrs. Lehman will object at this point, but if they do, see the suggestions in Chapter 8.

Situation 2

You are a reservationist for Best Western Olympus Hotel in Salt Lake City, Utah. Mr. Byron Carson calls up to book two double rooms, one for him and his wife Ann and one for Mr. and Mrs. Martin Warwick. You have quoted a rate of $84.00 per room. But you have also suggested they consider an available two-bedroom suite with a parlor at a rate of $130.00 per night. Mr. Carson seems to have difficulty making up his mind between two separate rooms or the two-bedroom suite. Help him out by recommending!

Close: "Mr. Carson, you would be happy with our regular rooms, but I am sure that you, Mrs. Carson, and the Warwicks would be even more satisfied with our two-bedroom suite. You would have two separate bedrooms plus the parlor, and you would save $38.00 per night."

Summary: At this point, you just pause and wait for Mr. Carson to respond. Then you make the booking according to his reply. Most of the time, the client will accept your recommendation and the sale is closed.

The Summary Close

The **Summary Close** is effective when a prospect has agreed with your sales points or responded positively to a series of trial closes. The most meaningful benefits should be emphasized, using the customer's own words when possible.

Situation 1

Maria and Luis Garcia have been discussing Collette Tours California Coast Tour and Globus Tours California Vacation with you. They seem to be having a difficult time deciding between the two tours, so you help them by summarizing your discussion with them. No concern has been expressed about the cost. Therefore, avoid that issue and concentrate on their needs as expressed when you qualified them.

Close: "I sense that you are having difficulty deciding between these two tours. Both have excellent qualities, but let's review your requests, and perhaps that will make it easier for you to decide."

"Maria, you mentioned that you love boat cruises and the Globus tour has a cruise of San Francisco Bay, a cruise to Catalina Island, and a cruise of San Diego harbor."

"You have both mentioned that you really appreciate excellent accommodations. Both tours have very good accommodations, but I think the Globus tour gets the nod in this category."

"Luis, you mentioned that you are looking for a small- to medium-size city in California with an Hispanic setting. Santa Barbara is the epitome of your search."

"Maria, you really want to see the San Diego Zoo. The Globus tour does not include this, but I can arrange this for you if you can stay in San Diego for one extra day at the end of the tour. An extra night can be arranged with Globus, and Gray Line of San Diego has a tour of the San Diego Zoo."

"Which of the two tours do you feel best meets your requests?"

Summary: Yes, your closing question is a choice question, but you have set it up with the Summary Close. Is there any doubt that they will choose the Globus tour in this case? Also, you have solved the deficiency problem of not having the San Diego Zoo included by selling-up. You sold an extra night in San Diego plus the Gray Line tour of the San Diego Zoo.

Note: You have been addressing the clients by their first names, so you must know them well or they asked you to address them by their first names during the introduction process. Otherwise you would address them formally, using the appropriate title of Mr., Miss, Mrs., Ms, Dr., Rev., Lt., or the like.

Situation 2

Mrs. Bertha Gaunt wants to travel through the Canadian Rockies by train. You have been discussing two possibilities. The first possibility is taking the Via Rail train from Edmonton—Jasper—Kamloops—Hope—Vancouver. The second possibility is taking a Rocky Mountaineer Rail Tour from Calgary—Banff—Lake Louise—Kamloops—Hope—Vancouver.

Close: "Mrs. Gaunt, there is definitely a great difference in the price of taking the Via Rail train to Vancouver and taking the Rocky Mountaineer. However, I think if you review your requests, you will agree that the Rocky Mountaineer Rail Tour meets more of your needs."

"You can depart from Calgary and see Banff, Lake Louise, the Spiral Tunnels, the Kicking Horse River, the Columbia River, and the Shuswap Lakes."

"You mentioned that the main purpose of you taking this trip is to see the Canadian Rockies. On the Rocky Mountaineer, you see the entire trip during daylight, whereas on the Via Rail train, you pass through most of the mountains during the night."

"On the Rocky Mountaineer, you get to sleep in a comfortable motel. On the Via Rail train, you sleep in a tiny roomette."

"On the Via Rail train, you get to spend 9 daylight hours traveling through the mountains. On the Rocky Mountaineer, you spend 16 daylight hours traveling through the mountains."

"Considering that you have been looking forward to seeing the Canadian Rockies for more than 10 years Mrs. Gaunt, do you think you should treat yourself to the best available experience?"

Summary: Pause, and let Mrs. Gaunt answer your question. I would be very surprised if she did not respond with permission to go ahead with the booking.

The Minor Points Close

The **Minor Points Close** works well for big sales. Many people are hesitant to make a buying decision regarding expensive items. In this situation, get the customer to agree with parts of your sales proposal and gradually lead them toward accepting the entire package.

Situation 1

Hilda Kurz, Denise Ganier, and Lorena Morales have been discussing Collette Tours California Coast Tour and Globus Tours California Vacation with you. Although the three young ladies all want to take an escorted tour of the California Coast, it seems to be very difficult to get them to agree on which tour to take. Hilda is adamant that the lower price is paramount, Denise insists that she wants the tour with superior hotels, and Lorena seems to prefer the tour with the three boat cruises. You decide to use the Minor Points Close by taking a three-step approach. First, you have each person list the five most important things she wants on her tour. Second, have each rank her five points in priority and give you her list. The result was the following list. Third, proceed toward closing by satisfying the highest priority items.

	Hilda	*Denise*	*Lorena*
1.	PRICE, PRICE, PRICE	excellent hotels	boat cruises
2.	boat cruises	Hollywood	17 Mile Drive
3.	Hollywood	17 Mile Drive	Santa Barbara
4.	Yosemite National Park	Santa Barbara	Yosemite National Park
5.	17 Mile Drive	Capistrano	San Diego Zoo

With this list in hand, proceed toward closing.

Close: The first step is to handle the price issue. If Hilda does not show some flexibility regarding price, there is no choice! You point out that although the Globus tour is $226.13 more based on two people sharing, it is only $90.00 more when three people are sharing. "Hilda, considering that the Globus tour includes three more meals and the three boat cruises that you want to take, don't you think that it is a good value for the extra $90.00?" Now you have Hilda's new first priority, the three boat cruises on the Globus side. Lorena's first priority was also the boat cruises. Denise's first priority was for excellent accommodations, and Globus had the edge in that category. The 17 Mile Drive is included on both tours so it is easy to get the women to decide that that is not a deciding factor. Denise and Lorena both had Santa Barbara as priorities which is also offered in the Globus tour.

The last step is to get the three traveling companions to agree that it is not possible to satisfy all their desires in either one of the two tours, but they must agree that the Globus tour satisfies their top priorities. Pause, listen, and watch for any response. If the response is positive or even neutral, say, "I suggest that we check to see whether they have any space available." Then start the reservation process by picking up the phone. If there is any objection, handle it with the procedures discussed in Chapter 8.

Summary: You could solve some of the deficiencies and sell-up by booking extra time at the beginning of the tour and selling Gray Line of San Francisco's Yosemite National Park. You could sell them a rent-a-car while they are in Long Beach, and they could explore Hollywood after their cruise to Catalina Island while they are staying in Long Beach. Or, you could sell them Star Line's Tour, City Stars Tour of Hollywood, instead of taking the Catalina Island Cruise. By selling them an extra day in San Diego, you could add Gray Line of San Diego's San Diego Zoo Tour or perhaps their Zoo and Sea World Tour. By selling-up, you could actually meet each of the client's five priorities.

Situation 2

Oscar Montoya requests a rail trip including the following stopovers listed in brackets: Washington—Jacksonville [3], New Orleans [3], San Antonio [2], Tucson [2], Palm Springs [3], and terminating in Los Angeles. He has 14 days to complete the trip. You book the trip and obtain a fare quote from Amtrak of $1,243.00. However, due to the travel time by rail and because most of the rail sectors operate on only 3 days per week, the trip would take at least 18 days.

Mr. Montoya insists that he has a maximum of 14 days, so you suggest that he travel by air instead of by rail. You book it by air, and the itinerary fits into the 14 days that Mr. Montoya has available. But the fare quote is $2,414.00. Mr. Montoya is extremely dismayed that it is going to cost almost twice as much to go by air, and he really wanted to experience rail travel.

Close: "Mr. Montoya, we have a problem. To do the trip you want by rail takes more time than you have available. To do it by air costs more than you are willing to pay. Could we eliminate two of the stopovers you requested so that we could fit the rail itinerary into the time you have available?" His reply is that he had to make those stopovers.

"Let's look at your request point by point. First, you have 14 days maximum, and that cannot be extended. Second, you must have stopovers in each of the cities requested. Third, the airfare of $2,414.00 is more than you can afford. Fourth, you prefer to travel by train." Mr. Montoya replied affirmatively to each of the four points. You reply, "Mr. Montoya, this is a difficult problem to resolve, but perhaps I can resolve your dilemma by using some combination of rail and air travel. Do you want me to try that?" He replies that he would appreciate that. You explain that it will take some time to explore this possibility and make an appointment to see him the next morning at 10:00 A.M. The result is the following itinerary:

18 AUG	US302	WASHINGTON	2:10 pm	JACKSONVILLE	4:03 pm	Y
20 AUG	US5611	JACKSONVILLE	11:40 am	NEW ORLEANS	2:00 pm	Y
22 AUG	AM 1	NEW ORLEANS	1:45 pm	SAN ANTONIO	4:45 am +1	RM
26 AUG	AM 1	SAN ANTONIO	5:35 am	TUCSON	9:44 pm	C
28 AUG	AM 1	TUCSON	9:44 pm	PALM SPRINGS	3:53 am + 1	RM
31 AUG	AM 1	PALM SPRINGS	3:53 am	LOS ANGELES	7:10 am	RM

10:00 A.M. The Next Morning

"Good Morning Mr. Montoya. I have excellent news for you. The above itinerary fits nicely into the time that you have available. (pause) It has all of the stopovers that you have requested. (pause) The total cost is $1,290.33, a saving of $1,123.67 as compared to doing the entire trip by air. (pause) As you can see, most of the trip is by train as you preferred." (pause)

"Mr. Montoya, do you prefer to pay for your tickets with your credit card or by check?"

Summary: After each of the four Minor Points were made, I would pause for Mr. Montoya's approval. These could be verbal or might just be body language like a nod of the head. Because there were no objections or questions, move directly to the close by asking a question about how he would like to pay. Notice that in this case, the Assumed Sold Close was used in combination with the Minor Points Close.

Working out the revised itinerary took over two hours. It is not the kind of work that you would like to do with the customer sitting at your desk. That is why an appointment with Mr. Montoya was made for the next day so that there would be enough time to work on it. Allow yourself more time than you expect it to take to allow for unforeseen problems and for other callers whether by telephone or in person.

The T-Account Close

The **T-Account Close** is really a variation of the Summary Close. When a decision obviously has not only benefits but also some disadvantages, divide a sheet of paper in half. List the benefits and advantages on the left side of the paper and the disadvantages on the right side. Customers appreciate the logic and fairness of this method. Help the client with the advantage side and ask them for the disadvantages. Overcome the objections if necessary.

When a customer has so many criteria and it is impossible for you to provide all of them in a single offering, get the customer to give each one a priority. Then use the T-Account Close to prove that your proposal has the priority items on the left side of the T-Account.

Situation 1

Ms. Vera Brown has been discussing Collette Tours California Coast Tour and Globus Tours California Coast Vacation with you. She seems to be having a difficult time choosing between the two tours and you do not have a clear idea of which one would be better for her, so you decide to use the T-Account Close.

Close: "Ms. Brown, you seem to be having difficulty choosing between these two tours. I will list the advantages and disadvantages of each tour. If you check mark the ones that are important to you, it should help you decide which one has the most advantages and least disadvantages for you." (See Figure 6-3 and Figure 6-4.)

"Ms. Brown, you have selected more positive factors for the Collette tour and fewer disadvantages, so it would seem to be the better choice for you. I think we should check to see whether there is any space available for your preferred date of travel." You pick up the telephone to check whether space is available and offer to hold it for her. (You know that "holding space for her" is the same as a booking, but it is a softer sell.) It is very unlikely that she would have an objection to you checking whether space were available in this situation, but if she did, you would follow the suggestions in Chapter 8.

Collette California Coast Tour

Advantages	Disadvantages
✓ Yosemite National Park	__ Fewer meals than Globus tour
__ San Diego Zoo	✓ No boat cruises
✓ Less expensive than Globus	✓ Doesn't go to Santa Barbara
✓ Capistrano	__ Hotels not as good as Globus
✓ Mann's Chinese Theatre	
✓ "Stars Walk of Fame"	

FIGURE 6-3

Collette California Coast Tour T-Account.

FIGURE 6-4

Globus California Coast
Vacation T-Account.

Globus California Coast Vacation

Advantages	Disadvantages
__ 14 meals included	✓ more expensive
✓ 3 boat cruises	✓ doesn't include Hollywood
✓ Santa Barbara	__ doesn't include San Diego Zoo
__ superior hotels	✓ doesn't include Yosemite
✓ Capistrano	
__ steam-train—redwood country	

In this example the T-Account Close has been combined with the Choice Close. However, if you feel that you have the right tour, product, or service for the customer, you can use the T-Account Close, using just one item emphasizing that it has more advantages than disadvantages.

Summary: In the rare occurrence that the check marks turned out to be equal for the two products being offered, I would revert to the I Would Recommend Close, state the reason why, and close. By listening closely to Ms. Brown's conversation while she was checking the advantages and disadvantages of each tour, you should be able to pick up something that would give the balance to one tour or the other. Or you could decide based on the feedback that you have had from previous customers.

Situation 2

Luigi Micozzi would like to take an adventure on a remote river in pristine wilderness. He has heard that Wilderness Odysseys of Alexandria, Virginia, have adventure-ecotours to the Pigeon River in northern Canada. When he asked about the price, he was surprised how much it cost. The salesperson decided to use a T-Account Close.

Advantages	Disadvantages
unique experience	cost
pristine wilderness	long trip to get there
professional environmental interpretation	
small group—personal attention	
native culture	
river safety and navigation excellence	

Close: "As you can see Mr. Micozzi, this is a unique experience that is very professionally delivered in one of a very few pristine environments left. You can understand that the cost of conducting such a trip for small groups with detailed personal attention would be more than tours carried out for a busload. Value for money paid is what you will find on this adventure. (pause) Which departure date would you prefer?"

Summary: After each point on the T-Account, you would pause and look for a positive response, either verbally or by body language. After a short pause, the question about the preferred departure date should close the sale.

Closing to Resistance Close

The **Closing to Resistance Close** is used when a customer has a major objection that you have successfully overcome. One example would be when a customer states that he or she does not have the money right now and you close by suggesting the use of a credit card or time payments (if possible).

Situation 1

Mr. and Mrs. George Mandel have been discussing Collette Tours California Coast Tour and Globus Tours California Vacation Tour with you. They like the Globus Tour but prefer a tour of only one week, departing from San Francisco because they will be staying with family in San Francisco. You discern two problems. First they want a shorter tour than nine days. Second, they don't want San Francisco included because they will be staying with relatives there.

Close: "Mr. and Mrs. Mandel, I have a solution for your problem. Globus will allow you to join the tour on Day 3 on Monday, and this would also reduce the price of the tour by $347.00 per person. Considering that this is exactly what you are looking for, I will give them a call to check whether they have space for the date you have requested."

Summary: It is unlikely that Mr. and Mrs. Mandel would resist your offer to check whether space is available, considering that you have overcome their problem. If there is space available, obtain their permission to hold it for them. (In our terminology, this is a booking.) In the unlikely event that they would resist your offer to check whether space is available, use the techniques explained in Chapter 8.

Situation 2

You have been trying to close a deal on a Fly-Cruise for Miss Kathy Ward and Miss Sheila Ingram. Both young ladies are enthralled about the idea of taking a cruise but find the price prohibitive. They are considering just flying to the Caribbean and staying in resorts on three different islands. You decide to do a cost comparison to show that the Fly-Cruise is good value for money paid and hope to overcome their resistance. (See Figure 6-5.)

COST OF SEVEN-DAY CRUISE COMPARED WITH INDEPENDENT TRAVEL

Item	7-Day Fly-Cruise	Item	7-Day Independent Tour
Outside Cabin Cat HH	$2,273.00	Share Double or Twin	$1,241.10
Meals: 6 per Day Included		Meals: (Low Estimate)	462.84
Transfers in San Juan	24.00	Transfers Round Trip	20.35
Government Fees and Taxes	45.07	Entertainment	140.00
Air Add-on SEA-SJU	579.00	Airfare SEA-SJU	1,063.50
Taxes and Other Charges		Taxes and Other Charges	38.45
Port Charges	25.00		
Total	$2,946.07	Total for 1 Destination Only	$2,966.24
		Additional Airfare for the Same Itinerary as the Cruise	624.65
		Extra Transfers	122.10
Total for the Air-Sea Package	$2,946.07	Total for Air-Land Tour	$3,712.99

FIGURE 6-5   Air-sea package versus independent travel.

Close: "At first look, it might seem that the cruise is more expensive, but when you consider that all of the meals and entertainment are included, you can see that the cruise is better value for money paid. (pause) I will check whether space available."

Summary: When you state that "the cruise is better value for money paid," pause, look for body language, and listen for verbal approval. If you discern approval, the objection has been overcome. Go for the reservation! This is a good way to use the Closing to Resistance Close.

The Shortage Close

The **Shortage Close** utilizes the suggestion that there may not be any space available. Shortage of space is the strongest closing aid. The salesperson indicates that it might not be possible to obtain the space the customer would like to have. Then the salesperson offers to check on the computer or telephone whether space is available. If there is, an offer to reserve it for the customer is usually all that is required to close the deal. This close works very well for tours, special events, accommodations, and various modes of transportation.

A scarcity of items that the customer wants to buy can also help to close the deal when merchandise is involved. It works especially well when only one of a kind is available.

Situation 1

Dr. and Mrs. Ian Robinson have been discussing Collette Tours California Coast Tour and Globus Tours California Vacation with you. They mention that they would like to start their tour on July 18. Today is Apri 15. You decide to use the Shortage Close.

Close: "Dr. and Mrs. Robinson, I don't know if I can get space on either of those tours. July 18 is right in the middle of peak season, and these two tour companies are the most popular of all for the California Coast. Which one would you like me to try first to check whether any space is left?"

Summary: This is one of the easiest closes of all. If people think there is any chance that they cannot get it, they want it even more. You can often close the deal in 2 minutes or less, whereas some of the other techniques may take 20 minutes or more. High season, holidays, booking on short notice, or even low or discount prices for low season could give concern whether there might be space available.

Situation 2

Mr. and Mrs. Peter Shuler and their children Andy (age 11) and Louise (age 9) call Glacier Park Lodge in Montana to obtain rates for next July 1–8. It is only September 7, almost a year in advance, so they are just planning ahead and not thinking of making a reservation at this time. You are a reservationist for Glacier Park Lodge.

Close: "Mr. Shuler, do you realize that the days you are asking about include the July 4th holiday? We are usually sold out more than a year in advance for that week. If you would like, I could check to see whether anything is available. (pause) Wow, you are in luck! There are two rooms left. Would you like to reserve two rooms or one?"

Summary: Do you have any doubt that Mr. Shuler would resist this close?

The Special Deal Close

The **Special Deal Close** can be used to nudge prospects into making a buying decision now when otherwise they would be inclined to postpone a buying decision. Of course, this technique is only successful when the offer is really a special deal. One good example would be for a special event when advance tickets are less expensive than tickets at the door.

Situation 1

Mr. and Mrs. Dieter Hoffman have been discussing Collette Tours California Coast Tour and Globus Tours California Vacation with you. Both clients are senior citizens. They are free to travel at any time, but cost is a serious concern. You have received a flier advertising a $200.00 discount for seniors for their last departure on October 23.

Close: "Mr. and Mrs. Hoffman, if we are lucky, I can save you $400.00 if you are willing to travel on October 23. Globus has a senior discount on that date only. Would you like me to check whether any space is available for that departure?"

Summary: The combination of the possibility of saving $400.00 and the possibility that space might be limited provides a strong motivation to make a quick decision. Expressing the total saving of $400.00 for the couple probably has more clout than expressing the $200.00 on a per person basis.

Situation 2

You are a reservationist for Northwest Airlines. Mr. Abe Vandenberg calls you on June 16 to request the lowest airfare from Los Angeles to Toronto for travel starting on June 30 and returning on July 19. You offer a special promotional fare of $334.04, but Mr. Vandenberg seems reluctant to make a booking at the present time.

Close: "Mr. Vandenberg, I should advise you that there are only three seats left at that price. On Friday the price goes up to $525.46, and there are only a few seats available at that price. Once they are gone, the full coach fare would apply and that is approximately $1,600.00 including taxes. I strongly suggest that you book one of the seats at $334.04 before they are gone."

Summary: How long do you think it will take Mr. Vandenberg to make up his mind? I bet he is willing to give you his credit card number immediately to guarantee his reservation. But be careful to verify that Mr. Vandenberg will be able to travel on the flights you have discussed because the fare will probably be nonrefundable if he is unable to travel.

The Option Close

The **Option Close** is probably the easiest one to complete because their is no pressure on the customer. It can be used for any goods or services that you can hold for a customer for a certain length of time with no obligation. Often the customer wants to "talk it over" with someone else before making a final decision to buy. However, if he or she does not buy the space or item now, it may not be available after they have talked it over with someone else.

If you can hold the space or item until they have an opportunity to discuss it, they are assured that the space or item will be available for them. However, they are not obligated to pay at this point. "Options" are always **time-limited**. When the **option date** is up, the customer has to make a final decision.

Situation 1

Lise Lapièrre has been discussing Collette Tours California Coast Tour and Globus Tours California Vacation Tour with you for herself and her husband, Jacques. She seems to be set on the Collette tour because it includes the mountains of Yosemite National Park plus the two attractions in Hollywood. However, when you offer to book it for her, she resists, saying that she would never make a commitment like that before discussing it with Jacques.

Close: "Mrs. Lapièrre, I am sure that you would have to discuss this choice with your husband, but I would hate to have you go home, discuss it, make a decision, and then find out tomorrow that it is no longer available. Collette Tours has a five-day option period. This means I could book it for you now without any obligation for five days. This would give you and Mr. Lapièrre sufficient time to consider it, and in the meantime you know that the space for you is reserved if you decide that it is the right choice for both of you. If you and Mr. Lapièrre decide that you prefer the Globus tour, we can change it. If it is okay with you, I will phone to see if Collette Tours has space available and if so, I will hold it for you." (For Collette Tours, holding it for you and making a reservation are the same thing, but for the customer it is a soft sell.)

Summary: Why would Mrs. Lapièrre not agree to take the **option**? She has nothing to lose and an excellent chance to convince her husband to take the tour she wants to take. The Option Close is the easiest one to make. There is little if any pressure on the client except that she will feel obligated to get back to you to confirm or change the reservation. Notice, I said change not cancel. If this is not the right choice for Mr. and Mrs. Lapièrre, you will find out what is the right choice and book that. Make sure that you make a definite appointment with the client to confirm or change the reservation. Get a date, time, and place to firm things up.

Situation 2

I take the Situation 2 example from the Special Deal Close and show you how you could use the Option Close if the Special Deal Close did not work. You are a reservationist for Northwest Airlines. Mr. Abe Vandenberg calls you on June 16 to request the lowest airfare from Los Angeles to Toronto for travel starting on June 30 and returning on July 19. You offer a special promotional fare of $334.04, but Mr. Vandenberg seems reluctant to make a booking at the present time.

Close: "Mr. Vandenberg, I should advise you that there are only three seats left at that price. On Friday the price goes up to $525.46, and there are only a few seats available at that price. Once they are gone, the full coach fare would apply, and that is approximately $1,600.00 including taxes. I strongly suggest that you book one of the seats at $334.04 before they are gone."

Mr. Vandenberg understands the chance he is taking of the fare going up if he does not book now, but he also realizes that the ticket would be totally nonrefundable if he is not able to go. He has not asked his boss for the time off yet and does not want to book until he has talked to his boss tomorrow.

"Mr. Vandenberg, we have a solution for your problem. Northwest Airlines will give you a 24-hour option. This means I can book it for you now at the lowest price and you are not obligated to pay anything for 24 hours. If your boss approves your vacation request, we can issue the ticket tomorrow. If these dates cannot be worked out, let us know tomorrow and we will work out the best deal we can get for the dates that are approved." Pause and listen for a verbal approval. Even silence is a tacit approval. Complete the booking.

Summary: The Option Close has made a difficult booking into an easy booking. Mr. Vandenberg has nothing to lose. He is guaranteed the lowest possible airfare if he can get the time off. He has time to talk to the boss regarding his request. If he is not able to get the time off, he is not obligated to pay anything. For Northwest Airlines, we have the booking. If he cannot go when he is booked, we ask him to call back so that we can make a booking for other dates.

The Assumed Sold Close

The **Assumed Sold Close** is used when the salesperson takes the position that the prospect is going to buy and begins to process the order. This is particularly effective when the prospect has answered the first qualifying question in his or her opening remarks. You already know the answer to *where*? For any type of service that has to be booked, the salesperson goes to the reservation computer or telephone and starts the reservation process, asking the customer for the required information, including dates, times, the number of people, names, and so on. Other versions of the Assumed Sold Close include starting to fill in an order form or counting out the required number of tickets. The Assumed Sold Close requires a lot of confidence and a little acting ability by the salesperson. It also requires good observation and listening skills to perceive an early closing signal. It can be used any time you discern the customer is going to buy. Words like, "I need," or "I have to," or "I have to be in Houston on Tuesday" can be responded to with, "Would you like to put it on your credit card or do you prefer to pay cash?"

This technique is especially appropriate for special events, attractions, tours, transportation, and accommodations sector.

Situation 1

Ms. Martha Clarke and Ms. Clare Myers have been discussing Collette Tours California Coast Tour with you. As you mentioned the various features, the following comments were made:

- Yosemite National Park—In unison, "Wonderful!"
- San Diego Zoo—Clare: "I bet you can't wait to see the panda bears, Martha."
- Hearst Castle—Clare: "That will be a highlight for both of us, Martha."
- Solvang—Martha: "I have always wanted to go to Denmark. Perhaps Solvang will give us a taste of what it is like."
- Mann's Chinese Theatre and the "Stars Walk of Fame"—Clare: "Martha, can you imagine what the girls in our bridge club will say when we tell them we've been to Hollywood?"

Close: "Because this is exactly the tour you desire, I suggest we book it before someone else gets your places." You watch carefully as you pick up the phone or go to the reservations computer. If you do not see any overt objection, you proceed with the reservation.

Summary: Assumed Sold closes are usually used for smaller purchases like tickets for a special event, an attraction, or local sightseeing. However, for larger or more complex sales, if you receive positive feedback at every step, why shouldn't you assume that the client is going to book? If the client is going to book, stop fooling around and book it.

Situation 2

A client was taking an extended trip to the Orient. He often, perhaps foolishly, did not take medical insurance when he traveled. But this time, because of the distance and the cost of emergency travel from the destinations back home, he thought he had better consider it. He went to the auto club and approached one of my former students to check out the details of the coverage and the cost. He did not have his mind made up to buy the insurance, but like most prospects, he just went in to ask a few questions.

Close: Warren did an exemplary job of qualifying the client, and by the time he had the answers to the client's questions, Warren had the policy all filled in. "Just sign here, Mr. Cunningham and you are all set." Warren was very convincing in his sales points, and Mr. Cunningham probably would have purchased the insurance anyway, but at this point he would have been embarrassed not to sign on the dotted line. The use of the Assumed Sold Close certainly sped up the process.

Summary: The Assumed Sold Close is by far the quickest close and can save you a great deal of time during a busy day. If there is no reason to believe that the prospect is not going to buy, why not take a positive attitude that he or she is going to buy and proceed in a straight line for the sale? It takes confidence and a little acting ability. It often edges a person who might tend to procrastinate to make an early decision.

CLOSING BY TYPE OF PROSPECT

Prospects can be divided into three types of people: dominant people, dependent people, and detached people.

Dominant people attempt to assert themselves over others and are motivated by self-esteem needs. They want to be looked up to by others. They expect a salesperson to be seasoned and firm. A Summary Close or a Special Deal Close often works well with dominant people. The Assumed Sold Close and the Minor Points Close do not work well for dominant people.

Dependent people are friendly, warm, and thoughtful. The Choice Close, Minor Points Close, and the Assumed Sold Close work well for dependent people.

Detached people are cold, businesslike, and may seem unfriendly. These people are concerned with facts and logic. They resist emotional appeals. The Summary Close, the T-Account Close, the Minor Points Close, and the Special Deal Close are effective with detached people.

CLOSE TO THE DECISION-MAKER

When selling to more than one customer, determine who is the **decision-maker** and sell to that person. "You want to reach the person who has the largest say in selecting a product or service. Men usually exert a larger say in buying insurance . . . while women are most likely to have a deciding vote in home furnishings. Perhaps both carry equal weight in purchasing a car or home. College-age students affect the choice of university, even if parents are footing the bills, and children have a lot to say about things like breakfast cereals, fast food, and toys."[2] "Better than half of those surveyed (55%) reported that the travel decision was a joint one. Another 30% said that the female made the decision, with the remaining 15% being credited to male influence."[3] Observe closely. Decide which partner is the decision-maker. And, close to the decision-maker.

When selling to groups, there is always a key person in the decision-making process. Determine who this person is before scheduling an appointment to discuss your proposal. The decision-maker could be the president, the chief executive officer, the past president, the social director, the secretary, or any other person of rank. But there is always one person who has more say in a decision than anyone else. Determine who this person is by asking questions. Talk to the secretary, receptionist, long-term members, executive members, and by observation when you are visiting the organization's facilities. Convince the decision-maker and he or she will close the sale for you.

SUMMARY OF THE CLOSING PROCESS

Closing is the process of asking a question that solicits an answer that gives the salesperson consent to complete the sale.

The customer has only three choices:

1. To accept—the deal is closed. Complete the booking!

2. To remain silent—gives consent or tacit approval. Complete the booking!

3. To object. If the customer objects to your attempt to book it, determine the reason for the objection. Handle the objection, and close again.

Notes

1. Richard F. Wendel and Walter Gorman, *Selling—Personal Preparation, Persuasion, Strategy,* 3rd ed. (New York: Random House Business Division), 387.

2. Robert T. Reilly, *Travel and Tourism Marketing Techniques,* 2nd ed. (Albany, NY: Delmar Learning, 1988), 24.

3. Robert T. Reilly, *Travel and Tourism Marketing Techniques* (Wheaton, IL: Merton House Publishing Co., 1980), 13.

Discussion Questions

1. Define the term *closing*.

2. Define the term *trial close*.

3. List 10 closing signals.

4. Describe seven situations when it is not a good time to close.

5. Name 10 closing techniques.

CHAPTER 7

Selling Techniques Using the Telephone

OBJECTIVES

After studying this chapter, you should be able to:

● Name the two principal types of telephone sales calls

● List two categories of incoming calls

● List five categories of outgoing calls

● Demonstrate effective use of a multiline telephone system

● List the six details you need to complete a credit card transaction over the telephone

● Complete a booking form with all of the information required to make a booking

● Respond to a phone call for information and turn it into a sales opportunity

● List four basic systems of word spelling used in the tourism industry

● Recite the symphonic alphabet

KEY TERMS

predisposed to buy	price-break information	hot calls
space-limited	read between the lines	psyched-up
seat sales	credit card authorization	follow-up call
fly-cruise	cold calls	symphonic alphabet

Even though Alexander Graham Bell's invention was first demonstrated in 1877, it still remains the most effective sales aid in the office. The telephone enables you to contact or be contacted by customers and prospects virtually anywhere in the world instantaneously. It allows continuous dialogue, including exchanges of ideas and opinions, discussion of topics of common interest, and—most important to a salesperson—an opportunity to persuade a prospect to make a buying decision.

There are a number of different types of sales possibilities using the telephone, but they can be categorized into two principal types: incoming and outgoing calls.

INCOMING CALLS

Most people would visualize an employee at his or her desk poised to receive an incoming call. Incoming calls are usually responses to advertising or publicity. The caller could be at one of two completely different stages of the buying process. He or she may be **predisposed to buy** and be calling to place an order. On the other hand, the caller's interest might just have been only slightly aroused, and he or she could be calling "just for some information."

Sometimes it is possible to tell that a caller is predisposed to buy by his or her opening statement. For example, he or she might say, "I would like to order . . ." or "I would like to make a reservation for . . ." or "I have to be in Los Angeles on Tuesday." In these situations it is obvious that the customer wants to buy. In other cases, it may not be so obvious that the caller has contacted you to place an order, but the procedure is clear. Qualify!

If the answers are straightforward and there are no interruptions, the caller has contacted you to place an order. You have the qualifying information you require to close the sale. So, close! Any closing technique could be used, but for these predisposed-to-buy situations, the Assumed Sold Close would seem to be the natural selection. However, if there were a number of possibilities, the Choice Close might be most effective.

Callers Predisposed to Buy

The most important concern when servicing callers predisposed to buy is to be fully prepared. Calls from customers predisposed to buy can happen at almost any time in the various sectors of the tourism business. In the Accommodations sector and the Food and Beverage sector, people often react whenever the spirit moves them. However, good advertising and promotions can incite people to respond instantaneously to a special value offer or unique event.

The timing of advertisements and promotions for attractions can prompt spectacular responses. Sometimes these can be coordinated with special events and other attractions. Some attractions thrive in peak conditions, and others provide indoor alternatives when the weather makes outdoor attractions less attractive.

Adventure and recreation advertisements and promotions, coordinated with programs that feature complimentary activities, can generate a dramatic number of incoming calls. Special events, meetings, and conventions can often generate numerous incoming calls for reservations before the deadline of a special price for advanced reservations.

Instant responses to advertising in the Transportation sector are a normal response to time-limited and **space-limited** spectacular **seat sales**.

Tour operators can usually obtain a significant response to advertisements and promotions that tie into popular entertainment. For example, a **fly-cruise** that advertises on *The Love Boat—The Next Wave* television show would have a large number of qualified prospects in the audience.

Any sector of the tourism industry can obtain a large number of calls whenever there is a time- or space-limited price special. The crucial factor when servicing callers predisposed to buy is to be fully prepared. Often firms do not have sufficient staff on duty to handle the responses to advertising programs or promotions.

Many companies, including airlines, do not have sufficient telephone lines to handle additional calls generated by a promotion. Money spent to arouse interest is lost when customers hang up because of frustration with long waits. The negative impression will likely carry over to future situations. In such cases, money spent for promotions actually has an adverse affect on sales.

Not only do you need an adequate number of telephone lines and staff to handle responses, staff must have the product knowledge to answer questions, point out the benefits, and close sales regarding advertised specials. Airlines used to be notorious for advertising spectacular seat sale fares in the weekend travel sections before informing travel agents that such an event was taking place. The phone lines to the airlines would be jammed for hours. People would call travel agencies, and their normal weekend staff would be insufficient for the extra demand. Also, once a caller did get through to the agent, usually the customer would know more about the special fare from the advertisement than would the agent.

Hopefully with improvements to Global Distribution Systems (GDSs), travel agents would now have full access to **price-break information** as soon as it would be available to the public. However, because the airlines are seeking the element of surprise over their competitors, seat sales will continue to be surprise announcements on weekends, catching many agencies short staffed. The most logical position would be to have additional staff on call in case of the extra demand created by seat sales or other extraordinary circumstances.

With an adequate number of telephone lines open and sufficient staff ready to receive incoming calls, the next task is to make certain that staff have the resources to do their job efficiently. First, each staff member should have a copy of the advertisement in front of them with the customer benefits highlighted. Terms and conditions should also be highlighted. Notes regarding quick access to the rules, fares, and general information in the Global Distribution System should be readily available. If time and resources permit, a file folder with additional background information and sales aids should be within arm's length. In any case you will need a booking form to take down the required information. (See Figure 7-1.)

There are probably almost as many different booking forms as there are travel and tourism organizations that need to use them. Many companies have forms with little boxes for each item of information required. These forms are often difficult to fill in while you are talking to a customer in person or especially on the telephone.

The sample booking form shown in Figure 7-1 has lines for the required information. Without lines, many people tend to scribble all over the page and usually have to rewrite everything as soon as they hang up the phone. Most people find that they can usually complete the form shown while talking on the telephone with a customer, carriers, hotels, and so on, neatly enough that it doesn't have to be rewritten.

The sample booking form shown in Figure 7-1 would be appropriate for some sectors of the tourism business but would need to be modified for others. Simply delete information not required and add spaces for additional information required. Use a personal computer to custom design a form appropriate for your business. Regardless of the nature of the information required on a booking form, the accuracy of the information is paramount.

Steps in Servicing Callers Predisposed to Buy

1. Greet the caller pleasantly identifying yourself and your company or organization. Try to "smile through the phone." (See Figure 7-2.) This may seem corny, but your disposition affects your tone of voice and is apparent at the other end of the phone.

2. Obtain the name of the client and use it soon and often. If possible, write it down to help reinforce it in your mind and for future reference. At this point, you do not need the

Name: _____   Date: _____

Name: _____

Name: _____

Name: _____

Address: _____

_____

Phone: (Home) _____   (Work) _____

No. of Passengers: _____   Class of Service: _____

Destination: _____

Departure: _____

Return: _____

Special Requests: _____

_____

Locator/Reservation No.: _____   Reservationist: _____

Require:

Hotel: Yes ❏   No ❏ _____

_____

Car: Yes ❏   No ❏ _____

Insurance: Yes ❏   No ❏ _____

Date	Flight No.	dp	From	ar	To	Class	Status

Arrangements Regarding Tickets: _____

Form of Payment: Cash ❏   Check ❏   Credit Card: _____

On Mailing List: Yes ❏   No ❏

FIGURE 7-1 Sample booking form.

FIGURE 7-2
Smile through the phone. (© PhotoDisc/ Getty Images)

complete name or names of the entire party, only the name by which the caller wants to be addressed.

3. Be an acute listener and make notes, both written and mental, of what the customer is requesting. **Read between the lines** of what the customer is saying in order to obtain a complete picture of what he or she wants. Then restate his or her request in your own words to make sure that you fully understood the request.

4. Obtain the qualifying information and insert it on the booking form or order form.

5. Ask a closing question to obtain consent to close the sale.

6. This is the stage where you need detailed and accurate information regarding the customers, including full names with the correct spelling.

7. Do whatever is necessary to complete the sale. Make the reservation in the computer or by telephone, or take the goods from the inventory.

8. Make arrangements for follow-up. This could involve tickets, confirmations, or goods by mail, or arrangements for pick up either at your office, at the airport, or at the tourism site, or for delivery.

9. "Thank you for calling _____. It has been a pleasure to serve you. I look forward to_____."

Examples of Remarks

"I look forward to . . .

. . . meeting you next Friday at 2:00 P.M."

. . . seeing you at your office on Tuesday at 10:00 A.M."

. . . delivering your tickets as soon as they arrive."

. . . meeting your husband when you come to pick up the tickets."

Callers Phoning Just for Some Informaiton

The vast majority of callers do not have making a booking or placing an order on their mind when they call a tourism organization. Often, an advertisement, promotions, word-of-mouth publicity, or even a seemingly unrelated event sparks the interest of a tourist to seek information.

Handling these calls requires more skill than do those of callers predisposed to buy. You have no idea when to expect such calls. They may tap all of the knowledge and experience that you have. Even more likely, they will request information that you do not have readily at hand. Organization is the key. Have information arranged in a logical manner so that it can be retrieved with dispatch. For complex bookings that include transportation plus accommodations and other arrangements, book the transportation first. If the customer accepts the transportation arrangements, he or she is going. Then you can take some time to arrange other details and make an appointment to call back or for an office visit to go over the entire itinerary.

The sales process using the telephone follows the same steps as when you are selling in person, but there are two principal differences. In a face-to-face sales presentation, the salesperson can appeal to all the senses by employing a number of sensory aids, including brochures, photographs, facial expressions, gestures, and other physical symbols. The person selling over the telephone must rely on his or her voice and skill with words to project his or her personality and ideas. The other principal difference in a telephone sales situation, particularly with a prospect who calls just for some information, is that it is easy for him or her to terminate the call once he or she has received the information that prompted the call.

USING ONE'S VOICE AND LANGUAGE SKILLS EFFECTIVELY

Information about the product or service must be communicated using words that evoke word pictures. Appeal to the same senses that you would use if the client were at your desk by using words that have a powerful emotional appeal.

The first key to effective telephone sales is to be a good listener. Limit your own talking so that the caller can articulate the questions he or she has in mind. Concentrate on what the customer wants and needs. Ignore outside distractions. Try to eliminate as many of them as possible. For example, turn the sound system down. Close windows if noise is coming from outside and alert others in the office that you will be busy on an important call.

Take notes, concentrating on relevant details. Try to concentrate on the principal ideas that the prospect is articulating. Listen for overtones and try to read between the lines. When you are not sure, ask questions to obtain the whole picture. Do not become irritated or distracted by the prospect's mannerisms. Concentrate on the ideas expressed and the questions asked.

Once you feel that you understand the prospect's questions or problems, restate them in your own words to demonstrate that you have been effectively listening and that you understand the customer's position.

At this point, you must start answering the prospect's questions, but not too quickly! If you provide all of the information that the caller wants before you have finished qualifying, the caller will say "Thank you very much" and terminate the call.

The second principal difference in a telephone sales situation is that you need to control the conversation and move the customer toward a buying decision. Asking questions helps to give the call direction and provides you with the qualifying information you need to make an effective recommendation.

As in any sales situation, once you have the qualifying information you need, make a recommendation and ask a closing question. If there is no reason to believe that the caller is not going to buy, the Assumed Sold Close might be used. You could proceed with a question regarding which form of payment the prospect would like to use. Be sure to offer a choice of the forms of payment you can accept. If you can only accept certain credit cards, offer only them specifically as a choice rather than an open option of check or credit card.

If there is some hesitancy by the prospect, the Option Close can be used to persuade the customer to allow you to make a booking. If there is some indecision regarding which one the customer prefers, the Choice Close could be the most effective one. If there is still indecision, the I Would Recommend Close would be appropriate.

Arrangements for follow-up are even more crucial for telephone sales than for face-to-face sales. If the prospect ever hangs up before you obtain his or her name and phone number, it is very unlikely that he or she will ever become a customer. Sometimes it is necessary to schedule another phone call to provide additional information or to confirm arrangements. Other times it is necessary to schedule an office appointment to finalize arrangements, pick up tickets, or to make a payment.

Credit Card Transactions over the Telephone

More and more, tourism organizations are demanding payment at the time of reservations. This makes it difficult to close sales over the telephone. Many tourism organizations will accept credit card transactions over the telephone, which makes it possible to close the sale over the telephone when payment is required at the time of booking. The salesperson will require the following information:

1. Name of the credit card.
2. Name of the financial institution.
3. Card number.
4. Expiration date.
5. Name of the customer as it appears on the card.
6. Then call the financial institution for a **credit card authorization** number (unless you have a Credit Card Authorization Machine). If you do not have a Credit Card Authorization Machine, consider purchasing one. The time it will save will make it very worthwhile.

Without a signed credit card authorization slip, a company is at risk that the customer may reject the charge to his or her account, leaving the vendor with an unpaid account. Most tourism companies will take this risk with known, regular customers and for advance bookings for which tickets will not be delivered until some time after the credit card charges have cleared.

For customers who are not well known or are placing credit card orders for tourism arrangements or products for immediate delivery, it is strongly recommended you insist that they come in to the office to sign the credit card authorization before a ticket or merchandise is released. (See Figure 7-3.)

OUTGOING CALLS

Most people would not picture tourism industry employees making outgoing phone calls to generate sales. However, these calls can be important sources of business. Outgoing telephone sales calls can be categorized into five types:

- cold calls for new business
- hot calls for repeat or specialized business

1. ACKNOWLEDGE RECEIPT OF TICKET(S) AND/OR COUPONS FOR RELATED CHARGES DESCRIBED HEREON. PAYMENT IN FULL TO BE MADE WHEN BILLED OR IN EXTENDED PAYMENTS IN ACCORDANCE WITH STANDARD POLICY OF COMPANY ISSUING CARD AND AS REFLECTED IN APPLICABLE TARIFFS.

J'ACCUSE RÉCEPTION DES BILLETS OU COUPONS CORRESPONDANT AUX DÉBITS CI-CONTRE. LE PAIEMENT POURRA ÊTRE EFFECTUÉ SOIT INTEGRALEMENT DÉS LA FACTURATION SOIT EN VERSEMENTS ÉCHELONNÉS AUX CONDITIONS FIXEES PAR LA SOCIÉTE EMETTRICE DE LA CARTE ET STIPULÉES AUX RÉGIEMENTS TARIFAIRES APPLICABLES.

X *Jim Ashcroft*

UNIVERSAL CREDIT CARD CHARGE FORM/BORDEREAU DE DÉBIT UNIVERSEL — CARTES DE CRÉDIT

AIRLINE CODE / CODE Cie AÉR.

1. CONTRACTOR INVOICE COPY / FACTURE DU CONTRACTANT

15 MAR 02

DATE OF ISSUE/DATE D'ÉMISSION

IF EXTENDED PAYMENT APPLICABLE, CIRCLE NO. OF MONTHS. ENTOURER LE NOMBRE DE MENSUALITÉS, EN CAS DE PAIEMENTS ÉCHELONNES.

3 6 9 12____

DATE AND PLACE OF ISSUE

ABC TRAVEL
ALBUQUERQUE, NM
69-7-5551-0
15 MAR 02
HBK

LIEU ET DATE D'ÉMISSION

NAME OF PASSENGER OTHER THAN CARDHOLDER / NOM DU PASSAGER SAUF S'IL EST TITULAIRE DE LA CARTE	OTATO NO. / Nº D'OTATO	CONNECTION OF PASSENGER WITH SUBSCRIBER / RELATION ENTRE PASSAGER ET SOUSCRIPTEUR	APPROVAL CODE / REF. DE L'ACCORD
ASHCROFT/DEBBIE (UM10)		DAUGHTER	4872

COMPLETE ROUTING/ITINÉRAIRE COMPLET	FARE BASIS / BASE TARIFAIRE	CARRIER / TRANSPORTEUR
ALBUQUERQUE		
MINNEAPOLIS		NW
ALBUQUERQUE		NW

AIRLINE/CieAÉR. FORM SERIAL NO./Nº DU BILLET
012-6278-365-439

TICKETS NOT TRANSFERABLE
NO CASH REFUNDS
BILLETS INCESSIBLES
AUCUN REMBOURSEMENT EN ESPÈCES

CREDIT CARD NAME/CODE / NOM OU CODE DE LA CARTE: CA

CAPITAL ONE
5555-1234-5678-0555
10/07
JAMES B. ASHCROFT

FARE/TARIF	TOTAL	ROUTE CODE / INDICATIF DU PARCOURS
USD 359.06	USD 397.50	
TAX/TAXE USD 38.44		
EQUIV.AMT.PD./CONTRE-VAL.VERSEE		

FIGURE 7-3 Credit card authorization form.

- calls to obtain new accounts
- calls to obtain group business
- follow-up calls to obtain referrals and repeat business

Cold Calls

Cold calls are phone calls to a list of phone numbers at which you have no idea whether the respondents have any interest in your product or service. In the tourism business, cold calls are usually unproductive because a large proportion of people called are not qualified prospects and much time is wasted.

Hot Calls

Hot calls are phone calls to prospects who can benefit from the product or service that you have to offer. With increasingly sophisticated computer systems, it is possible to pinpoint prospects with very specific interests. These could be customers who have purchased similar products or services before or perhaps customers who have indicated an interest during follow-up calls after previous sales.

Calls to Obtain New Accounts

Calls to obtain new accounts usually are aimed at businesses. There is usually a reason to believe that the company called is a good prospect. This could be that you had received a referral from a satisfied customer. It could be because they are a new company within your geographical region or because you are able to offer some specialized service that your competitors are unable to offer.

Calls to Obtain Group Business

Group business very seldom comes to you. You have to go after it. The first step is to determine which types of groups could possibly use your services. Next, make a list of specific groups of each type. For example, a hunting and fishing lodge could have a list of fishing and hunting clubs and a separate list of companies that would be the right size to use the lodge during off-peak times for business meetings or retreats. If you have a number of groups to contact, it is probably a good idea to save your best prospects until you have tried your approach on others. You will have an opportunity to learn from errors and you will be able to polish your delivery. Know whom to ask for. If your call is a referral, ask the person who referred you whom you should speak to. If it is a cold call, ask the receptionist or secretary for the name of the person who handles the types of business you are seeking. Build a rapport with secretaries. Get to know their names and keep them in your card files. Make them aware of the importance of your proposal to his or her boss and organization. Find out an appropriate time to call this person, prepare your presentation, and call back.

Organize your call. Make a list of facts that you will need and of questions you wish to ask. Write down the ideas you want to present in the form of benefits they can provide to the individual you are calling and to the organization he or she represents.

Call at a convenient time. If you know the customer in advance, note the times when he or she is usually in the office. Know the habits of your customers and whether they are more receptive in the morning or afternoon. Do they work on weekends or evenings?

Generally, local calls are most likely to get through between 11:00 A.M. and 3:30 P.M. Lunchtime cuts into this period and varies for different organizations and individuals. Make a note of when people will be unavailable. Long-distance lines are most likely to be free around 2:00 P.M.

Avoid calling just before lunch or close to closing time. If you are contemplating calling someone at home, make sure that this is acceptable. Make sure that you do not call too early, too late, or at meal times. If you are calling long-distance, make sure that you make an allowance for differences in time zones and check to see if daylight saving time is in effect. (See Figure 7-4.)

International Standard Time Chart

Standard Time: Legal time for each country fixed by law and based on the theoretical division of the world's surface into 24 zones each of 15° longitude with certain deviations due to frontiers or local option.
Daylight Savings Time (DST): Modified (advanced) legal time adopted by certain countries for part of year, especially during local summer.

△ — Arizona and parts of Indiana do not observe DST.
‡ — Province of Saskatchewan and certain Canadian cities remain on Standard Time all year.
★ — Except Broken Hill, N.S.W.; follows South Australia times.
■ — Certain States of Brazil do not observe DST.
E — Estimated Date Based On Previous Year.
* — Listed are MAJOR cities for each zone.
▽ — Serbia and Montenegro
• — Change from last issue.

Country	Standard Time — Hours from GMT	Standard Time — Time at 1200 hrs GMT	Daylight Saving Time — Hours from GMT	Daylight Saving Time — Effective Period (first and last day)
Afghanistan	+4 1/2	16 30		
Albania	+1	13 00	+2	Mar. 28, 1999E—Oct. 31, 1999E
Algeria	+1	13 00		
American Samoa	−11	01 00		
Andorra	+1	13 00	+2	Mar. 28, 1999E—Oct. 31, 1999E
Angola	+1	13 00		
Argentina	−3	09 00		
Armenia	+4	16 00	+5	Mar. 28, 1999E—Oct. 31, 1999E
Aruba	−4	08 00		
Australia				
Lord Howe Is.	+10 1/2	22 30	+11	Oct. 31, 1999—Mar. 25, 2000
New South Wales, Australian Capitol Territory (A.C.T) ★	+10	22 00	+11	Oct. 31, 1999—Mar. 26, 2000
Victoria	+10	22 00	+11	Oct. 31, 1999—Mar. 25, 2000
Northern Territory	+9 1/2	21 30		
Queensland	+10	22 00		
South Australia and Broken Hill	+9 1/2	21 30	+10 1/2	Oct. 31, 1999—Mar. 25, 2000
Tasmania	+10	22 00	+11	Oct. 03, 1999—Mar. 25, 2000
Western Australia	+8	20 00		
Austria	+1	13 00	+2	Mar. 28, 1999—Oct.31, 1999
Azerbaijan	+4	16 00	+5	Mar. 28, 1999E—Oct. 31, 1999E
Bahamas (excluding Turks and Caicos Islands)	−5	07 00	−4	Apr. 04, 1999E—Oct. 31, 1999E
Bahrain Island	+3	15 00		
Bangladesh	+6	18 00		
Barbados	−4	08 00		
Belarus	+2	14 00	+3	Mar. 28, 1999E—Oct. 31, 1999E
Belgium	+1	13 00	+2	Mar. 28, 1999—Oct. 31, 1999
Belize	−6	06 00		
Benin Peoples Rep. (Dahomey)	+1	13 00		
Bermuda	−4	08 00	−3	Apr. 04, 1999E—Oct. 31, 1999E
Bhutan	+6	18 00		
Bolivia	−4	08 00		
Bosnia Herzegovina	+1	13 00	+2	Mar. 28, 1999E—Oct. 31, 1999E
Botswana	+2	14 00		
Brazil ■ East (Including All Coast and Brasilia)	−3	09 00	−2	Oct. 03, 1999E—Feb. 26, 2000E
West	−4	08 00	−3	Oct. 03, 1999E—Feb. 26, 2000E
Territory of Acre	−5	07 00		
Fernando De Noronha	−2	10 00		
British Virgin Islands	−4	08 00		
Brunei Darussalam	+8	20 00		
Bulgaria	+2	14 00	+3	Mar. 28, 1999E—Oct. 30, 1999E
Burkina Faso	GMT	12 00		
Burundi	+2	14 00		
Cambodia	+7	19 00		
Cameroon, Republic Of	+1	13 00		
Canada ‡ — Newfoundland	−3 1/2	08 30	−2 1/2	Apr. 04, 1999—Oct. 31, 1999
Atlantic	−4	08 00	−3	Apr. 04, 1999—Oct. 31, 1999
Eastern	−5	07 00	−4	Apr. 04, 1999—Oct. 31, 1999
Central	−6	06 00	−5	Apr. 04, 1999—Oct. 31, 1999
Mountain	−7	05 00	−6	Apr. 04, 1999—Oct. 31, 1999
Pacific	−8	04 00	−7	Apr. 04, 1999—Oct. 31, 1999
Yukon Territory	−8	04 00	−7	Apr. 04, 1999—Oct. 31, 1999
Cape Verde Islands	−1	11 00		
Cayman Islands	−5	07 00		
Central African Republic	+1	13 00		
Chad	+1	13 00		
Chile				
Continental	−4	08 00	−3	Oct. 10, 1999E—Mar. 18, 2000E
Easter Island	−6	06 00	−5	Oct. 10, 1999E—Mar. 18, 2000E
China, People's Republic Of	+8	20 00		
Cocos (Keeling) Islands	+6 1/2	18 30		
Colombia	−5	07 00		
Comoros (see Mayotte)				
Congo	+1	13 00		
Congo, (Dem Rep of)				
Kinshasa, Mbandaka	+1	13 00		
Kasai, Kivu, Shaba	+2	14 00		
Cook Islands	−10	02 00		
Costa Rica	−6	06 00		
Cote d'Ivoire	GMT	12 00		
Croatia	+1	13 00	+2	Mar. 28, 1999E—Oct. 31, 1999E
Cuba	−5	07 00	−4	Mar. 28, 1999E—Oct. 31, 1999
Cyprus	+2	14 00	+3	Mar. 28, 1999—Oct. 31, 1999
Czech Republic	+1	13 00	+2	Mar. 28, 1999E—Oct. 31, 1999E
Denmark	+1	13 00	+2	Mar. 28, 1999—Oct. 31, 1999
Djibouti	+3	15 00		
Dominican Republic	−4	08 00		
Ecuador				
Continental	−5	07 00		
Galapagos Is.	−6	06 00		
Egypt	+2	14 00	+3	Apr. 30, 1999—Sep. 30, 1999
El Salvador	−6	06 00		
Equatorial Guinea	+1	13 00		
Eritrea	+3	15 00		
Estonia	+2	14 00	+3	Mar. 28,1999—Oct. 31, 1999
Ethiopia	+3	15 00		
Falkland Islands	−4	08 00	−3	Sep. 12, 1999E—Apr. 15, 2000E
Faroe Island	GMT	12 00	+1	Mar. 28, 1999E—Oct. 31, 1999E
Fiji	+12	23 59	+13	Nov. 07, 1999—Feb. 27, 2000
Finland	+2	14 00	+3	Mar. 28, 1999—Oct. 31, 1999
France	+1	13 00	+2	Mar. 28, 1999—Oct. 31, 1999
French Guiana	−3	09 00		
French Polynesia				
Gambier Is.	−9	03 00		
Marquesas Is.	−9 1/2	02 30		
Society Is., Tubual Is., Tuamotu Is., Tahiti	−10	02 00		
Gabon	+1	13 00		
Gambia	GMT	12 00		
Georgia	+4	16 00	+5	Mar. 28, 1999—Oct. 31, 1999
Germany	+1	13 00	+2	Mar. 28, 1999—Oct. 31, 1999
Ghana	GMT	12 00		
Gibraltar	+1	13 00	+2	Mar. 28, 1999E—Oct. 31, 1999E
Greece	+2	14 00	+3	Mar. 28, 1999—Oct. 31, 1999
Greenland				
Except Scoresbysund and Thule	−3	09 00	−2	Mar 27, 1999E—Oct. 30, 1999E
Scoresbysund	−1	11 00	GMT	Mar. 28, 1999E—Oct. 31, 1999E
Thule	−4	08 00	−3	Apr. 04, 1999E—Oct. 31, 1999E
Guadeloupe (incl. St. Barthelemy, Northern St. Martin)	−4	08 00		
Guam	+10	22 00		
Guatemala	−6	06 00		
Guinea	GMT	12 00		
Guinea-Bissau	GMT	12 00		
Guyana	−4	08 00		
Haiti	−5	07 00		
Honduras	−6	06 00		
Hong Kong	+8	20 00		
Hungary	+1	13 00	+2	Mar. 28, 1999E—Oct. 31, 1999E
Iceland	GMT	12 00		
India (incl. Andaman Is.)	+5 1/2	17 30		
Indonesia				
Central	+8	20 00		
East	+9	21 00		
West (Jakarta)	+7	19 00		
Iran (The Islamic Rep. of)	+3 1/2	15 30	+4 1/2	Mar 22 1999—Sep. 21, 1999
Iraq	+3	15 00	+4	Apr. 01, 1999E—Oct. 01, 1999E
Ireland, Rep. of	GMT	12 00	+1	Mar. 28, 1999—Oct. 31, 1999
Israel	+2	14 00	+3	Apr. 02, 1999—Sep. 03, 1999
Italy	+1	13 00	+2	Mar. 28, 1999—Oct. 31, 1999
Jamaica	−5	07 00		
Japan	+9	21 00		
Johnston Is.	−10	02 00		
Jordan	+3	15 00		
Kampuchea, Dem. (see Cambodia)				
Kazakstan				
West	+4	16 00	+5	Mar. 28, 1999E—Oct. 30, 1999E
Central	+5	17 00	+6	Mar. 28, 1999E—Oct. 30, 1999E
East	+6	18 00	+7	Mar. 28, 1999E—Oct. 30, 1999E
Kenya	+3	15 00		
Kiribati, Rep. Of	+12	23 59		
Canton, Enderbury Islands	+13	01 00		
Christmas Is.	+14	02 00		
Korea, Democratic People's Rep. Of	+9	21 00		
Korea, Republic Of	+9	21 00		
Kuwait	+3	15 00		
Kyrgyz Rep.	+5	17 00	+6	Mar. 28, 1999E—Oct. 31, 1999E
Laos	+7	19 00		
Latvia	+2	14 00	+3	Mar. 28, 1999E—Oct. 31, 1999E
Lebanon	+2	14 00	+3	Mar. 28, 1999—Oct. 30, 1999
Leeward Islands				
Antigua, Dominica, Montserrat, St. Christopher, St. Kitts, Nevis, Anguilla	−4	08 00		
Lesotho	+2	14 00		
Liberia	GMT	12 00		
Libyan Arab Jamahiriya	+2	14 00		
Liechtenstein	+1	13 00	+2	Mar. 28, 1999—Oct. 31, 1999
Lithuania	+1	13 00	+2	Mar. 28, 1999—Oct. 31, 1999
Luxembourg	+1	13 00	+2	Mar. 28, 1999—Oct. 31, 1999
Macau	+8	20 00		
Macedonia	+1	13 00	+2	Mar. 28, 1999—Oct. 31, 1999
Madagascar	+3	15 00		
Malawi	+2	14 00		
Malaysia	+8	20 00		
Maldives	+5	17 00		
Mali	GMT	12 00		
Malta	+1	13 00	+2	Mar. 28, 1999—Oct. 31, 1999
Martinique	−4	08 00		
Mauritania	GMT	12 00		
Mauritius	+4	16 00		
Mayotte	+3	15 00		
Mexico*				
Except Baja California Norte, Baja California Sur, Chihuahua, Nayarit, Sinaloa, Sonora	−6	06 00	−5	Apr. 04, 1999E—Oct. 31, 1999E
Baja California Sur and N. Pacific Coast (States of Nayarit and Sinaloa) — Chihuahua, Culican, La Paz, Mazathlan	−7	05 00	−6	Apr. 04, 1999E—Oct. 31, 1999E
Baja California Norte (Above 28th Parallel) — Mexicali, Tijuana	−8	04 00	−7	Apr. 04, 1999E—Oct. 31, 1999E
Sonora	−7	05 00		
Midway Island	−11	01 00		
Moldova, Republic of	+2	14 00	+3	Mar. 28, 1999E—Oct. 31, 1999E
Monaco	+1	13 00	+2	Mar. 28, 1999—Oct. 31, 1999
Mongolia (Ulan Bator)	+8	20 00		
Morocco	GMT	12 00		
Mozambique	+2	14 00		
Myanmar	+6 1/2	18 30		
Namibia	+1	13 00	+2	Sep. 05, 1999E—Apr. 02, 2000E
Nauru, Republic Of	+12	23 59		
Nepal	+5 3/4	17 45		
Netherlands	+1	13 00	+2	Mar. 28, 1999—Oct. 31, 1999
Netherlands Antilles (incl. Southern St. Maarten)	−4	08 00		
New Caledonia	+11	23 00		
New Zealand (Excluding Chatham Is.)	+12	23 59	+13	Oct. 03, 1999—Mar. 19, 2000
Chatham Is.	+12 3/4	00 45	+13 3/4	Oct. 03, 1999—Mar. 19, 2000
Nicaragua	−6	06 00		
Niger	+1	13 00		
Nigeria	+1	13 00		
Niue Island	−11	01 00		
Norfolk Island	+11 1/2	23 30		
Norway	+1	13 00	+2	Mar. 28,1999—Oct. 31, 1999
Oman	+4	16 00		

FIGURE 7-4

International Standard Time Chart. *(Reprinted by special permission from the OAG® Air Cargo Guide. Copyright © 1999, Reed Elsevier Inc. All rights reserved.)*

What to Do If You Call at an Inopportune Time

"Learn to listen for busy signals. Not the buzzing kind that comes from your phone, but the kinds that tell you the person you're calling is busy or preoccupied."[1]

Often you can tell by the tone of voice, mannerisms, or subtle hints that your party would rather talk later. Ask if you can call back at a better time. You'll have better results when the person you're calling can give you full attention. "Also, your thoughtfulness will be appreciated and the person will be more inclined to act favorably toward you."[2]

A positive, confident mental attitude is essential to making an effective sales call. Getting yourself **psyched-up** before you call can project this positive attitude right through the phone and into your prospect's mind.

The first 15 seconds of your call are crucial. Make sure that you address your prospect by name. Identify yourself and the company or organization you represent. Establish rapport by being interested and knowledgeable about your prospect's business or organization. Sometimes this will require considerable research.

Capture your prospect's attention with a proposal that cannot be ignored or with an interest-creating comment. This is easier said than done. But it is certainly worth spending considerable time to come up with a captivating phrase. It could relate to something that will generate profits, save on costs, be a catalyst for fun, or enhance your contact's image with his or her peers or group.

One thing that calls to obtain new business accounts or to obtain a group booking have in common is that neither is usually completed by a single telephone call. Often a face-to-face meeting needs to be set up to discuss details. This may be conducted over a business lunch. Other times it may be important for the client to see your facilities, or it might be important for you to see your prospect's facilities.

After a face-to-face meeting, the telephone should be used to say thank you for the opportunity to meet and to reconfirm further procedures that will be taken. Telephone calls can be made at most anytime to report on progress, to solve problems, or to speed up the exchange of information.

The Follow-Up Call

The fifth type of outgoing business telephone call is the **follow-up call** after a sale has been completed. These calls can provide several benefits. First, they can be used to make sure that the product and service was satisfactory. Second, they provide an opportunity to ask for referrals, a valuable source of new business. Third, they can be used to determine when the customer might need additional services.

Ask if they have thought about where they would like to travel on their next vacation. Then find out approximately when they would like to travel. Ask if there is any information that they would like you to research for them. Make notes in your desk calendar regarding when you should research the information requested, and when you should forward it to them. Schedule a follow-up call several days after you would expect the clients to receive the information that you have sent.

WORD SPELLING

Some letters can sound like others over the telephone. The letter *F* sounds like the letter *S*. It is often difficult to differentiate among *B*, *V*, or *P*; and the letter *M* can sound like an *N*. Many people cannot discern the difference between William and Lillian over the telephone.

For names, addresses, and file locators or reservation numbers, tourism professionals usually use word spelling to make sure the listener gets the letters correctly. Sometimes a word is substituted for each letter spelled out. For example, "Is the spelling of your family name, *P* as in *papa*, *E* as in *echo*, *W* as in *whiskey*?"

Other times, the name is spelled out in the normal manner except for the "troublesome" letters. For example, "Is your family name spelled, *J-O-H-N-S*, *T* as in tango, *O-N*, *E* as in *echo*?" For people who speak English as a second language, it is better to word spell every letter.

There are four basic systems of word spelling used in the tourism industry. (See Figure 7-5.)

- The first is the **symphonic alphabet** that is used by most international air carriers.

- The second is the Domestic Airlines word spelling system used by many of the domestic airlines in the U.S.A.

- The third is the Telephone Operators system traditionally used by telephone operators in the U.S.A.

- The fourth is the International Place Names system that is useful with international customers who speak English as a second language.

The Symphonic Alphabet

Most international air carriers use the symphonic alphabet. English is the international language in the airline industry. The symphonic alphabet uses standardized words that are very distinct for the sound of the letter indicated. Because the same word is used worldwide, there is little chance of being misunderstood. It is important for

Letter	Symphonic Alphabet	Domestic Airlines	Telephone Operators	International Place Names
A	Alpha	Adam	Alice	Athens
B	Bravo	Boston	Bertha	Berlin
C	Charlie	Chicago	Charles	California
D	Delta	Detroit	David	Dublin
E	Echo	Edward	Edward	England
F	Foxtrot	Frank	Frank	France
G	Gulf	George	George	Glasgow
H	Hotel	Henry	Henry	Hamburg
I	India	Ida	Ida	Italy
J	Julliette	John	James	Jordan
K	Kilo	King	Kate	Kingston
L	Lima	Lincoln	Louise	London
M	Mother	Mary	Mary	Madrid
N	November	New York	Nellie	Naples
O	Oscar	Ocean	Oliver	Oslo
P	Papa	Peter	Peter	Paris
Q	Queen	Queen	Quaker	Québec
R	Romeo	Robert	Robert	Romania
S	Sierra	Sugar	Samuel	Sweden
T	Tango	Thomas	Thomas	Tokyo
U	Uniform	Union	Utah	Ukraine
V	Victor	Victor	Victor	Victoria
W	Whiskey	William	William	Washington
X	X-ray	X-ray	X-ray	Xanthos*
Y	Yankee	Young	Young	York
Z	Zulu	Zero	Zebra	Zurich

* Better stick with X-ray.

FIGURE 7-5   Word spelling

anyone involved in international tourism to commit the symphonic alphabet to memory for use with other professionals in the tourism industry.

Domestic Airlines System of Word Spelling

Before the symphonic alphabet was designed, domestic airlines in the U.S.A. had developed their own word-spelling alphabet. Many domestic carriers still use this system. People working in other sectors of the tourism industry who deal mostly with the Domestic Airline System of word spelling are probably familiar with this system.

Tourism industry employees who speak English as a first language and who know the symphonic alphabet should not have any problem understanding the Domestic Airline System of word spelling.

Telephone Operators System of Word Spelling

Telephone operators in the U.S.A. have used their own word spelling system for many years. Their system is based on people's first names and place names, and other common words. These words are very distinctive for the letters they represent and are widely understood by their customers. This system may not be effective with international clientele or business contacts.

International Place Names System of Word Spelling

The problem with the symphonic alphabet is that many customers who are not involved with the airline industry or international tourism may not understand the words used. This is even more likely if they speak English as a second language. The International Place Names system of word spelling is very easy for people who speak any language to understand. Simply select international place names that you are sure the listener will understand. For example, *F* as in Frankfurt, *S* as in Sweden, *B* as in Berlin, *V* as in Victoria, *P* as in Paris, *M* as in Madrid, *N* as in New York. Place names should be selected according to the language and origin of the person to whom you are speaking, but make sure the pronunciation you are using is one to which he or she is accustomed. For example, if you were using *N* as in Naples, it would be alright for someone who speaks English as a first language, but it should be pronounced Napoli (NAH-poh-lee) for someone who speaks Italian as a first language.

There are two pitfalls to avoid when using international place names for word spelling. First, avoid names that are spelled with different first letters in other languages. For example, Canada would not be a good example for the letter *C* because in many languages,

Canada is spelled with a *K*. Second, avoid names that are completely different in various languages. For example, Germany is known as Deutschland by the people who live there and as Allemagne by their neighbors in France.

As an industry, it is recommended that we use the symphonic alphabet that is used by most international carriers. With customers who are not familiar with this system and who are speaking English as a second language, the fourth system, which uses international place names, is preferable.

SUMMARY

The telephone can be your most valuable sales aid. More people respond to advertisements and promotions by telephone than by any other means. The key to success in handling these calls is to be prepared for them and to be organized to handle them efficiently.

By using outgoing telephone calls, you can visit as many customers in one hour as you could personally call on in a day. Success from outgoing calls depends upon calling key people at the right time. Organize your call to cover important benefits to the customer efficiently and get yourself psyched-up to deliver your message with enthusiasm that will get your prospect turned on.

Notes

1. *Today's Way To Operate*, Trans Canada Telephone System, Ottawa, Ontario, Canada, 1982.
2. Ibid.

Discussion Questions

1. Name the two principle types of telephone sales.
2. What are the two categories of incoming calls?
3. What are the five categories of outgoing calls?
4. List the six pieces of information you need to complete a credit card transaction over the telephone.
5. List the information required to complete a booking form for transportation.
6. What additional booking information is required if your customer is traveling to or from an international destination?

7. What additional booking information may be required if a customer requires other services in addition to basic transportation?

8. List four basic systems of word spelling used in the tourism industry.

9. Recite the symphonic alphabet.

10. Make up your own International Place Name word spelling alphabet.

Overcoming Objections

OBJECTIVES

After studying this chapter, you should be able to:

● Identify and overcome objections due to time considerations

● Identify and overcome objections due to financial considerations

● Determine whether the recommendation satisfied the prospect's needs

● Recommend another proposal that better meets the prospect's needs

● Determine whether the customer misunderstood the salesperson's proposal, and if so, clarify the proposal

KEY TERMS

A + PS = MS	sell down
NAQP	split payment

STEP 8: OVERCOMING OBJECTIONS

Recognize resistance due to lack of credibility of the salesperson and suggest ways of overcoming this problem. Listen. Do not interrupt when customers are stating their objections to your recommendations. If you do not completely understand their objections, probe to obtain a clear understanding of the customer's problems with your recommendation.

When you fully understand the nature of their objections, it is necessary to evaluate the situation to determine whether there is a misunderstanding between you and the client about your perception of the client's requirements or the client's comprehension of your proposal. If so, keep asking questions until you truly understand each other.

Then determine whether you should stay with your proposal and further explain its benefits to the customer, make a new recommendation based upon your more complete comprehension of the client's needs, or meet the customer half way by sticking to your original recommendation but modifying it to more closely satisfy the customer's needs.

It is really frustrating, but no matter how hard you try, it seems you are unable to close many deals when you know that the prospects are really interested in what you are offering. But they walk away without giving you the opportunity to make the sale. There is a formula for closing more sales:

$$A + PS = MS$$
ATTITUDE + PROBLEM SOLVING = MORE SALES

Before setting a strategy for increasing sales, determine how many contacts with prospects you are converting into sales. Anyone who has worked in the tourism industry realizes that many people do not approach the salesperson with the idea that they are going to buy a service or product.

They contact you just for some information. Out of five prospects that contact you just for some information, how many do you convert into sales? If you are not sure, start keeping score. Keep a piece of paper or a file card with one side for telephone contacts and the other for personal contacts. After each contact, mark down *S* (for sales) if you made the sale, or *L* (for losses) if you did not make the sale. Follow an *L* by a brief comment about why you think you did not make the sale. (See Figure 8-1.)

On the In-Office Record of Sales and Losses for personal contacts note that the salesperson closed 6 out of 11 prospects. The booking for Arnott regarding a Holland America cruise was still to be decided and a follow-up appointment had been scheduled for October 7 at 2:00 P.M. If this were typical for a period of a month or more, you could conclude that this salesperson was good but had some room for improvement. Two of the *L*s were **NAQP**s (not a qualified prospect), so you would not be concerned about them.

For the caller, Guenette, the salesperson should ponder whether he or she was not skillful enough at determining the date or whether the prospect really did not know the dates. To determine the dates for a prospect who is reluctant to reveal them, state that the prices vary on different dates and you would not want to misquote the price. Start with a season. Would you want to go during the winter? If the customer does not want to go during the winter, he or she will correct you.

Once you have a season, suggest a month. If you would like to go on February 17, the price will be $1,719.00. If this date is not a possibility, the customer will correct you. Suggest another date. Soon you

IN-OFFICE RECORD OF SALES AND LOSSES		S	L	SEP. 27, 2002
Name	Request	S	L	Comment
Melnyk, R.	2 A, STT PKG	✓		10 day DIT
Walker, E.	2 A, 1 C, ITC		✓	2 wk Hawaii, follow-up too slow
Muños, T. M.	1 A, ALB-LAX	✓		air only, ?car/accom
Schultz, B.	4 A, BOS-WAS C	✓		AMTRAK
Arnott, D.	3 A, Holland America Cruise	?		OCT 7, 2:00 pm
Sinclair, M.	2 A, Via Rail		✓	NAQP — project
Guenette, S.	Collette Tour — HI-VISTAS		✓	didn't know dates
Sanchez, W.	1 A, ALB-PHX + Hotel	✓		OK
Blunt, S.	2 A, 1 SR, 1 CH, ALB-MSY	✓		Check re: tours
Ploski, F.	2 A, 2 C, Disney World	✓		OK
Allard, C.	Cunard World Cruise		✓	NAQP — cost

FIGURE 8-1

In-office record of sales and losses

will arrive at a date on which he or she could travel. At this point use the Option Close with the suggestion that if the date is not the one they prefer, you can change it.

If the caller, Guenette, really did not know the date he or she could travel because someone else actually authorizes vacation time, two approaches can be taken. First, "If you had your choice, when would you prefer to go?" If you receive an answer to this question, use the Option Close: "If your employer does not approve the date, we can change the reservation."

Second, you could ask, "When will your employer announce your vacation dates?" When you receive an answer to this question, make an appointment either by telephone or preferably for an office visit to complete the booking. Remember, always make appointments for a precise date, time, and place.

Now refer to the Record of Sales and Losses for telephone contacts. (See Figure 8-2.) Here the salesperson closed four out of ten prospects. For a single day, this is not a significant difference from the 6 out of 11 prospects for personal contacts. But if this pattern was constant over a period of a month or more, perhaps there is a flaw in the salesperson's telephone sales technique.

RECORD OF SALES AND LOSSES BY TELEPHONE		S	L	SEP. 27, 2002
Name	**Request**	**S**	**L**	**Comment**
Cloutier, L.	2A, Hawaii		✓	gave too much info
Garcia, L.	wanted posters		✓	NAQP
Cheung, H.	2A, NYC-HKG		✓	hung up
Mack, F.	2A, NCL	✓		cruise
Wilson, S.	2A, MBJ ITC		✓	has to talk it over with . . .
Butler, T. M.	1A,NYC-SFO	✓		+ hotel (moderate)
Simon, P.	RQ photo of Eiffel Tower		✓	NAQP
Krahn, G.	2A, NYC-SEA		✓	AMTRAK, not avail.
Moregno, R.	2A, honeymoon STT	✓		Blue Beard's Castle
Hernandez, T.	4A, NYC-AMS	✓		FIT with EURAIL

FIGURE 8-2

Record of sales and losses for prospects by telephone

The two NAQPs would not be a cause for concern. For prospect Cloutier, the salesperson realized her mistake in giving out too much information before qualifying. Prospect Cheung hung up before the salesperson could attempt a close. He probably received all the information he needed before the salesperson had qualified him. In this case, the salesperson probably gives out too much information, before qualifying, when answering telephone calls.

Prospect Wilson was a different problem. The salesperson realized that Wilson was a qualified prospect. She either used the wrong closing technique or was not skillful enough at using the Option Close to convince the client to make a buying decision. Fine-tuning her explanation of how an option allows her to hold space for the customer with no obligation is to the customer's advantage. If the customer understood that the option was to her advantage, confirmed space with no obligation, you would have converted this L (loss) to a S (sale).

You couldn't provide prospect Krahn with the service requested. But you might have been able to close the sale by suggesting other dates or by booking air or motor coach transportation.

Over a period of time your Record of Sales and Losses will indicate your busy days, and busy times of day, and conversely your relatively quiet periods. This can help you plan when to schedule your follow-up calls and other administrative chores.

Every time you fail to make the sale, analyze what happened. Did you make a mistake? Was there something else you could have done to close the deal? Was the person who contacted you an NAQP?

If you sell to less than one out of five prospects, you are not even closing the sales for clients who have already made up their minds to purchase the tourism product or service that you are discussing! About one in five prospects knows the product or service they desire and when they want it. If you are not closing sales with these people, you are not even asking for the sale!

If you are closing sales with two out of five, you have developed some sales skills but have the potential to double your sales and hopefully your income. Whether you are paid a salary, commission, or a combination of both, your paycheck is directly related to your sales. If there is more revenue coming in, your employer can afford to pay you more. If you keep score, you can justify a request for a pay increase.

If you are booking three out of five, you are a good salesperson. But you have room for improvement. However, it is impossible to "get them all." About one out of five or six contacts is not a qualified prospect. Prospects may need information for a school project, be passing time while a friend is busy shopping, or dreaming about a tourism experience that is light years away in terms of budget and time availability.

To improve sales, you must start with a positive attitude! If only one out of five or six contacts is not a qualified prospect, logic dictates that it is possible to book the others. If people approach you for information about tourism, they must have a desire to experience a tourism product! If they really want to have a tourism experience, why don't they let you close the deal?

The answer is that they really do want to have the tourism experience but they have a problem. Help them solve their problems and you will be able to close the sales!

Prospects who will be sharing the tourism experience with someone else want to talk it over with him or her before making a purchase. Reply, "I am sure you do need to consult Martha before you make a final decision, but I do not want you to be disappointed if space will not be available. I suggest that we check to see whether space is available and hold it until you talk it over with Martha. If it is not what you want, we can change it."

Use the word *change* rather than *cancel*. If the customer decides that he or she does not want the product or service that you sold, you can change it. Some clients have a problem making up their mind between possible choices. I say "between," because you should have offered only two choices to satisfy their needs. If you offered more than two choices, then you caused the confusion.

"Which of these two would you prefer?" If they can not decide, help them! "I would recommend this one because . . ." If there is no objection to your recommendation, check whether it is available and offer to hold the space for them. (Within the industry, offering to hold space for someone is exactly the same as making a reservation or booking. But to the customer, holding space makes it sound like less of an obligation.) If they object, find out why and decide whether you should counter the objection, or offer them something else that would avoid their objection.

Other problems may be financially based. Some clients may be able to afford your recommendation but are not convinced that it is a good value. Cost comparisons are good for this type of problem. For example, compare the cost of normal transportation charges to the promotional fare. (See Figure 8-3.)

The customer thought the promotional fare of $599.50 was high. Realizing that there were only seven seats available at that price and knowing that if he delays his decision, he might have to pay $2,438.00 would probably help him to make a decision to buy now.

Another point of comparison—the cost of touring independently compared to the package price you are recommending. (See Figure 8-4.) For the same services, the Collette Tour would save your customers $176.13 per person, which you would express as a saving of $352.26 for the total cost for both of you (to maximize the saving). The Collette Tour saves them money. It would also leave the driving to them, so they could keep their eyes on the scenery instead of on the road. The services of a professional tour escort cannot be overstated. The information about the places that they will visit will be invaluable and probably not be available if they travel on their own. Also, the tour escort can provide them with information regarding their personal preferences regarding the types of restaurants, entertainment, and attractions your clients prefer. Tours are always the most time-efficient way to garner the most out of a vacation. People who tour on their own waste a lot of valuable vacation time planning what they are

---

AVAILABILITY ON DELTA AIRLINES AS OF DEC. 5, 2002

Date	dp	From	ar	To	Lowest Fare
JAN 11	8:35a	New York	11:33a	Los Angeles	$599.50
JAN 23	1:00p	Los Angeles	9:20p	New York	including taxes

Seats available at lowest fare: **7**

Full Coach Fare
$2,438.00
including taxes

Seats available at the full coach fare: **138**

FIGURE 8-3
Promotional fare compared with full coach fare

INDEPENDENT TOUR TO COMPARE WITH COLLETTE CALIFORNIA COAST TOUR

Note: All costs are per person based on two people sharing the rental car and twin rooms in all hotels, including taxes and baggage handling. Meals include tax and tips but do not include alcoholic beverages.

Hertz mid-sized car 1 week, pickup at San Francisco Airport, unlimited mileage, Collision Damage Waiver, Personal Accident Insurance, drop off at San Diego Airport	$ 212.81	**Oct 23—Day 5**	
		Breakfast: Casa Munras Garden Hotel	$ 13.30
Gasoline and oil	$ 55.00	Hearst Castle Tour	$ 15.40
		Hotel: Danish Country Inn, Solvang	$ 82.50
		Dinner: Bit 'O Denmark Restaurant	$ 15.00
Oct 19—Day 1			
Hotel: Sir Francis Drake, San Francisco	$ 98.22	**Oct 24—Day 6**	
		Breakfast: Bit 'O Denmark Restaurant	$ 7.59
Dinner: Sir Francis Drake Hotel	$ 31.25	Dinner: Beverly Hills Hilton	$ 31.25
		Hotel: Westin Bonaventure, Los Angeles	$ 106.03
Oct 20—Day 2			
Gray Line Tour of San Francisco	$ 31.00		
Hotel: Sir Francis Drake, San Francisco	$ 94.22	**Oct 25—Day 7**	
		Breakfast: Westin Bonaventure	$ 13.60
		Tour: Mission San Juan Capistrano	$ 6.50
Oct 21—Day 3		Hotel: U.S. Grant, San Diego	$ 127.50
Yosemite National Park entrance fee	$ 10.00	Dinner: U.S. Grant Hotel	$ 25.00
Hotel: Tenaya Lodge	$ 81.95	Tour: by tram of San Diego Zoo	$ 22.00
Dinner: Tenaya Lodge	$ 27.15		
		Oct 26—Day 8	
Oct 22—Day 4		Breakfast U.S. Grant Hotel	$ 12.25
Breakfast: Tenaya Lodge	$ 12.16	Hotel: U.S. Grant Hotel, San Diego	$ 127.50
Hotel: Casa Munras Garden Hotel, Monterey	$ 88.15		
Dinner: Whaling Station Restaurant	$ 27.80	Total cost of traveling independently	$1,375.13
		Cost of Collette's California Coast Tour (per person)	$1,199.00

FIGURE 8-4

Independent tour to compare with Collette California Coast tour.

going to do instead of enjoying what they could be doing. The tour operator has spent a great deal of time to ensure that the tour represents the best value to the consumer.

The advantages of selling a tour are even more significant for the salesperson. To sell a tour it takes the salesperson one or two minutes on the telephone or reservations computer. To plan and book an independent tour for a client would probably take anywhere from 4 to 12 hours for a one or two week holiday, often longer.

A third cost comparison to make is between weekend or off-season rates and the regular rates. Perhaps a sale can be made at this level.

A fourth comparison is to show what is included in your recommendation for a best available tour versus what the customer would receive for a lower-priced budget tour. Compare Trafalgar's Best of Switzerland (see Figure 8-5) with Cosmos's Grand Tour of Switzerland (see Figure 8-6). Both tours are good value for their price and are fairly represented in their brochures. Trafalgar promotes itself as "First Class Fully Escorted." Cosmos promotes itself as the "World's Best Budget Touring."

Trafalgar's Best of Switzerland includes buffet breakfasts each day. Cosmos's Grand Tour of Switzerland includes continental breakfasts of bread or rolls, butter, jam, and coffee. Trafalgar includes five dinners, whereas Cosmos includes four. The main difference in meal service is that the quality of the restaurants would be better with Trafalgar. But the principal difference between Trafalgar and Cosmos is the quality of the hotels.

Trafalgar uses first-class hotel accommodations. Cosmos uses tourist class and superior tourist class hotels. These are terms not usually used in North America, but they would definitely be deemed budget. In Zürich, Cosmos uses a first-class hotel, but it is "only 20 minutes away by train"!

I do not want to imply that Cosmos's Grand Tour of Switzerland is not a good tour, especially considering value for money paid—as they market it, the "World's Best Budget Touring." The point I am making is that there is a significant difference in the quality of the two tours. It is easier to sell the lower priced tour, but will your client be satisfied? Qualify your prospects carefully and sell them the tour that is appropriate for their needs.

For other clients, whether the tourism product is affordable could be the problem. The first response of many salespeople is to **sell down**, proposing:

- a less expensive product or service
- a shorter tour, stay, or adventure
- a destination or attraction that is closer to where the tourist is now and that has similar attributes

(continues on page 144)

Best of Switzerland

Touring: Zurich • St. Moritz • Italian Lakes • Zermatt • Montreux • Geneva • Interlaken • Lucerne

Why not take a cruise on Lake Lucerne!

Truly a scenic spectacular of lakes, valleys and soaring mountain peaks. There are stunning mountain passes and dining experiences as you explore the Swiss cantons and the elegant resorts and cities.

● Overnight stays
( ). No. of nights

Time to splash out on a Rolex!

Day 1 Depart Canada Overnight flight to Zurich.

Day 2 Arrive Zurich We transfer you to your hotel on arrival in Zurich. This afternoon, an *orientation tour* of this lakeside city reveals its charm and beauty. This evening, we enjoy a *welcome drink* with our Tour Director.

Day 3 Zurich – St. Moritz Snow-capped mountains and sparkling lakes surround us on our morning drive to the tiny Principality of *Liechtenstein* where we visit its capital, *Vaduz*. We continue via *Klosters*, favourite ski-resort of the British Royal family, and spectacular *Davos*. Next it's up the *Fluela Pass* (when open), past picturesque Susch to *St. Moritz* - home of the international jet-set. Tonight, we enjoy dinner at our hotel. **(BB D)**

Day 4 St. Moritz – Italian Lakes (Baveno) This morning we ascend the *Julier Pass* and continue our drive along the *San Bernadino Route* to Bellinzona. We continue to *Lake Maggiore* and via *Locarno* into Italy and the beautiful resort of *Baveno* for the night. Later, why not take a cruise across the lake to picturesque Borromean Islands? Dinner is at our hotel. **(BB D)**

Day 5 Italian Lakes (Baveno) – Zermatt This morning we drive to pretty *Stresa* and then towards the majestic *Simplon Pass*, 6,600 feet high. Later, we reach Tasch to board 114 the *electric mini-buses and taxis*

which take us up to the picturesque village of *Zermatt*. This evening dinner is at our hotel. **(BB D)**

Day 6 Zermatt at leisure – Geneva Time to relax this morning before we drive through the *Rhône Valley* to Lake Geneva where we view Byron's *Castle of Chillon*. We continue to *Montreux* and see the major sights. Next via Lausanne to

You'll see the imposing Chillon Castle on Lake Geneva at Montreux.

Geneva where *orientation* shows us the Reformation Monument, United Nations' Building and the Jet d'Eau Fountain. Tonight, why not dine on fine cuisine with views of Mont Blanc? **(BB)**

Day 7 Geneva – Lucerne (2) This morning via *Berne*, where we see the famous bears, we stop in the resort of *Interlaken*. On to *Brienz*

to see the traditional *craft of wood-carving* with time to purchase a piece or two! Then over the *Brünig Pass* to lakeside *Lucerne* in its beautiful setting for two nights. This evening dinner is at our hotel. **(BB D)**

Day 8 Lucerne orientation & at leisure After breakfast we enjoy an *orientation tour* around this medieval city highlighting the *Lion Monument* and Chapel Bridge. Later with time at leisure perhaps take an excursion to a nearby mountain, or join in the fun of a Swiss folklore show. Or you may choose to explore the old city for watches, cuckoo clocks and delicious Swiss chocolates. **(BB D)**

Day 9 Lucerne – Zurich – Canada After breakfast, it's farewell as we transfer to Zurich Airport for our return flight to Canada. **(BB)**

FIGURE 8-5 Trafalgar's "Best of Switzerland." *(Courtesy of Trafalgar Tours)*

Enjoy a Wealth of First Class Included Features

Daily Sightseeing Highlights

ZURICH Orientation including the medieval Old Town.

LIECHTENSTEIN Visit the capital of the tiny principality, Vaduz.

LOCARNO See this beautiful resort on Lake Maggiore.

STRESA Visit this lovely lakeside reosrt.

ZERMATT Ascent by electric mini-bus and taxi to your Zermatt hotel. View the Matterhorn (weather permitting).

LAKE GENEVA View the Castle of Chillon.

MONTREUX Sightseeing showing the major sights.

GENEVA Orientation including the Jet d'Eau Fountain. View Mont Blanc (weather permitting).

BERNE Visit the Bear Pits.

INTERLAKEN Visit the lakeside resort near the Jungfrau.

BRIENZ See local wood-carvers at work.

LUCERNE Orientation including the Lion Monument and the walled Old Town.

Spectacular Scenic Drives

- The Fluela and Julier Passes
- The Engadine Valley and Maloja Pass
- The Italian Lake District
- Along the shores of Lake Maggiore
- The Simplon Pass
- The Rhône Valley
- Along the shores of Lake Geneva
- The Bernese Oberland and Brünig Passes

Superior Transportation

- You'll tour by luxury air-conditioned motorcoach with reclining seats and washroom
- Zurich Airport Transfers are provided on Days 2 and 9

Europe's Leading Guides

- The services of one of Trafalgar's professional multi-lingual Tour Directors on tour

Dining Highlights

- A welcome drink with your Tour Director in Zurich
- 7 Buffet breakfasts (BB)
- 5 three-course dinners (D)
- 12 meals in total – see day by day itinerary

First Class Hotels

You'll stay in twin-bedded rooms with private facilities at these superb hotels:

Zurich: Renaissance
St. Moritz: Belvedere
Italian Lakes (Baveno): Splendid
Zermatt: Alpenroyal
Geneva: Cornavin
Lucerne (2): Flora

All hotel service charges and tips, baggage handling fees and local taxes included.

For a comprehensive list of the hotel facilities on this tour please see pages 185-188.

All this plus a stylish travel bag and wallet containing comprehensive tour documents and helpful information.

See the hundred foot high Jet d'Eau fountain on Lake Geneva

---

9 days from C$1335

Package ID SWBOA

Departure Ref	Departs Toronto	Returns Toronto
Land: C$1335		Land+Air*: C$2200
SWBOA/201	Fri 7 Apr	Sat 15 Apr
SWBOA/202	Fri 14 Apr	Sat 22 Apr
SWBOA/203	Fri 21 Apr	Sat 29 Apr
SWBOA/204	Fri 28 Apr	Sat 6 May
SWBOA/205	Fri 5 May	Sat 13 May
SWBOA/206	Fri 12 May	Sat 20 May
Land: C$1335		Land+Air*: C$2320
SWBOA/207	Fri 19 May	Sat 27 May
SWBOA/208	Fri 26 May	Sat 3 Jun
SWBOA/209	Fri 2 Jun	Sat 10 Jun
SWBOA/210	Fri 9 Jun	Sat 17 Jun
Land: C$1335		Land+Air*: C$2485
SWBOA/211	Fri 16 Jun	Sat 24 Jun
SWBOA/212	Fri 23 Jun	Sat 1 Jul
SWBOA/213	Fri 30 Jun	Sat 8 Jul
SWBOA/214	Fri 7 Jul	Sat 15 Jul
SWBOA/215	Fri 14 Jul	Sat 22 Jul
SWBOA/216	Fri 21 Jul	Sat 29 Jul
SWBOA/217	Fri 28 Jul	Sat 5 Aug
SWBOA/218	Fri 4 Aug	Sat 12 Aug
SWBOA/219	Fri 11 Aug	Sat 19 Aug
SWBOA/220	Fri 18 Aug	Sat 26 Aug
SWBOA/221	Fri 25 Aug	Sat 2 Sep
SWBOA/222	Fri 1 Sep	Sat 9 Sep
SWBOA/223	Fri 8 Sep	Sat 16 Sep
Land: C$1335		Land+Air*: C$2320
SWBOA/224	Fri 15 Sep	Sat 23 Sep
SWBOA/225	Fri 22 Sep	Sat 30 Sep
SWBOA/226	Fri 29 Sep	Sat 7 Oct
SWBOA/227	Fri 6 Oct	Sat 14 Oct
SWBOA/228	Fri 13 Oct	Sat 21 Oct
SWBOA/229	Fri 20 Oct	Sat 28 Oct
SWBOA/230	Fri 27 Oct	Sat 4 Nov

Single room supplement	C$240
Triple room reduction	C$50
Child reduction	C$200

Please note: This tour visits **France** for a short period.

* Plus applicable departure taxes

LEISURESHOPPER   LSA/V:TTC/I:SWBOA

COSTSAVER

For a similar tour featuring excellent tourist class hotels ask for Trafalgar's CostSaver 2000 brochure. See page 58.

Please ask your Travel Agent for a copy

Action Discount
SAVE C$35
per person
See Pages 22/23 for more details

Skybargain Fares

The above 'Land+Air' prices are from Toronto. For details and special low add-on fares from other Canadian cities, see page 24.

Airport Transfers

Transfers on arrival will be provided only for passengers who have booked their flights on a Trafalgar recommended airline and advised Trafalgar of their flight dates. Transfers from Zurich Airport will operate at 09.00, 11.00 and 12.30. Passengers arriving later should make their own way to the first hotel. Return transfers from the last hotel will arrive at the Airport at 08.30.

115

FIGURE 8-5   *(concluded) (Courtesy of Trafalgar Tours)*

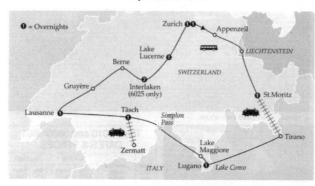

COSMOS

WORLD'S BEST BUDGET TOURING   ESCORTED

Grand Tour of Switzerland

Featuring the Bernina Express Train

Tour **6020** — 9 days incl.air, or 8 days Zurich/Zurich
Tour **6025** — with Interlaken extension - 16 days incl.air, or
15 days Zurich/Zurich

❶ = Overnights

ALL THIS IS INCLUDED

■ Scheduled transatlantic flights and airport transfers in Zurich if Cosmos issues the tickets; see page 13

■ Services of a professional tour director

■ Hotels listed below or equivalent; see also page 9. Rooms with private bath or shower, hotel taxes, porterage, tips, and service charges

■ Continental breakfasts (B) and dinners (D) as detailed in the tour description

■ Touring by private first-class air-conditioned motorcoach

■ The Bernina Express Train; Mountain Train Täsch-Zermatt

■ Visits to Appenzell, Liechtenstein, St. Moritz, Lugano, a chocolate factory at Caslano, Lake Maggiore, Täsch, Zermatt, Lausanne, Gruyère village, Berne, Interlaken, Lucerne

■ Scenic highlights: Julier Pass, Engadine Valley, Swiss-Italian Lake District, Simplon Pass, the Bernese Oberland

■ Tour 6025 only: Jungfraujoch excursion. Value $115

■ Portfolio of travel documents

▼ LAUSANNE, ON THE NORTHERN SHORE OF LAKE GENEVA   ▼ ALPHORN BLOWERS

Day 1, Fri. BOARD YOUR OVERNIGHT TRANSATLANTIC FLIGHT.

Day 2, Sat. ARRIVAL IN ZURICH, SWITZERLAND. Check into your hotel in Zurich/Regensdorf. The rest of the day is free for you to explore Zurich, which is only 20 minutes away by train. Tonight meet your tour director and fellow travelers.

Day 3, Sun. ZURICH-ST. MORITZ. A sensational drive today through some of Switzerland's most famed cantons. First by way of the market town of Herisau, then stop in Appenzell to see the old town center with its Town Hall. Further east to the minute principality of Liechtenstein. A scenic drive through "Heidiland" to the Rhine Valley before starting the ascent of the mighty Julier Pass. Soon you'll be in the heart of Switzerland's largest canton, the Grisons. Here see some of the world's best alpine views before arriving in St. Moritz. (B)

Day 4, Mon. ST. MORITZ-BERNINA EXPRESS TRAIN TO TIRANO, ITALY-LUGANO, SWITZERLAND. Enjoy the highlight of the whole tour and a wonderful way of crossing the Alps. One of Europe's most spectacular train rides begins in St. Moritz and takes you across the lofty Bernina Pass via the Swiss Poschiavo area to Tirano in the Italian Valtellina. Here rejoin your coach for the journey to the shores of Lake Lugano. (B,D)

Day 5, Tue. LUGANO-LAKE MAGGIORE-TÄSCH. Morning break in Lugano with a visit to a chocolate factory in nearby Caslano. Afterwards return to Italy to savor the luminous atmosphere of Lake Maggiore. Time for an optional visit to Isola Bella, a magnificently located palace and garden island. Then back into Switzerland via the scenic Simplon Pass. Overnight in the village of Täsch. (B,D)

Day 6, Wed. TÄSCH-ZERMATT-LAUSANNE. This morning an excursion by train to Zermatt, the famous resort beneath the Matterhorn. In the afternoon motor through the vineyards and apricot groves of the lower Rhône Valley to Lake Geneva before arriving in Lausanne on its northern shore. (B)

Day 7, Thu. LAUSANNE-LAKE LUCERNE. Stop awhile in Gruyère, then on to Switzerland's beautiful capital, Berne, a charming town with arcaded shops, carved fountains, and towers. Included sightseeing features the Bear Pit and the monumental Federal Palace. Then by way of the shores of Lake Thun to Interlaken. After a visit continue over Brünig Pass to Lake Lucerne. Time for an optional folklore evening in Lucerne. (B,D)

Day 8, Fri. LAKE LUCERNE-ZURICH. One of Switzerland's finest cities nestled amid its snow-capped alps, surrounded by its lake, and embellished by the clear mountain waters of the River Reuss. Your sightseeing takes in the main highlights. A grand selection of optional activities completes the day. The most popular options are a half-day excursion to the 10,000-foot-high Mount Titlis, and a boat cruise on Lake Lucerne. In the late afternoon an easy drive back to Zurich for an overnight in nearby Regensdorf. (B)

Day 9, Sat. YOUR HOMEBOUND FLIGHT ARRIVES THE SAME DAY. (B)

➤ If you need a visa for Italy, please secure a multiple-entry visa.

94 **CA**

FIGURE 8-6   Cosmos "Grand Tour of Switzerland." *(Copyright 1999, COSMOS®)*

▲ *ON TOP OF THE WORLD — THE JUNGFRAUJOCH*

Tour 6025

Days 1, Fri. to 6, Wed. Like tour 6020.

Day 7, Thu. LAUSANNE-INTERLAKEN. Stop awhile in Gruyère, then on to Switzerland's beautiful capital, Berne, a charming town with arcaded shops, carved fountains, and towers. Included sightseeing features the Bear Pit and the monumental Federal Palace. Then by way of the shores of Lake Thun to Interlaken staying at the hotel Central Continental for the next 7 nights. (B)

Days 8, Fri. to 13, Wed. IN INTERLAKEN-INCLUDED JUNGFRAUJOCH EXCURSION. It's all pure picture-postcard. Interlaken has just about everything anyone could want on holiday. It lies beneath the towering Jungfrau and between two sparkling lakes. The undoubted highlight of your stay is the train journey to the Jungfraujoch — Top of Europe. Start the train journey from Interlaken and travel through some breathtaking alpine scenery with views of some of Switzerland's best-known peaks. Closer to the summit go through the Eiger Mountain by tunnel to reach the world's highest rail station at an altitude of 11,332 feet. Now you are in a world of glaciers, and on a clear day you can see as far as the Vosges Mountains in France and the hills of the Black Forest in Germany. The view from the Belvedere Sphinx terrace — the highest one in Europe — will span nearly the whole of Alpine Switzerland. You also have the opportunity of viewing the longest glacier in Europe, the Grosser Aletschgletscher. It really is a unique and unforgettable experience. (B daily)

Day 14, Thu. MORNING IN INTERLAKEN. AFTERNOON TO LAKE LUCERNE. (B,D)

Day 15, Fri. LUCERNE-ZURICH. Day at leisure in Lucerne as day 8 of tour 6020.

Day 16, Sat. YOUR HOMEBOUND FLIGHT ARRIVES THE SAME DAY. (B)

▲ *INTERLAKEN. HOTEL CENTRAL CONTINENTAL*

YOUR HOTEL IN INTERLAKEN is the Central Continental (ST), located on the banks of the River Aare and only 100 yards from the Interlaken-West railway station and the boat-landing stage. The Central is also within easy reach of all that matters in Interlaken. It is a family-run hotel and has recently been refurbished. The elegant restaurant is renowned for its good food. The hotel bar and cozy tavern vie with each other in offering a wide variety of drinks and cocktails. The sun terrace affords a unique view of the Jungfrau mountain. All rooms with private facilities including satellite TV, telephone and mountain view. For single supplement see the Dates & Prices box.

Tours 6020 and 6025 DATES & PRICES

Departure number	Leave CAN. or join Zurich next day		Tour 6020		Tour 6025	
			9 days CAN./ CAN. C$	8 days Zurich/ Zurich C$	16 days CAN./ CAN. C$	15 days Zurich/ Zurich C$
0325	Fri	24 Mar	1884	849	2464	1429
0401	Fri	31 Mar	1914	879	2474	1439
0408	Fri	07 Apr	1914	879	2474	1439
0415	Fri	14 Apr	1914	879	2474	1439
0422	Fri	21 Apr	1804	879	2364	1439
0429	Fri	28 Apr	1804	879	2364	1439
0506	Fri	05 May	1934	899	2514	1479
0513	Fri	12 May	1934	899	2514	1479
0520	Fri	19 May	1964	929	2564	1529
0527	Fri	26 May	1964	929	2564	1529
0603	Fri	02 Jun	2224	929	2824	1529
0610	Fri	09 Jun	2224	929	2824	1529
0617	Fri	16 Jun	2224	929	2824	1529
0624	Fri	23 Jun	2224	929	2824	1529
0701	Fri	30 Jun	2224	929	2824	1529
0708	Fri	07 Jul	2224	929	2824	1529
0715	Fri	14 Jul	2224	929	2824	1529
0722	Fri	21 Jul	2224	929	2824	1529
0729	Fri	28 Jul	2224	929	2824	1529
0805	Fri	04 Aug	2224	929	2824	1529
0812	Fri	11 Aug	2224	929	2824	1529
0819	Fri	18 Aug	2224	929	2824	1529
0826	Fri	25 Aug	2224	929	2824	1529
0902	Fri	01 Sep	2224	929	2814	1519
0909	Fri	08 Sep	2224	929	2814	1519
0916	Fri	15 Sep	2019	899	2599	1479
0923	Fri	22 Sep	2019	899	2599	1479
0930	Fri	29 Sep	2019	899	2595	1475
1007	Fri	06 Oct	1999	879	2559	1439
1014	Fri	13 Oct	1999	879	2559	1439
1021	Fri	20 Oct	1884	849	—	—

For any airfare supplement from your departure city, see page 15.

To cover various departure and arrival taxes, $27 per person (subject to change) will be added to your air-inclusive invoice.

Single room supplement: tour 6020 $259; tour 6025 $356; guaranteed shares (not available for tour 6025: see page 5; no triple room reduction.

Tour 6025: Supplement per person for half-board in Interlaken $216

COSMOS HOTELS

ZURICH Trend (F) at Regensdorf. **ST. MORITZ** Bären (ST) or Belvedere (ST), **LUGANO** Beha (T) or Post Simplon (T) or Calipso (T), **TÄSCH** Walliserhof (ST) or Touring (T) at Visp, **LAUSANNE** City (ST) or Golden Pass (ST) at Montreux, **LAKE LUCERNE** Löwen (T) at Lungern or Turist (T) at Flüelen

FIGURE 8-6   *(concluded) (Copyright 1999, COSMOS®)*

For some, this might be the only solution to their problem. But do not sell down too quickly! Determine how strong the desire is for the tourism product or experience originally requested before selling down. You might make an easy sale now but have a very disappointed client afterwards. Although a form of selling down, changing the dates could reduce the cost to a low season rate and may still give the clients the experience they desire.

The desire for the higher-priced product or service may be strong, and if you can find a solution to how the customer could afford it, the prospect will be sold. Consider the following ideas:

- A **split payment**—using cash or a check for part of the payment, with the rest on a credit card.

- Better for many would be a bank loan with a much lower rate of interest for extended payments. Your banker will be very pleased with your referrals for holiday loans.

- There are some people who firmly refuse to purchase anything on credit. For them, the solution is to set a budget. By setting a budget to save so much per month to cover the shortfall, the customer might delay the tourism experience but ultimately get what he or she wants. If possible, set up a payment plan through your company but be sure that all payments are received before the supplier's due dates.

For many who are hesitant to go into debt to obtain what they really want, explaining that prices may increase or that space may not be available may be all that is needed to close the deal.

Many salespeople create problems for themselves by offering the least expensive product or service available. For some clients, this makes for an easy close, but it might be their last business with you if they are not satisfied.

Other prospects may not allow you to book them because they do not believe that they can get what they want for the price you are offering. Before you make a recommendation, carefully determine the quality that the client prefers. Avoid technical terms such as "deluxe," "first class," or "star systems" because they are not standardized and most clients are not sure what they mean.

More complaints concern accommodations than any other aspect in the tourism business. You should probe for preferences before recommending accommodations. It can be useful to find out which accommodations the client has used on previous trips. Then determine his or her level of satisfaction with the accommodations used in the past. With this information on hand, it may be easy to select appropriate accommodations for this trip.

Otherwise, ask, "Would you prefer very good or moderate accommodations?" If the client chooses very good, you know that he or she is a very discerning customer and price is not the most important criterion. If the client indicates moderate, you can be sure that the mid-price range is the answer and that top quality is not expected. Budget accommodations may not satisfy this client.

If you do not get a positive response to either very good or moderate, reluctantly offer a third choice, budget! If the client chooses budget, you know that price is a high concern and high quality cannot be expected.

Sometimes customers cannot make up their minds because they have too many objectives to be satisfied in a single offering. Suggest that they list the things they would like to have in their tourism arrangements in order of importance. Satisfy the high priorities and close the deal!

The biggest problem clients can present is not knowing when they can experience the tourism product that you are trying to sell. The client may not know his or her holiday schedule. Specifically ask, "When would you like to go if you had your choice?" If you obtain an answer, suggest holding the space, and if necessary later, changing the reservation. Use the word *change*, not *cancel*.

If you are unable to even get approximate dates, ask, "When will you know the dates for your holiday?" If you can obtain the answer to this, make a definite appointment for a follow-up, preferably in the office, but possibly by telephone. Nail it down. Get a date and time.

If you are trying hard and feel that you are still missing possible sales, the problem could be you. I do not mean to embarrass anyone, but you may be doing things that interfere with a client's trust that you can do the job he or she requires. Examples include an untidy desk, unprofessional dress or language, mannerisms, or behavior.

One problem that many young people in the tourism industry encounter is convincing much older clients that they have the knowledge and experience to provide the professional service these clients require. This is a difficult problem to overcome. A few things that will help include dressing and speaking in a professional manner, displaying your graduation diploma or certificate from an approved tourism program, and any industry certification for continuing education.

Do a good job of qualifying your clients so that your recommendations do meet their needs. Do not give any information of which you are not sure or that you cannot verify. Express an air of confidence and say that you will research his or her request and be back with the answer shortly. There are all kinds of printed and people resources in the tourism industry both within and outside your office from whom you can obtain authoritative answers.

STEP 9: CLOSING AGAIN

Once you have identified the client's problem, help him or her to solve it. Now it is time to close again. Look for the closing signals presented in Chapter 6 and use the most appropriate closing technique.

SUMMARY

If a prospect asks a serious question about tourism, he or she really wants to have a tourism experience. If he or she resists your attempt to close the deal, he or she has a problem. If you can identify the problem and help the customer solve it, you will be able to close the deal!

Some clients' problems are more difficult than others, but they can be overcome! Analyze the situation every time you are unable to close the sale, and identify the problem that the customer had. Start thinking of how you could fine-tune your problem-solving techniques to make the sale next time. Good luck; keep score; and keep trying!

Discussion Questions

1. What are some of the objections customers might have to making a deal now? How would you handle these objections?

2. What are some of the objections customers might have regarding financial considerations? How would you handle these objections?

3. If a customer would not allow you to close, what type of questions would you ask to determine whether your recommendation met his or her needs?

4. Under which circumstances would you abandon your original recommendation and make a different proposal that would better meet your prospect's needs?

5. List three examples of resistance due to the lack of credibility of the salesperson and suggest ways of overcoming each problem.

CHAPTER 9

Selling-Up

OBJECTIVES

After studying this chapter, you should be able to:

● Define *selling-up* and *upgrading*

● Provide examples of selling-up in all eight sectors of the tourism industry

● Explain 12 more opportunities for selling-up

● Explain 15 selling points that will help a client to accept a higher-priced tourism product or service

KEY TERMS

selling-up	selling additional services	per diem
upgrading	club class	cruise-and-stay

STEP 10: SELLING-UP

Selling-up is increasing the amount of the sale either by **upgrading** or **selling additional services** or both. Upgrading is a specialized type of selling-up focused on selling a higher-quality product—for example, selling first-class or business-class air transportation rather than coach class. In the accommodations sector, it could be selling an ocean view room or a suite rather than a garden view room.

In the fast-food business, selling additional services is where the real selling is done. If you ask people what McDonald's restaurants sell, they will invariably reply, "Hamburgers." But, have you ever been sold a hamburger at McDonald's? They just take your orders for the hamburger.

147

What they sell you are fries, milk shakes, desserts, and any number of additional items. Order a hamburger at Wendy's, and they will invariably try to sell you a Combo that includes fries and a beverage. If you order a Combo, they will always offer you a Biggie (a larger size) for *only* 49 cents more. Notice the emphasis on the word *only*!

In travel agencies, people come in to buy basic items such as air tickets and tours. The real selling occurs when the salesperson sells additional services such as hotel accommodations, or a car rental, or an upgraded transportation ticket for a higher class of service. You can learn a lot from the other sectors of the tourism industry, and they can learn a lot from the travel trade sector. We can all learn from McDonald's and Wendy's.

Selling-up can be done during the qualifying process or even when closing the sale, if it fits naturally into the sales discussion. However, it is usually done after the customer has made a definite decision to buy the primary product or service you have been discussing. If customers mention anything about higher-quality accommodations or service before you do, they want it. Sell the higher-priced product or service and close the sale now!

What type of selling-up you do depends upon which sector of the tourism industry and in which branch of that sector you are working. I will present a number of ideas for selling-up for specific sectors. However, some of the ideas I am presenting under a certain sector can be adapted to other sectors as well, either as presented or with some modifications.

The Accommodations Sector

In addition to the examples of selling-up in the Accommodations sector already mentioned, try these ideas.

Convince the customer of the value of having a suite rather than just a room. Selling points would include the extra comfort of having more space, plus the advantage that some members of the party could go to bed earlier than others or some could get up earlier than others without disturbing anyone. Some could watch TV while others read or work. Most suites have two televisions, which makes it possible for children to watch one program while adults can watch another.

When selling-up to a room with kitchen facilities, you can point out the convenience of being able to keep drinks cold or having hot coffee or tea in your room. The economy of being able to have some meals in the room rather than having the expense of consuming all meals at restaurants will help create acceptance of the additional cost of the accommodations.

Accommodations with special facilities like a whirlpool or water-beds can be sold as an opportunity to experience something one might not have at home. Also, clients can be persuaded to pay a little more for accommodations in a historical property or one that is otherwise unique to the destination rather than the type of lodging available most anywhere. A good example of this would be the Fantasyland Hotel in West Edmonton Mall, one of the world's most unique hotels. It is located in the West Edmonton Mall, the world's largest shopping and entertainment complex, with more than 800 stores and services.

One of the Fantasyland Hotel's most unique rooms is the classic Roman Room (see Figure 9-1). The classic Roman Room sweeps the client away to the time of Anthony and Cleopatra. White marble statues will surround them. They can enjoy the luxury of a round velvet covered bed, silk draperies, and an authentic Roman bath.

Another unique experience could be a stay in the African Room (see Figure 9-2). After an exciting safari, clients can take refuge in a luxurious dwelling complete with cheetah-designed carpeting, bamboo furniture, and zebra covered queen-size bed, a bunk bed, and a full-size jacuzzi. It's a theme room the whole family can enjoy! Fantasyland Hotel includes 113 themed rooms. A sales kit including slides of the theme rooms provides you with the opportunity for selling-up for a unique experience. People will buy and pay more for unique experiences.

FIGURE 9-1

Roman Room. *(Courtesy of Fantasyland Hotel at West Edmonton Mall, Edmonton, Alberta, Canada)*

FIGURE 9-2

African Room. *(Courtesy of Fantasyland Hotel at West Edmonton Mall, Edmonton, Alberta, Canada)*

The Adventure and Recreation Sectors

If you are selling in the Adventure and Recreation sector, you could sell either a longer duration or a package that has more included. Consider adding transportation either from your access gateway or all the way from the client's departure point. Many of the points made for tour operators and wholesalers in the Travel Trade sector would also be applicable to the Adventure and Recreation sector. (See Figure 9-3.)

The Attractions Sector

Most locations in the Attractions sector have a gift shop. Make sure that it is stocked with quality items that are truly related to the attraction. Structure the tourist's experience so that the tourist will travel through the gift shop before leaving the facility. If a tour is included, make sure that the tourist has sufficient time to observe what is available in the gift shop.

Attractions can also increase their sales by featuring special events that complement the attraction. A luau in Hawaii can provide a more personal experience than a stage show. (See Figure 9-4.)

The Events and Conferences Sector

For conferences, conventions, exhibitions, and trade shows, the obvious way to sell-up would be to convince the customers to purchase

FIGURE 9-3
Snorkeling at the Chankanaab Reef.
(© PhotoDisc/Getty Images)

FIGURE 9-4
A luau in Hawaii. (© PhotoDisc/Getty Images)

more space. Providing ideas to draw more potential customers would enhance your chances of selling more space. New business could be obtained by asking those signed up to recommend other companies or organizations that could benefit from the event.

Use market research to determine the sources of your present customers. For fairs, festivals, special events, and marketplaces, ask visitors for suggestions of how to reach others from their area. Determine what drew their attention? What was the most important factor that made them decide to come? When the results are analyzed, use the knowledge gained to do the things that worked well with other markets.

The Food and Beverage Sector

A restaurant owner named Joseph had someone else act as the maître d' to meet customers cordially at the door, check their reservation, escort them to their table, introduce them to their waiter, and distribute menus.

The maître d' would then allow enough time to browse through the menu and could tell by the conversation and body language of the patrons when they were almost ready to make decisions. Enter Joseph. He would approach each table at the precise buying moment. He would greet everyone by name with an enthusiastic welcome. If he did not know a name, he would ask for it, and then promptly use it. The next time that person visited the restaurant, Joseph would remember the name.

Joseph would describe the specialties of the day and specialties of the house in such mouth-watering terms that people felt they had to try them. Inevitably, they would order a special hors d'oeuvre, dessert, drink specialty, or special main course that they had not previously contemplated.

Once decisions were made, he would recommend the most appropriate wine to accompany the meal in such glowing terms that patrons almost always purchased one a few notches above their normal choice. Then Joseph would make a gracious and friendly exit, explaining that Chantel (or Mario) would be right over to take their order. Be assured, the servers would be ready for Joseph's cue. He would move immediately to the next table where people were at the decision-making process of what to order.

Joseph is a master salesperson. He does not waste time doing things other staff can do. He devotes all his time to selling-up without losing any time doing other tasks. Needless to say, he does it in a very pleasing public relations manner.

Another salesperson had Joseph's technique perfected. This time it was not in the restaurant business or any other sector of the tourism industry. But it was a delight to watch. Denise Goulet was in the market to purchase a new television. The salesperson was Dexter.

Dexter qualified Denise quickly and well. Dexter demonstrated why a particular model met all her needs better than the others and closed the deal. As soon as Denise had made up her mind, Dexter introduced her to his assistant, who efficiently wrote up the sale, obtained the merchandise, and made arrangements for payment. While these details were taking place, Dexter had closed three more rather large sales. Dexter is a master salesperson. His time is not wasted doing paperwork or routine details. He sells, and that's all!

In your business, do not allow your top salespeople to waste a minute filling out invoices, chasing down merchandise, or even collecting payments. Let them sell! People learning the business can do the other jobs, and with the right guidance, they will eventually learn to do the job as well as Joseph or Dexter. Who do you think will have more fun on the job and earn more money—Joseph and Dexter, or the unnamed people doing those other tasks? Welcome to a career in sales!

The Tourism Services Sector

Much of the selling in the Tourism Services sector is indirect selling because often it is not the people working in this sector who actually collect the money. However, there are many opportunities for selling-up. When people come to information centers to request information on one topic, probe to find out what else they might be interested in. Inquire whether they are aware of other attractions and services available. If so, offer to phone to check whether space is available or put the tourist in direct contact with the provider of the product or service.

In retail operations, the salesperson can often suggest additional items that could be purchased as gifts for Christmas, birthdays, and so on. Explain the advantages and benefits of similar but more expensive items than those that a customer is interested in purchasing.

In duty-free shops (see Figure 9-5), people usually feel restricted by the duty-free allowances. However, it is legal to take back more than the duty-free allowance as long as it is declared and the appropriate duty and taxes are paid. Salespeople in duty-free shops should be aware of any items that would still be less expensive in spite of the taxes payable in particular countries. Sometimes additional items will be worth paying the duty.

Because of the North America Free Trade Agreement (NAFTA), there is no duty payable on goods produced in Canada, the United States of America, or Mexico for travel within this area. However, there may be other taxes applicable, so it is wise to know the comparative values of transporting goods over the normal limit.

Most people go to duty-free shops to buy duty-free liquor and cigarettes. But duty-free shops carry many other items that could be attractive to a customer from another country. A salesperson could simply ask if particular items are available in a tourist's home country or state. Often this will stimulate the customer to take something home for friends or relatives that they cannot obtain at home.

FIGURE 9-5

Emerson Duty Free Shop. *(Courtesy of the Emerson Duty Free Shop)*

For auto clubs, additional revenue can be obtained by directing the tourist to the travel agency office of the auto club for additional services. Similarly, everyone in the travel agency of the auto club should be asking their client if he or she is a member of the auto club. If not, they should sell the advantages of becoming a member, distribute promotional literature, and ask if the client would like to speak to someone in the membership department for more information.

The Transportation Sector

In the Transportation sector, most salespeople just assume that every prospect wants the least expensive fare possible. However, for approximately 10 to 15 percent of the traveling public, convenience and comfort are more important than price. Salespeople in a travel agency should always ask, "Would you prefer first class or coach?" for air transportation. Or, if you were discussing rail transportation, "Would you prefer **club class** or coach?"

One could persuade a big or tall person that he or she would be much more comfortable in a first-class air seat with more width and legroom and a wider seat than the cramped facilities offered in economy/coach class.

For rail service on Via Rail, one can sell-up to club class by pointing out the following benefits:

1. Passengers can relax in the first-class lounge with free non-alcoholic beverages while waiting for the train.

2. Club passengers are preboarded before coach passengers.

3. Free newspapers are offered in club class but not in coach class.

4. Meals are included in club class.

5. A complimentary aperitif and after dinner liqueur or other drink is included in club class as well as wine with the meal.

For people traveling overnight by train, you should always try to sell-up to include sleeping accommodations, stressing the discomfort of sitting up all night in a coach.

For passengers traveling by ship, the advantages of a more expensive cabin or stateroom include more space, better location, and the benefit of being able to see out from an outside cabin. In a travel agency, an agent had drawn lines on the floor to show how small an economy cabin was on a ship. This was an effective aid for selling-up to a larger size stateroom.

This would vary with the ship being sold, but the salesperson could use one that is frequently sold. The difference in what is being recommended to a particular customer should be described.

People will often request a smaller rental car than the car they drive at home. Salespeople can sell-up by stressing the small difference in cost per day for a larger car and more comfort. If there is more than one person sharing the car, show how little the difference in price is per person per day. A good sales point for people traveling from place to place is that in a smaller car there might be enough room for the passengers, but will there be room for the luggage?

With recreational vehicles, selling-up can be done emphasizing the extra comfort and facilities available in a more expensive unit. Emphasize that the vehicle will not only be their means of transportation but it will also be their home for the duration of the trip.

When transferring tourists from the airport, rail station, bus station, or cruise port to their accommodations, taxi drivers should always offer to provide a city tour for their customers. A city tour by taxi can be tailored to the exact interests and time restraints of the tourist. Also, a city tour by taxi can be very cost-effective if there are three to five passengers.

However, this can only be done where it is legal and if the driver is qualified as a guide. In many cities, only certain transportation companies are licensed to provide tours. Customers and drivers should always settle on the price before getting into the taxi. Be sure to determine whether the price is per person or for everyone in the party. Get this written down, particularly if the driver is speaking English as a second language.

The Travel Trade Sector

When selling tours or transportation, you can sell local sight-seeing. Most local sight-seeing companies will pay a commission to other members of the tourism industry for selling their local sight-seeing, boat tours, transfers, and other services. If you do not have reciprocal sales agreements with other tourism industry suppliers, make it a priority for today. You can sell their products and services at a profit. And they can sell your products and services. Also, you can sell car rentals at the destination or stopover points.

Whenever you are selling a tour, always explain the value of an extended stay. The **per diem** (or daily cost) of a one-week stay includes transportation, transfers, and a number of other expenses in addition to accommodations. A second week would cost little extra except for the accommodations, therefore lowering the per diem cost. (See Figure 9-6.)

FIGURE 9-6

Cost of a one-week versus a two-week tour per diem. *(Courtesy World of Vacations)*

One of the easiest ways to sell-up is to sell a longer tour. When you look at the prices of World of Vacations inclusive tour charter to Barceló Parque del Lago Hotel in San José, Costa Rica, from Toronto, the second week is always a bargain compared to the first week. The most spectacular comparison is for departures between March 9 and March 15. The first week costs $1,279.00. The second week costs *only* $80.00 more, just $11.43 per diem! Taking a two-week holiday is *only* $97.07 per diem as compared to $182.71 per diem for a one-week vacation. This should be a very easy opportunity to sell-up unless the client just cannot take a two-week vacation.

Tour guides can often increase their tips by offering to provide individuals advice regarding restaurants, entertainment, special events, shopping, or any other special interest or product.

Whenever a customer has a risk of financial loss, the salesperson has a legal obligation to offer insurance. For example, always offer cancellation insurance for protection from losses due to unused services due to illness, accidents, or bad weather. Other benefits of travel protection that can be covered include trip interruption protection, emergency medical/dental coverage, emergency medical transportation, baggage insurance, baggage delay, travel accident, and trip inconvenience coverage.

Comprehensive travel protection plans provide insurance for all or most of the items just listed, usually at a lower price than if the individual coverages were purchased separately. Selling insurance provides the traveler with peace of mind, removes the liability from the salesperson for not disclosing possible risks, and pays excellent commission. Usually, the commissions from selling the insurance are higher than the commissions for selling the transportation. (See Figure 9-7.)

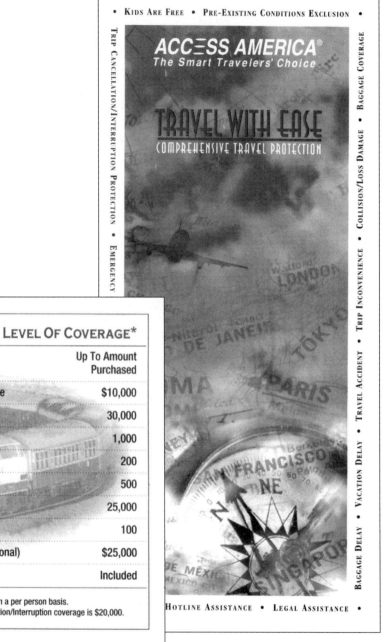

FIGURE 9-7

Always offer travel insurance. (© World Access Service Corporation)

TWELVE MORE OPPORTUNITIES FOR SELLING-UP

Travel agents have the opportunity to sell-up almost everything already mentioned, but I ask you to consider these 12 additional opportunities for selling-up. Many of these can also be used by tour operators and wholesalers either in direct sales or by having their sales representatives emphasize the opportunities to travel agents. Most transportation companies sell tours using their services, and many of these ideas will also work for them.

1. Combine a vacation with a business trip. Then suggest that they might take their family along. Use family plan fares or special promotional fares to create acceptance.

2. Sell a side trip or stopover.

3. Persuade travelers who are going to be visiting friends or relatives to take a tour, stopover, or side trip before and/or after their visit.

4. Persuade travelers who will be visiting friends or relatives to take them along on a tour.

5. Convince singles to bring along a friend to save money and to have more fun.

6. Persuade a couple to bring along another couple to save money (sharing a car rental or a suite in a hotel) and to have more fun.

7. If a customer is buying a prepaid ticket to bring friends or relatives to the U.S.A. or Canada, sell travel arrangements for the visitors to see America.

8. A cruise could be added to a land package.

9. A land package can be added to a cruise purchase. Some cruise lines have **cruise-and-stay** packages. For others, you could always make arrangements for a land package either at the beginning or the end of a cruise.

10. Always sell transportation to and from the starting point of a tour.

11. If the departure is early in the morning or the return is late in the day, sell accommodations close to the airport, rail station, or port.

12. Make a combination of two or more of the opportunities for selling-up presented in this chapter.

Traditionally, many organizations in the tourism industries have operated in isolation from their colleagues in other sectors. If you do not have the arrangements to make commissions from selling each other's services now, establish cooperative relationships and make the necessary agreements to sell each other's services to increase your mutual sales.

FIFTEEN SELLING POINTS THAT WILL HELP A CLIENT TO ACCEPT A HIGHER-PRICED TOURISM PRODUCT

The biggest problem of selling-up is price resistance. The following 15 sales points should help you to convince a customer to accept a higher-priced tourism product.

1. It provides extra comfort.

2. It is more relaxing.

3. It is more convenient.

4. There is less hassle (trouble-free).

5. There is more enjoyment.

6. Use your client's own statements to show that the higher-priced item has more of what they want (or more of what interests them).

7. If applicable, mention it is a once-in-a-lifetime opportunity.

8. Tell them, "You deserve it!" or "You deserve to spoil yourself!"

9. Convince the customer that your offer is value for money paid. For example, the value of a cruise compared to a land package when one considers all of the inclusive features.

10. It will be difficult to obtain this quality at this price again.

11. If you wait, it will probably go up in price to the point where it may be impossible for you to go.

12. A more memorable vacation or honeymoon.

13. Appeal to financial needs. The difference in the cost is very little when considered as a proportion of the total expenditure or as an extra cost per person per day. Compare the extra per diem cost to show how little it is considering the added pleasure it would provide.

14. Appeal to safety needs. Stress that you cannot guarantee safety anywhere, but that you recommend companies and services that have a good safety record.

15. Traveling with a high-quality company will provide you with more confidence that you have made the right decision.

Discussion Questions

1. Define *selling-up*.

2. Explain the similarities and differences between selling-up and upgrading.

3. List three examples of selling-up in each of the eight sectors of tourism.

4. What are the 12 additional opportunities for selling-up?

5. List 15 selling points that would help you to convince a client to accept a higher-priced tourism product or service.

CHAPTER 10

Customer Service

OBJECTIVES

After studying this chapter, you should be able to:

- Describe sources from which you can retrieve information to advise clients regarding:
    a. which airport and which terminal your clients will be using for departure and arrival
    b. the documentation required for an international trip
    c. health measures required and additional health measures recommended for an international trip
    d. customs regulations regarding what you can take into and out of a foreign country
    e. customs regulations regarding what can be brought home from a foreign country
    f. the availability of duty-free shopping at international airports and surface border crossings
    g. the most efficient way to make transfers between transportation terminals and accommodations
    h. local transportation at the destination
    i. check-in times and procedures for transportation, tours, and accommodations
    j. passengers' free baggage allowance
- Advise outgoing and incoming tourists regarding the best means of handling and exchanging currency
- Advise customers what is and what is not included in their purchase
- Assist clients in establishing a budget for their trip
- Advise clients regarding tips, gratuities, and service charges
- Advise passengers regarding the need to reconfirm international flights
- Advise clients of the importance of having appropriate travel insurance
- Discuss the criteria for good novelties, gifts or favors for customers

KEY TERMS

transfer

runaround

check-in time

weight system

piece system

collision damage waiver
   (CDW)

loss damage waiver (LDW)

inclusive tour

independent tour

net rates

STEP 11: PROVIDING CUSTOMER SERVICE

Many salespeople in the tourism industry waste time and confuse the customer by giving too much information between the qualifying and closing steps of the sales process. Once the customer has made a buying decision and you know the details regarding his or her tourism arrangements, now is the time to provide all the information the client will require to have a pleasant, safe, and trouble-free tourism experience.

YOU HAVE TO TELL YOUR CLIENT

In the tourism industry, you will often be servicing international visitors. Their needs for information can be much more complex than those of domestic travelers. If you are the primary provider of the major tourist services for an international visitor, you will have to provide all or at least most of the following information.

For domestic travelers, only some of the information will be applicable. If you were working as a supplier of individual services—for example, at one particular tourist attraction, special event, or duty-free shop, or the like—you would not routinely be expected to provide all the information presented here. However, you should be prepared to answer questions regarding any of the topics presented here.

Which Airport and Which Terminal?

If there is more than one airport in any of the cities from which a client is departing, connecting, or arriving, it is essential that the salesperson make it absolutely clear to the passenger which airport is being used. This is especially true if it is necessary to transfer from one airport to another.

Cities in the U.S.A. with more than one airport include:

- Chicago
- Detroit
- Houston

- The Los Angeles area
- New York
- The San Francisco area
- Washington

In Canada, cities with more than one airport include:

- Edmonton
- Montréal
- Toronto

In Asia, cities with more than one airport include:

- Singapore
- Taipei
- Tokyo

In Europe, cities with more than one airport include:

- Berlin
- Brussels
- Bucharest
- Frankfurt
- Glasgow
- London
- Milan
- Moscow
- Paris
- Rome
- Zürich

In South America, cities with more than one airport include:

- Buenos Aires
- São Paulo

If there is more than one terminal in an airport from which the passenger is departing, connecting, or arriving, it is also vital that you make sure that your client understands which terminal he or she must use. If a connection requires a transfer from one terminal to another, this must also be clear to the customer. This information should be given orally to the client when the reservations have been completed, but even more important, it should be clearly stated on the client's printed itinerary.

If a change from one terminal or airport to another is necessary, the passenger should be advised of the easiest and least expensive means to make the **transfer** and also how much time will be required. Travel agents and people working in the airline industry will be able to access information about airports, terminals, and transfers between airports or terminals from their Global Distribution System. Workers in other sectors of the tourism industry should request this information from the travel agent or airline reservationist with whom they are making the reservations for their clients.

Documentation Required

Documentation required may include a passport, visas, tourist card(s), proof of citizenship, and proof of identity. What is required depends upon a traveler's country of citizenship and the countries to which he or she is traveling or transiting.

Information regarding documentation required is available in the Global Distribution Systems used by travel agents and employees in the transportation sector. It is also included in a publication entitled, the *Travel Information Manual*. It is often referred to as "the *TIM*." A consortium of international airlines publishes it. To order a subscription contact:

> *Travel Information Manual (TIM)*
> Subscriptions Dept.
> P.O. Box 49
> 1170 AA Badhoevedorp
> The Netherlands, Europe
> Phone: 31-(0)20-403-7923
> Fax: 31-(0)20-403-7978
> E-mail: lentinga@iata.org

Health Measures Required and Advised

For tourists coming from or transiting through countries with endemic areas of certain communicable diseases, inoculations may be required to enter that country or return to their own country. Inoculations normally required for passengers arriving from endemic areas are usually restricted to cholera and yellow fever. Inoculations or medication not required but advised, for the protection of the tourist, may be just as important as the ones required by governments. Advise clients to consult their doctor or medical officer of health before leaving their home country. Advise tourists to obtain information from their local medical officer of health. Remember that you are not a doctor. Give information but not advice on suggested inoculations or medicine. A useful Internet site for information about additional measures advised is maintained by the Centers for Disease Control and Prevention, at

<http://www.cdc.gov/travel>. This listing will provide you with a list of areas from which to choose. For example, if you choose tropical South America, it will add "tropsam.htm" to the Web site address (<http://www.cdc.gov/travel/tropsam.htm>).

Yellow fever is the only inoculation required by governments to travel to and from destinations in this region, but the Centers' Web site advises travelers to obtain protection from hepatitis A, hepatitis B, rabies, typhoid, plus booster doses for tetanus, diphtheria, and measles.

North Americans are used to advice about not drinking the water or eating certain foods when they travel to some other countries. However, many are surprised to learn some foreign tourists have diarrhea and other problems with the food in the U.S.A. or Canada.

The problem is usually not one arising from lack of cleanliness, but just different bacteria to which their systems have not yet adjusted. But, it is just as important that they receive prompt medical attention as it would be for you if you had similar problems in a foreign country.

Avoiding Hazards of Destinations Visited

You should give general advice regarding avoiding hazards of destinations to be visited. These types of advice might include warning drivers traveling in British Columbia that they must stop to allow pedestrians to cross the street. Or in other destinations, tourists must be warned to take precautions regarding wild animals. For example, a tourist from South America tried to entice a wild bear into a hotel in the Rocky Mountains! If her travel counselor had provided her with the "You are in Bear Country" warning in "Keep the Wild in Wildlife" brochure, she probably would never have put herself and other hotel guests and employees in such danger. This brochure is published by Parks Canada to educate the public, "How to Safely Enjoy and Help Protect Wildlife." Tourists should also be advised to take precautions regarding potentially dangerous situations in adventure travel such as white-water rafting. (See Figure 10-1.)

Give advice regarding whether the water is safe to drink. In the cities of Canada and the United States this is rarely a problem, but it could be in rural areas or on camping or adventure holidays.

Advise clients regarding any dangers that may be more prevalent in the destination country than in one's own country. Examples of this would be big city crime, or terrorist target areas, or the dangers in some areas regarding wild animals.

Customs Regulations and Duties

Items allowed and items restricted when entering another country should be pointed out to an international traveler. Regulations

FIGURE 10-1

Keep the Wild in Wildlife brochure. (Courtesy of Parks Canada)

regarding the type and amount of goods that your clients will be able to bring back to their own country should also be pointed out. The United States Customs publishes a booklet called *Know Before You Go* (Figure 10-2), which details what one can bring into the United States. Canada has a similar booklet entitled *I Declare* (Figure 10-3).

FIGURE 10-2

Know Before You Go. (Courtesy of U.S. Customs Service)

FIGURE 10-3

I Declare. (Courtesy of Canada Customs and Revenue Agency)

Availability of duty-free shopping at the airport of departure and whether there is a duty-free shop at the passenger's destination is important information for most travelers. The availability of duty-free shops at airports is listed in the OAG. Clients should also be advised if there is duty-free shopping on board the aircraft. Travel agents and airline personnel can find this information in their Global Distribution System. Others in the tourism industry should enquire at the time they are making reservations for their client. For people leaving the country by surface vehicle, you could check with state or provincial tourist boards or the American or Canadian Automobile Association to determine if there is a duty-free shop at the border crossing.

Advise Clients Regarding Exchanging Foreign Currencies

Advise clients to use local currency. The only exception to this would be for cruise passengers who are only going to be in port for a few hours and are not expecting to do much shopping. In this case, check to see if U.S. dollars are accepted at a fair exchange rate. Carry just what you need in small denominations.

Advise tourists to take only the amount in cash that is covered by their apartment, or homeowners, or baggage insurance. This can vary greatly, from as little as $100.00 to $1,000.00 or more. For some travelers, particularly those who are in charge of groups, it could be very important to be covered for a higher amount of cash. For example, a tour conductor or group leader may have to carry a relatively large amount of cash for unexpected expenses for a group. For these people, it would be wise to shop around for a policy that covers a larger amount of cash.

In many places, there is a significant service charge for cashing traveler's cheques. For example, the service charge for cashing traveler's cheques in Hong Kong is $10 per check! Determine whether there is a charge and, if so, how much, from North American branches of banks available in the foreign country. If this is not possible, check with the tourist board.

In destinations with high service charges for cashing traveler's cheques, it is often preferable to obtain cash through an ATM (Automated Teller Machine) or even cash advances on credit cards. Advise your client to establish a positive balance on a credit card so that funds can be taken out in a foreign country without incurring interest charges. Some places charge extra if one uses credit cards. The relative merits of using traveler's cheques, credit cards, and cash advances is subject to change at any moment. Tourism salespeople should keep up with current trends and advise their clients accordingly for the specific destination.

Foreign tourists should obtain Canadian dollar traveler's cheques for travel within Canada and U.S. dollar traveler's cheques for travel within the U.S.A. In most other countries, many international currencies are exchanged at most branches of banks. Exchange rates are prominently posted in the front window of the bank with flags to indicate the exchange rate for each currency available.

International tourists should be advised that it is very difficult to exchange currencies other than U.S. or Canadian dollars in North America. Often only head offices of major banks exchange other major currencies. Many currencies are almost impossible to exchange. So, advise international visitors to the U.S.A. or Canada to exchange their money before arriving in North America.

Take at least enough local currency to cover your needs until the first banking day in the host country. If this is a small amount, it could be changed at the airport. Be sure to go early, because they are sometimes completely sold out of a currency when large groups are traveling. A group of Canadian college students were traveling to Mexico. Most of the students had obtained Mexican pesos in advance, but a few waited to purchase pesos at the airport. Three 747s were departing for Mexico within the hour, and the exchange office was sold out of pesos. Canadian dollars were not accepted locally except at banks. It was Saturday, and Monday was a bank holiday. The students who did not have Mexican currency could not go anywhere, and could only order food or drinks at the hotel to be charged to their room. Hotel prices were four or five times the rates the other students were paying!

If you require more than $100.00 to be exchanged, it is usually to your advantage to exchange your money through your bank. Most branches of banks in the United States or Canada have to execute these transactions through head offices, and that may require 3 to 10 days in advance, depending upon your destination. You should advise clients of any bank holidays during their trip. This information will be available from the tourist boards for the countries visited.

Advise your clients to use up change and small bills near the end of a trip. Often change, and sometimes, even small banknotes cannot be exchanged for local currency when tourists return home or move on to another country.

Advise Your Clients Regarding Inclusions and Exclusions of Their Purchases

You must advise customers regarding what is included and, conversely, what is not included in their purchase.

- Meals: Which ones are included in the price and which ones are at the tourist's expense?

- Taxes including state, provincial, and national taxes like the Canadian GST (Goods and Services Tax) or the VAT (Value Added Tax) imposed in the United Kingdom.

- Tourists should also be advised of how they can recover the GST on their purchases and, where applicable, the provincial sales taxes. This type of information is available from tourist boards.

- Tourists should be advised regarding air transportation and departure taxes, especially any that are not included in the ticket and subject to collection at airports as in Montréal and Vancouver. Travel agents and airline employees should be able to advise you regarding these charges. Ask at the time that you make reservations for your clients.

- Hotel taxes and service charges.

- Transfers, whether they are included or not. If they are included, the name of the company, how to contact them, and where to go to obtain the service. If they are not included, what choices are there? What are the differences in the cost and convenience in the alternatives? This information will be available in the Global Distribution System of the travel agent or airline reservations agent. (See Figure 10-4.)

FIGURE 10-4

Airport limousine service.

Advising Your Clients How to Establish a Budget for Their Trip

On a vacation, tourists will probably want to live somewhat above their normal means. In budget terms, their week may have seven Saturdays and no Mondays. You cannot suggest how much money a client should bring because there is such a difference in individual tastes and spending patterns. Advise the client to budget for the following items:

- Shopping—minimum, nothing; maximum, the amount allowed by customs in their country for returning passengers. They can usually bring back more than their duty-free allowance, but they must declare it and pay the necessary duties and taxes. If the customer is interested in shopping, add a few comments about the best values or unique items available at the destination and suggest reading materials for further information.

- Meals—budget according to what you would spend if you were traveling in your own area or country. Add or subtract a percentage to your total meal budget according to the difference in cost of living at the destination compared to what it would cost at home. If you are not sure which percentage to add or subtract, check with colleagues, clients who have recently returned from the destination, the tourist board, a carrier or tour operator serving the area.

- Entertainment—budget according to the same guidelines as given for meals except if they are planning specific expenditures for which you can obtain precise costs—for example, the Lido Show in Paris.

- Local transportation—Will the customer be using taxis, mass transit, or a car rental? If they will be traveling by taxi, advise the customer to inquire at the hotel or some other reliable resource what is the best routing to their destination. By requesting a particular routing, the passenger will be perceived as a knowledgeable passenger and be less likely to receive the **runaround**. It is a good idea for your clients to take a business card, matches, a postcard, or something with the name and address and phone number of the hotel or other destination at all times. If the tourist is going to be using mass transit, he or she should be given precise instructions regarding how the system works. Information on exact fares required, transfers, and connections should be given. Mass transit is not recommended for inexperienced travelers who do not have a good command of the language. When you do not know the details that your client needs, contact the tourist board of the country, state, or province that they will be visiting.

For any person from a different country, or even a different state or province, he or she should be given instructions regarding the difference in local laws and customs. For example, right turns are not allowed on a red light in the province of Québec, and motorists must stop for pedestrians in British Columbia. Give particular advice for British drivers and any others who are not used to driving on the right side of the road. One of the most important pieces of advice would be for making left turns. They are used to looking left, right, left, whereas when they are driving on the right side of the road, they should look right, left, right!

Tips, Gratuities, and Service Charges

Tips, gratuities, and service charges are more or less the same thing. They all are payment for services rendered. The word *tips* is derived from the expression "*to insure prompt service.*" Tips is the term used most often when the customer decides how much to pay for the service and usually pays the provider of the service personally. A gratuity is a more sophisticated word for tips. Service charge is the term used when the amount paid is set by the company providing the service. It may be prepaid by the customer as in the case of most hotels in the Caribbean region or automatically added to the bill as in many restaurants in Western Europe.

Travelers are often very concerned about the tipping customs in the countries that they will be visiting. Around the world the percentage for tips is generally between 10 and 20 percent, with 15 percent being the most common acceptable average. Tips in the United States usually range from 15 to 20 percent because service personnel are almost completely dependent upon their tips. In Canada, tips usually range between 10 and 15 percent because of the higher minimum wages. If the cost of the meal or service were very low, then it would be customary to tip 20 percent or more. For example, you would probably not leave a tip of less than $.25 for a cup of coffee costing $1.00.

It is very important that professionals working in the tourism industry in the U.S.A. and Canada give proper advice to international tourists. This is particularly true for tourists who come from the few countries that do not have tipping. These are usually communist countries like Cuba and China. In countries that used to be part of the Soviet Union, many travelers still may not be familiar with tipping practices in other countries. Japanese tourists are not accustomed to tipping for baggage handling.

Tourists coming from countries like most of those in Western Europe are sometimes used to a service charge automatically being added to a restaurant bill. They might not realize that a tip is expected. The following guidelines should help the travel counselor give appropriate advice.

You should inform tourists which services are included in the price of a tour. For example, gratuities are often included for meals that are included in a tour. But, tourists should be advised to tip for meals and beverages not included in the tour. Many European restaurants add a 15-percent service charge to the bill. You should advise tourists that no additional tip is required.

In Québec, a 15-percent service charge is added to almost all ski packages. No additional tip is necessary for baggage handling or meals. Would tips be required at the bar? Advise the tourist to scrutinize the bill to see if a service charge has been added. It is unnecessary to tip for the services included in the tour package if a service charge is included! Americans are often regarded as "big tippers" in many parts of the world. Often this is because they tip even though the service charges have already been added to their bill. Sometimes this is because the American customer does not realize that a service charge has already been added to his or her bill. Other times, it may just be because the customer appreciates the excellent service received and just wants to give the server a "little extra."

Traditionally, in communist countries or on ships operated by those countries, tips were not only unnecessary but were considered an insult! A personal gift, particularly something from your own country, was accepted as a personal token of friendship. Since the demise of the Soviet Union, things have really changed, and cash tips are certainly appreciated, especially in U.S. dollars. This is true in Russia and the former Eastern European Block.

Advise Clients When They Need to Check In before Departure

Clients should be advised how long they should check in before their flights, tours, or other travel arrangements. This information should also be on their printed itinerary. This information is available in the Global Distribution Systems for travel agents and airline personnel. Tour operators and wholesalers will have this information available for their own operations. It is usually printed in their brochures. If not, ask. In the accommodations sector, each property sets its own policy regarding **check-in time** and checkout times. Most require a guarantee if check-in is going to be after 6:00 P.M. The *Official Airline Guides* list the minimum check-in times for international flights.

Advise Clients to Reconfirm Return Flights on International Itineraries

Clients should be advised to contact the carrier to advise them of their telephone contact at their destination, in case there are schedule changes. Clients returning to international destinations should be advised to reconfirm their return flight at least 72 hours prior to their departure. Advise them that it is a good idea to do this upon arrival at their destination while waiting for their baggage.

Advise Clients Regarding Their Baggage Allowances

Clients should be advised concerning their free baggage allowance. Clients should also be advised of the excess baggage charges if the customer desires to take more than the free allowance. This is especially important if they have an international stopover and the baggage allowance on the next flight reverts to the **weight system**. Free baggage allowances vary between different destinations and also from one carrier to another. The two principal free baggage allowance systems are called the **piece system** and the weight system. The piece system allows a number of pieces of baggage with defined maximum dimensions determined by the formula width + length + height. For example, most transatlantic airlines allow two pieces of checked baggage, one with maximum dimensions of 55 inches and one with maximum dimensions of 62 inches plus a carry-on piece with maximum dimensions of 45 inches. Each of these three pieces can have a maximum of 70 pounds.

The weight system ignores the number of pieces but limits the free baggage allowance to a total limit by weight, often 44 pounds or 20 kilograms in coach class or 66 pounds or 30 kilograms in first class.

A business traveler knew that between North America and Europe that he was allowed to take three pieces of baggage with up to 70 pounds each. He wanted to take as many samples of his products as permitted within the free baggage allowance. He took the maximum 210 pounds. This was no problem to Amsterdam, but after a stopover, his limit reverted to the European allowance of a total of 44 pounds from Amsterdam to Athens. The excess baggage charge from Amsterdam to Athens was $1,004.20 in U.S. funds one way. The passenger sued both the travel agency and the airline. He won on both counts. The judge found the travel agent guilty for not properly advising the passenger and for filling in the ticket, Amsterdam to Athens, with *PC* in the baggage box, indicating that the piece system was in effect when actually the weight system was in effect. The judge found the airline negligent for accepting the ticket in New York, even though the baggage entry was completed incorrectly for the Amsterdam to Athens flight.

The situation could have been worse. If the passenger had one stopover on his return, the charge for excess baggage would have been double! If he had more than one stopover, the excess baggage charges would have been more than double! If he wanted to leave the samples in Greece, he might have had to pay large import duties and taxes or he might have had serious legal problems.

Explain the Terms of an Option

If you have booked a client on a flight or package on an option, the meaning and terms of the option should be clearly explained to the customer. The amount of deposit required, the due date for the deposit, and the consequences of not having it paid on time should be clearly stated. The client must know the balance due and the date it is required. Administrative charges for changing the reservation and cancellation charges should be clearly understood by the client before you forward payment to the supplier.

Travel Insurance

Advising your client regarding travel insurance is important. Whenever the client is at risk of losing money regarding a trip, it is the salesperson's obligation to offer insurance against losses. This includes, but is not limited to, cancellation insurance to cover the nonrefundable portions of payments made, flight insurance, medical insurance, and baggage insurance for losses not covered by the transportation ticket or personal insurance.

International tourists are not covered for medical costs or accidents when they travel to the United States or Canada. Medical insurance for visitors to the United States or Canada is available and should always be offered to your incoming clients.

Many American insurers do not cover clients outside the United States. Canadian health care covers expenses only to the limit they would be covered in one's province of residence. When traveling in the United States and some other countries, costs of medical care can be as much as four times the cost in Canada. Without extra insurance the traveler would be liable for the difference. So, for most international travelers, medical insurance is a must.

Double-check Flight Schedules

Always double-check flight numbers and times if reservations were made well in advance. This is especially important if they span the major schedule change dates of April or October. Notify the client if there are any changes in flight numbers or times.

Car Rentals

With regards to car rentals, advise the client of the extra costs including mileage or charges per kilometer, if applicable, and the exchange rate if they want the price converted from a foreign currency. Whenever quoting an equivalent amount from a foreign currency, always explain that this rate changes daily and sometimes more than once per day. The cost of the **collision damage waiver (CDW)**, referred to in some places as the **loss damage waiver (LDW)**, and whether it is necessary or not, local taxes, and the possible cost of fuel, if the tank is not returned full, must be explained. Charges for topping off the gas tank are often much more than the normal cost of gasoline.

PREPARING THE CUSTOMER'S PACKAGE

For an **inclusive tour**, the tour company will usually prepare the basic package and forward it to the travel agent. The salesperson will provide additional material to make it more useful to the client and to enhance the image of the agency. For example, hotel brochures could be added for the accommodations selected and brochures from the tourist board of the destination visited.

The transportation tickets along with a printed itinerary should be enclosed in a ticket jacket. Ask the client if extra copies of the itinerary will be required. Some companies prefer to replace the tour company's or airline's ticket jacket with their own in order to give their company a higher profile. Some of the information discussed earlier under "You Have to Tell Your Client" might be included on a printed form on your company's letterhead. Include selected materials from tourist boards.

If your reservations computer has the required information regarding health requirements and recommendations, print a copy and include it with the tickets. Insert recommendations from your local health unit to supplement the information available in your reservations computer. Enclose a copy of *Know Before You Go*, available from any U.S. customs office at no charge. When a customer is traveling to or from Canada, you can obtain the *I Declare* pamphlet at no charge from Canada customs.

List the immigration documentation required on the itinerary very clearly and point it out to the client. Include information regarding passports, visas, proof of citizenship, and proof of identity. Make sure that the client knows the difference between proof of citizenship and proof of identity! Proof of citizenship includes a birth certificate for a citizen born in the country of which he or she is a citizen, passport, or citizenship card. A citizen born in another country would need naturalization papers, a citizenship card, or a passport. A driver's license or Social Security card is not proof of citizenship. Proof of identity requires a government issued photo ID with a signature. Often travelers are asked for two documents proving their identification.

Vouchers, confirmations, and receipts for all prepaid services should be included. Clients feel very anxious about traveling without documentation when they have prepaid for a service. Many airlines have recently instituted a "travel without ticket" system called electronic tickets. A United Airlines representative indicated that in the first two years of using electronic tickets, acceptance by travelers has grown to 90 percent. However, many clients are still used to the traditional system of tickets and feel very anxious about traveling without documentation when they have prepaid for a service. Set them at ease by issuing your company voucher to verify the reservation and proof of payment. (See Figure 10-5.)

If you do not have vouchers, print all the required information on your company letterhead and sign it.

ABC TRAVEL & TOURISM   **VOUCHER No. 51157**
154 South Broadway, ROCHESTER MN 55904 Phone: (507)281-7000

To: _____United Airlines Inc._____, **Date:** 16 NOV 2000_____

Address: _O'Hare International Airport_____

_____CHICAGO, IL_____

Client(s): _Mr. Simon Goldberg_____

For: _____First Class Flights Round Trip_____

No. of Days/Nights: _____, **From:** Chicago/O'hare_____ **To:** New York/La Guardia

Conf. No.: Q5N5FA_____, **Prepaid Voucher:** __✓__, **or Confirmation Only:** __

Value: two thousand and two ————————————XX/100---$ _2,002_____.__

Comments: 04 DEC   UA 692 dp Chicago/ORD 9:00 a.m. ar New York/LGA 12:06 p.m.

_____08 DEC   UA 677 dp New York/LGA 4:00 p.m. ar Chicago/ORD 5:35 p.m.

Have a good trip Mr. Goldberg_____, **Signature:** _Rose Shapiro_

FIGURE 10-5   Completed voucher

For late bookings, documentation is usually picked up at the airport. Handle this situation the same as you would ticketless travel. Issue a voucher for exchange at the airport or type up the details on your letterhead. For services that are reserved but not prepaid, give the customer letters of introduction with confirmation numbers and contacts (e.g., the name of the reservationist who confirmed the booking for them and the date and time the reservation was made).

A bon voyage card could be enclosed with the package but is probably more effective if mailed to arrive a few days before departure. A friendly note with suggestions to make your client's trip more enjoyable could be included with the package but might be included with the bon voyage card. This could include reminders to reconfirm return flights for international trips, or any other item that could be forgotten in the rush to get ready for the trip. Advise travelers not to pack their passport or other documentation in their luggage! The passenger should always carry these items.

Tourist board brochures are usually informative and free. They make a good insertion in the customer's package.

When making hotel reservations, request several copies of the hotel brochure along with a written confirmation. Enclose the confirmation and one copy of the brochure with the tickets. Keep one or more copies of the hotel brochure in your sales kit for future customers. For inclusive tour packages, request a supply of hotel brochures directly from the hotel or chain for the properties that are included in your clients' tours. Hotel brochures give much more detail than the brief descriptions given in tour brochures.

Provide your client with a reading list. Hopefully, the client will have most of this information early in the sales process. For clients interested in a complex **independent tour**, they should be given a reading list at the time of the first inquiry. It will help them to clarify their requests and make your job much easier. For customers booking an inclusive tour, give them a reading list at the time of booking. However, photocopies of interesting articles or a recently discovered source of information of interest to the client could be included with the tickets.

For major purchases, companies will often include a small gift with the ticket package. This is discussed later under the heading "Novelties or Favors."

ETHICS IN SELLING TOURISM

Ethics is a discipline dealing with moral duty, conforming to right principles of conduct as accepted by a specific profession. In selling tourism, we have three publics that we must deal with ethically: our customers, our suppliers, and our colleagues—both coworkers and competitors.

The American Society of Travel Agents (ASTA) has developed a 13-point Code of Ethics that stands for "Integrity in Travel" for its members (Figure 10-6). ASTA is the largest organization of travel agents in the world.

AMERICAN SOCIETY OF TRAVEL AGENTS (ASTA)
CODE OF ETHICS

Preamble

We live in a world in which travel has become both increasingly important and complex in its variety of modes and choices. Travelers are faced with a myriad of alternatives as to transportation, accommodations and other travel services.

Travelers must depend on travel agencies and others in the industry to guide them honestly and competently. All ASTA members pledge themselves to conduct their business activities in a manner that promotes the ideal of integrity in travel and agree to act in accordance with the applicable sections of the following principles of the ASTA Code of Ethics. Complaints arising under this Code should be filed in writing with the ASTA Consumer Affairs Department.

ASTA has the following categories of membership: Active, Retail Travel Sellers, International, Individual, Allied, Travel School, Associate, Associate Independent, Senior and Honorary.

Responsibilities of All Active, Retail Travel Sellers, International Members (and) Associate members of such firms and Associate Independent and Individual —

Members:

1. **Accuracy.** ASTA members will be factual and accurate when providing information about their services and the services of any firm they represent. They will not use deceptive practices.

2. **Disclosure.** ASTA members will provide in writing, upon written request, complete details about the cost, restrictions, and other terms and conditions, of any travel service sold, including cancellation and service fee policies. Full details of the time, place, duration, and nature of any sales or promotional presentation the consumer will be required to attend in connection with his/her travel arrangements shall be disclosed in writing before any payment is accepted.

3. **Responsiveness.** ASTA members will promptly respond to their clients' complaints.

4. **Refunds.** ASTA members will remit any undisputed funds under their control within the specified time limit. Reasons for delay in providing funds will be given to the claimant promptly.

5. **Cooperation.** ASTA members will cooperate with any inquiry conducted by ASTA to resolve any dispute involving consumers or another member.

6. **Confidences.** ASTA members will not use improperly obtained client lists or other confidential information obtained from an employee's former employer.

7. **Confidentiality.** ASTA members will treat every client transaction confidentially and not disclose any information without permission of the client, unless required by law.

8. **Affiliation.** ASTA members will not falsely represent a person's affiliation with their firm.

9. **Conflict of Interest.** ASTA members will not allow any preferred relationship with a supplier to interfere with the interests of their clients.

10. **Compliance.** ASTA members shall abide by all federal, state and local laws and regulations.

Responsibilities of All Members:

1. **Notice.** ASTA members operating tours will promptly advise the agent or client who reserved the space of any change in itinerary, services, features, or price. If substantial changes are made that are within the control of the operator, the client will be allowed to cancel without penalty.

2. **Delivery.** ASTA members' operating tours will provide all components as stated in their brochure or written confirmation, or provide alternative services of equal or greater value, or provide appropriate compensation.

3. **Credentials.** An ASTA member shall not, in exchange for money or otherwise, provide travel agent credentials to any person as to whom there is no reasonable expectation that the person will engage in a bona fide effort to sell or manage the sale of travel services to the general public on behalf of the member through the period of validity of such credentials. This principle applies to the ASTA member and all affiliated or commonly controlled enterprises.

Conclusion

Adherence to the Principles of the Code of Ethics signifies competence, fair dealing, and high integrity. Failure to adhere to this Code may subject a member to disciplinary actions, as set forth in ASTA's Bylaws.

FIGURE 10-6   ASTA Code of Ethics. *(Courtesy of the American Society of Travel Agents)*

The United States Tour Operators Association (USTOA) believes that industry self-regulation is a more acceptable alternative than government imposed rules. In 1975, USTOA developed its own ethics code. In November 1978, USTOA produced an even more definitive industry-developed compendium of "Ethics in U.S. Tour Operations/Standards for Integrity." (See Figure 10-7.) Among USTOA's goals are consumer protection and education. USTOA informs the traveling public on how to be a better consumer. The organization has established a $1 million Consumer Protection Program to aid consumers and travel agents in the event of a USTOA member default.

FIGURE 10-7

Tour Operators' Code. (*Courtesy of the United States Tour Operators Association*)

Tour Operators' Code

Principles of Professional Conduct and Ethics

1. It is the responsibility of Active and Affiliated Active Tour Operator Members of the United States Tour Operators Association (USTOA) to conduct their business affairs forthrightly, with professional competence and factual accuracy.

2. Representations to the public and retailers shall be truthful, explicit, intelligible and avoid deception, and concealment or obscuring of material facts, conditions or requirements.

3. In advertising and quoting of prices for tours, the total deliverable price, including service charges and special charges, shall be stated clearly and readily determinable; and the pendency of any known condition or contingency, such as fares subject to Conference and/or Government approval, shall be openly and noticeably disclosed.

4. Advertising and explanation of tour features shall clearly state and identify the facilities, accommodations and services included; any substitutions of features or deviation from the advertised tour shall be communicated expeditiously and the cause thereof be explained to agents and/or clients involved.

5. Each Active and Affiliated Active Tour Operator Member of USTOA shall so arrange and conduct its business as to instill retailer, consumer and public confidence in such Member's financial stability, reliability and integrity, and shall avoid any conduct or action conducive to discrediting membership in USTOA as signifying allegiance to professional and financial "Integrity in Tourism."

Ethics Related to Your Customers

As a salesperson in tourism, you have three areas of concern regarding ethics related to your clients:

1. You are acting as your client's agent.

2. You must have confidence in your suppliers.

3. If something goes wrong, will your client be protected?

Acting as Your Client's Agent

As a salesperson in the tourism industry, you are acting as the client's agent. As an agent, you are obligated to obtain the product or service that will fulfill your customer's needs at the best available price. As the client's agent, you have failed if you sell something that does not meet the client's needs and expectations, even if it is less expensive than the alternatives.

Also, as the client's agent, if you sell products or services that the customer does not need, you are not acting in good faith. Likewise, if you do not obtain the best price for which the client is eligible, you are not performing as the client's agent. If you enter the client's requirements for air transportation, car rentals, and a number of other services into a Global Distribution System like Amadeus, Galileo, Sabre, or Worldspan, the GDS will do a search to obtain the best price according to your client's request.

If you sold a ticket for a tour at the regular adult price when a customer was eligible for a senior citizen's discount, this would not be ethical. Recently, I called Northwest Airlines for the fare from Los Angeles to Toronto, round trip. I was quoted a fare of $334.04 including the tax for the dates I required. The full coach fare was $1,600.00.

I think it would not have been ethical to sell me the full coach fare ticket at $1,600.00 without letting me know I was eligible for the promotional fare of $334.04. Of course there were a number of differences in the conditions regarding the two fares. But I thanked the Northwest agent for giving me the choice and explaining the difference in the rules regarding each fare.

Confidence in Your Suppliers

Do you have confidence in the suppliers' products that you sell? What has the feedback been from previous clients who have purchased the supplier's products? If you have not sold the supplier's products before, determine the feedback that your colleagues have received. Check with your coworkers and with friendly competitors.

If it is a new tour or company, check the quality of the ingredients. By ingredients, I mean the quality of the motor coaches, accommodations, and local sight-seeing included. Discuss these details openly with your client.

Your reputation, and the reputation of the company for whom you work, depends upon your selection of suppliers. How do the suppliers you have selected measure up when it comes to safety records, on-time performance, and customer satisfaction?

What Happens if Something Goes Wrong?

If something goes wrong, will your clients be protected? Hopefully, you have selected suppliers that have exemplary records of providing what they have promised. But, even with the best suppliers, something can occasionally go wrong. For example, the weather or a natural disaster could prevent part of a tour or even an entire tour from being delivered. Cruise ships have been known to catch on fire, run aground, or even sink. Are your client's lives as safe as possible according to the SOLAS (Safety of Life at Sea) principles? Are your client's funds protected? If the supplier cannot deliver what it has promised, will your client get his or her money back? For lesser problems, will customers be compensated reasonably?

In some states and provinces, travel and tourism companies are required to be licensed and bonded. In other jurisdictions, no licensing is required and bonding is voluntary. If a company is bonded, your client's funds are protected. Companies that are not bonded will not have any statement regarding bonding in their brochure. But, if a company has paid to be bonded, that fact will be prominently displayed in their brochure! If your supplier is not bonded, are you able and willing to guarantee your client's funds if your supplier is unable to provide the services promised?

I do not know the source of the next statement, but I certainly do believe it. If your client is satisfied with the way a problem is handled, he or she will tell an average of 8 people. If a client's problem is not resolved in a manner that is satisfactory to the customer, he or she will tell 20 others—and will never do business with you again.

In tourism, we rely on satisfied customers for repeat business and referrals. For referrals to come to you, you must first have a satisfied customer. If you ask a satisfied customer for referrals, you are much more likely to receive them.

Not to follow these principles when selling tourism is fatal. Selling an inferior product or service at a cheap price will make it easy to close a sale now. But, dissatisfied customers will guarantee you a quick exit from the tourism business. Dissatisfied clients will never be repeat customers. They will not refer any new customers to you. They will discourage many potential clients from doing business with you personally or with your company.

One mistake in recommending a supplier may undo all the good work you have done for years. Do your utmost to make sure that the supplier makes amends acceptable to the customer. If the supplier does not perform well here, take a loss, satisfy the customer, and discard the supplier.

Always follow up to see if the customer's complaint was satisfied to his or her satisfaction. If so, apologize for the inconvenience. State that you are pleased that the situation has been resolved and that you are looking forward to doing business with the customer in the near future.

If the mood is pleasant, turn the topic toward future travel. If you can obtain a possible tourism experience and approximate date, it gives you a good opportunity to properly prepare for the customer's next trip.

Two very good clients of ours had purchased a package tour to Palm Beach, Florida, for one week, which was to include a rental car for two days. The brochure had an asterisk in front of the statement describing the inclusion of the rental car. At the bottom of the page, an asterisk appeared followed by a statement that if the car was unavailable, the clients would receive a $79.00 rebate. When Mr. and Mrs. Stansky returned from Florida, they explained that the car was not available and requested the $79.00 refund. The travel counselor, Mike, explained that he would call that same day to request the refund. He telephoned immediately and followed up with a letter.

Ten days later Mrs. Stansky returned to the office to see if Mike had received the refund. Mike explained that he had not received it yet, so he called the tour company and was assured that it would be mailed that week. After another two weeks, Mr. and Mrs. Stansky returned to the travel agency to check whether the agency had received the refund yet. Now, Mike was really angry! He telephoned an executive in the company and stated that this was totally unacceptable. He was assured that this would receive the executive's personal attention. After another eight days, Mike received the refund check. Being embarrassed about the delay, Mike thought that he would personally deliver the refund check rather than mail it or telephone the clients. When he arrived at the door, Mike was informed by a neighbor that Mr. and Mrs. Stansky were away on a tour and would be back in approximately three weeks.

Mike immediately realized he had just lost two of his best clients over a relatively minor failure in service by a supplier. The following facts seemed apparent:

1. Mr. and Mrs. Stansky were entitled to the car rental for two days.

2. They did not receive the car rental for the two days and submitted the voucher for the car rental for a refund.

3. The brochure clearly stated that if the car rental was not available, the customer would receive a refund of $79.00.

4. Mr. and Mrs. Stansky made three trips to our office over 24 days to receive the refund to which they were clearly entitled.

5. After 32 days, the refund check arrived. (In retrospect, this was probably not that bad considering most tour company's accounting departments.)

6. When Mike went to deliver the refund check, Mr. and Mrs. Stansky were away on a major vacation.

7. They did not book this vacation through Mike. He had lost two of his best clients!

8. Mike made a stupid error in handling this situation!

What should Mike have done?

1. It was clear that Mr. and Mrs. Stansky were entitled to a $79.00 refund. Mike should have issued a refund check on the spot. He should have informed the tour company that he had refunded the customer the amount of $79.00. Mike should have requested the tour company to make the refund check payable to his company.

2. Mr. and Mrs. Stansky did not receive one of the important benefits of the tour. Mike should have apologized on the spot for their inconvenience. He should have offered some form of retribution over and beyond the tour company's refund to secure their good will—for example, a $25.00 gift certificate toward future travel (and try to get the tour company to do the same), flowers, and/or wine. (**Note:** The $25.00 gift certificate toward future travel would have the greatest value to the client and the least cost to your company.)

3. The agency could wait for the refund from the tour company. The clients could not! If the tour company failed to compensate Mike's company for the money refunded to Mr. and Mrs. Stansky, the tour company would be eliminated from the agency's supplier list.

Ethics Related to Your Suppliers

We also have an ethical obligation to our suppliers. Whether they provide commissionable products and services or competitive **net rates** to which we can apply a reasonable markup, our suppliers are the source of our income. If we are going to sell their products, we must support them.

Suppliers spend a great deal of money to provide us with promotional materials, special events, seminars, sales representatives, and familiarization trips. If we accept suppliers' generous support, we are obligated either to support the sale of their products or to inform them why we cannot fully support their services as they are, and to make suggestions for improvement so that we could support them.

Ethics Related to Your Colleagues

Last but not least is our ethical relationship with our colleagues. This would include the relationship we have with our coworkers and our competition.

In the sectors and subsectors of the tourism industry in which employees are paid strictly on commission, it would seem that our co-workers are our adversaries or competitors. This attitude is most destructive for both the company and its employees. First of all, the attitude of the employees pervades the atmosphere and becomes apparent to potential clients, and they will scramble for a less competitive, more helpful atmosphere.

Second, it deprives the salesperson of an extremely important support system. When you are away from your workstation, would it not be very helpful to you if your colleague could take a very positive attitude toward helping your client? Would it not be beneficial if you could provide information from your experience and expertise to assist your colleague in closing a sale?

Sales staff need to be indoctrinated with a philosophy of promoting the company first, working as a team, and assisting each other. The total result should be a bigger pie, and each individual's slice of the pie should be bigger.

In some cases one counselor can initiate a sale and another counselor could complete a large portion of the work. In these cases, a commission-splitting agreement could be made on an ad hoc basis or some policy could be determined by the company and its employees.

In companies where sales personnel are paid either on straight salary or a combination of salary plus commission, it is to everybody's benefit to build a team concept that embodies the philosophy that the customer comes first.

With regard to our competitors, it is also beneficial to retain an ethical relationship. With direct competitors within the same geographical region, competition is a beneficial situation for the customer. It promotes quality at competitive prices. Friendly competition can provide benefits for both parties. For example, many airlines that have been competing for many years with an unreasonable overcapacity have decided to agree on a code sharing agreement to share the market and promote each other's flights.

For example, Northwest has a code sharing agreement with KLM. Delta has code sharing agreements with Swiss Air, Austrian Airlines, and Sabena. United Airlines has code sharing agreements with Air Canada, British Airways, Quantas, and others. These are just a few examples of code sharing. The trend is to form partnerships and cooperate rather than compete.

Also two competitors promoting chartered flights, each with less than a 50-percent load factor, might find it mutually beneficial to share one chartered flight with a 90-percent load factor. Cooperation with competitors can turn a disastrous loss for each one into a profit situation for both.

In Hawaii, the entire tourism industry pulls together. Of course each company or organization tries to sell its products or services first. But if one does not have what the customer needs, it promotes other Hawaiian suppliers. The staff would help the customer find an organization that does have what the tourist needs. They give the tourist as much information as they have and put the tourist in direct contact with the provider of the service. Usually, they would telephone the organization for you.

The philosophy of the Hawaiian Tourism Industry:

1. We are brothers . . . we are Hawaiian!
2. We are brothers . . . we work in the tourism industry!
3. Tourists are our lifeblood!
4. If we increase tourism, we all benefit!
5. Help me brother! I will help you!
6. Aloha!

NOVELTIES OR FAVORS

Most businesses give items to customers to enhance their image or to serve as a constant reminder of the company's service. Such gift items are frequently called favors in Canada and novelties in the United States. These gift items may range from a pen or matchbox with the company logo, name, phone number, and address on it to an attractive carry-on bag. Wine or flowers can make a positive impact. It can be less expensive and have a personal impact if you deliver the wine (perhaps champagne) or flowers with the tickets.

The cost of favors or novelties must be commensurate with the value of the trip. You would not give away a free carry-on bag to a customer taking a short rail or air trip with no additional services. Similarly, you would not use an ordinary pen as a favor for a couple who had booked an expensive all-inclusive holiday or cruise.

Good favors or novelties should look classy, but be relatively inexpensive and be useful, have a long life, and be highly visible!

Discussion Questions

1. What are the various types of documentation sometimes required for international travel?

2. What advice would you have for outbound and inbound international tourists regarding the best means of handling and exchanging currency?

3. What advice would you give to tourists regarding establishing a budget for a trip?

4. How would you determine the check-in times for transportation and tours?

5. Discuss five criteria for good novelties or favors.

6. How would you explain the regulations regarding reconfirming return flights for international travel?

Follow-Up Procedures

OBJECTIVES

After studying this chapter, you should be able to:

● Describe the two most popular methods of follow-up used in the tourism industry

● List four advantages of doing your follow-up by telephone

● List five points to be covered in a follow-up telephone call

● Describe follow-up procedures for each of the eight sectors of the tourism industry

● Explain the importance of asking for referrals

KEY TERMS

head them off at the pass   captive audience
ecotours   guest comment cards

STEP 12: FOLLOW-UP PROCEDURES

Follow-up is the most neglected part of the sales process in the tourism industry, and yet it can be the most rewarding and fruitful. As with selling-up, the most effective methods for follow-up vary from one sector of the tourism industry to another.

For adventure and recreation packages and most types of tours, the salesperson should contact the customer within a week of his or her return, preferably the second or third day after the return. Customers are probably too tired and busy to be bothered the first day. After that, the sooner you contact them, the better.

Clients can be contacted by telephone or by mail. Follow-up by mail usually consists of a welcome back card with an evaluation form regarding their trip and a postage-paid return envelope. The welcome back card is good for public relations, but I believe there are important advantages in doing your follow-up by telephone:

1. It is more personal.

2. You can evaluate the reactions of your client personally.

3. The amount of feedback you receive will be significantly increased.

4. It is less expensive and faster.

When you are preparing the customer's package, be sure to note in your calendar the date your client(s) will be returning. When you present them with the ticket package, mention that you would like to call them after they get back to hear about their trip. Customers will usually be quite pleased that you are interested in their trips after the sale has been closed. If they approve, ask them when it would be convenient. Try to obtain a range of times to make it easier to fit into your schedule. Then mark your preferred time and date on your calendar. If you find at a later time that you will be unable to call them between the designated times, phone ahead of time.

If it is convenient for both you and the customer to conduct the follow-up call at that time, do it then. If not, reschedule the call for a time that is mutually convenient. Some weeks can be unpredictable, but usually you can tell which days and particularly which times of day will be less busy than others. By scheduling your follow-up calls, you are more impelled to do them. Calling customers at times that are convenient for them will usually ellicit more information.

Prepare a prompt sheet with the questions you wish to ask and space for the answers you will receive. (See Figure 11-1.)

Follow-up Sheet

Outline of Points to Be Covered

1. Welcome back—clients are usually pleased that you take the time and interest to contact them after their trip.

2. Make sure you have called at a convenient time.

3. Did they enjoy their trip? Your returning customers can be your best source of product knowledge. The information they give you is right up-to-date and from the customers' point of view.

CLIENT FOLLOW-UP SHEET

Date of Return: _____   From: _____

Date of Follow-up: _____   Time: _____

Client's Name: _____

Dates of Travel: _____   Phone No.: _____

Destinations/Services Provided: _____

_____

_____

How was your holiday? _____

_____

How would you rate it overall?   EX ❏   VG ❏   GOOD ❏   FAIR ❏   POOR ❏

   If you had a problem, what was the nature of your problem?

   _____

   _____

   If you had a problem, I will contact _____

   And get back to you by DATE: _____ TIME: _____

What were the best aspects of your holiday? _____

_____

_____

Would you give us permission to pass on your comments to future travelers? _____

_____

Is there anything we can do to improve our service for you? _____

_____

Have you thought about where you would like to go on your next vacation? _____

Where do you think you would like to travel? _____

When do you think you would like to take your next vacation? _____

Is there any information that you would like me to send you regarding your next vacation? _____

Additional Comments: _____

_____

FIGURE 11-1 Client follow-up sheet

4. If there were any problems, it gives you a chance to "**head them off at the pass**." It is better that you approached the client first, rather than let the problems fester to a boiling point and have the client burst into the office when you are busy with other clients. The worst scenario is that they might never tell you about their problems but tell everyone else with whom they meet and never return to give you a chance to rectify the problem or make another booking.

5. On the way back from a holiday, most clients like to look ahead to their next trip. Ask your clients if they have thought about their next trip. Find out approximately when they would like to go and mark it down in your calendar. Find out if there is any information that they would like you to send to them about their next destination. Determine when would be the most appropriate time to send them the information. Mark this down in your desk calendar. A few days after you would expect that they would have received it, mark down on your desk calendar to phone them to see if they have received your package. This would be your opener to discuss if the information was of interest to them and to start the qualifying process over again for their next booking. Forward promotional materials to the customers with plenty of lead time to confirm their next booking. Follow-up with a telephone call several days after you would expect the client to receive your mailing piece. Determine whether the client received the material and find out if it was helpful and of interest. If so, determine when the client would like to get together. Make a definite appointment including the date, time, and place.

For people working in adventure tours, **ecotours**, and any type of attraction, you should obtain follow-up information before the tourist leaves the sight. Follow-up questionnaires or cards can be handed out with a postage-paid envelope and a request to fill them out and mail them in. However, the problem with this method is that you will have a large number of nonresponses.

It is usually better if you have an opportunity to have a **captive audience** to have the customers fill in evaluation cards and hand them in on the spot. This can often be done on the bus, plane, or train on the last leg of the trip. If this is not possible, perhaps it could be done while waiting for a group meal to be served or at the end of the meal. Any other opportunity where the group is together and waiting for any reason would be a good time to complete an evaluation form. (See Figure 11-2.) Not only does this enhance your chances of obtaining an almost perfect rate of return, but it also makes the waiting time

ACTION TOURS EVALUATION FORM

Name of Tour: <u>Wonders of the Holy Roman Empire</u>   No. of Days: <u>18</u>

Departure Date: <u>JUL 9, 2002</u>   Starting Point: <u>Berlin</u>

Family Name: _____   First Name: _____

No. of Adults: _____, No. of Seniors (60+):_____, No. of Youths (13–18): _____,

No. of Children (2–12): _____, No. of Infants (under 2): _____

Which of the following would summarize your overall impression of the tour?

EXCELLENT ____ VERY GOOD ____ GOOD ____ FAIR ____ POOR ____

Which three inclusions of the tour did you like the best?

1. _____

2. _____

3. _____

Were there any inclusions in the tour that you did not like?

_____

_____

If you had a problem on the tour, what was the nature of your problem?

_____

_____

If you had a problem on our tour, how were our efforts to resolve the problem?

EXCELLENT ____ VERY GOOD ____ GOOD ____ FAIR ____ POOR ____

Is there anything that you want us to do after the tour is over? _____

_____

_____

Would you recommend our tour to others?   YES ____ NO ____ MAYBE ____

Do you have any particular people in mind? _____

Can we use your name as a satisfied customer when promoting our tour to others?

YES ____ NO ____ MAYBE ____

COMMENTS: _____

_____

_____

FIGURE 11-2 Evaluation form

seem shorter for your clients. Also, offering an incentive encourages customers to respond. For example, you might offer a prize or perhaps a discount on a future trip.

Always close the evaluation with a statement that you have really enjoyed serving them and that you look forward to the opportunity to serve them again. "If you know of anyone who would enjoy our services, we would appreciate your referral. Be sure to ask your referral to mention your name when they contact us." This will provide you an opportunity to track your success with referrals. It will also provide you an opportunity for public relations communications with both the previous customer who referred you new customers and a personal letter to the new customers with reference to the people who had referred them to you.

In the Accommodations sector, it is customary to have **guest comment cards** in the room, but the number filled in is usually relatively low. A significantly higher proportion of guests who have complaints will fill them in. This is beneficial for corrective measures but does not yield much positive feedback.

The Super 8 Motel guest comment card would probably elicit greater feedback than most because of its relatively brief check-off format making it easy and quick for the guest to complete. Yet it still provides space for comments. (See Figure 11-3.) If it is feasible, select a random sample of guests for a personal telephone call near the end of the guest's stay or shortly after he or she returns home to determine specific information regarding his or her stay.

In the Food and Beverage sector, follow-up should start earlier than in any other sector and should include all customers. The server should check back with the patron shortly after being served to ensure that everything is satisfactory. Before departure, the maître d' or some other supervisor should follow-up with questions regarding overall satisfaction and any other information that the management wants.

Most restaurants have comment cards on the table. The number that are filled in and the amount of information garnered is increased greatly by holding a drawing each month for a free meal for two. If this is routinely pointed out by the server, the percentage of responses can be phenomenal. Comment cards are also extremely useful in creating an effective mailing list for future promotions.

For the Attractions and Special Events sector, it is probably best to do some type of sampling to interview guests while they are on the site. Tourism services should obtain addresses of contacts and conduct surveys from time to time using a random sample of visitors. A questionnaire to be completed by the client should be designed to elicit the type of information desired.

In the Transportation sector, most people are cooperative about filling in evaluation forms while traveling on the last leg of their trip because they usually do not have anything else to do at the time.

WELCOME TO OUR SUPER 8 MOTEL. 7/98

Would you please help us judge how well we are meeting your needs? Please mark the block below the face that represents how you react to each of the following questions.

Site #: 5174
Strathmore, AB
CANADA

	☺	😐	☹	😟
YOUR ACCOMMODATIONS				
What was the APPEARANCE of the motel?	☐	☐	☐	☐
How CLEAN was your room?	☐	☐	☐	☐
Were you COMFORTABLE in your room?	☐	☐	☐	☐
What was the condition of your room's FURNISHINGS?	☐	☐	☐	☐
Was the BATHROOM clean?	☐	☐	☐	☐
How do you perceive our PRICE or VALUE relationship?	☐	☐	☐	☐
OUR SERVICES				
Were we FRIENDLY?	☐	☐	☐	☐
Were we EFFICIENT?	☐	☐	☐	☐
Were we RESPONSIVE TO YOUR NEEDS?	☐	☐	☐	☐
OVERALL, how do you rate our SUPER 8?	☐	☐	☐	☐
WOULD YOU VISIT THIS SUPER 8 MOTEL AGAIN?	☐ YES		☐ NO	

NAME:__________ ADDRESS: __________

CITY:__________ STATE or PROVINCE:__________ ZIP or POSTAL CODE: __________

PHONE NO.:__________ ROOM NO.:__________ ARRIVAL DATE: __________

COMMENTS: __________

FIGURE 11-3

Guest comment card. *(Courtesy Super 8 Motels, Inc.)*

In the Events and Conferences sector, it is common practice to have participants complete an evaluation form after each major session. Participants expect this, and the return rate is high and immediate.

Remember two major elements of your follow-up:

- Thank your clients for the opportunity to serve them and state that you are looking forward to assisting them with their next tourism arrangements.
- Ask your clients for referrals. If you have done a good job in arranging your clients' tourism experiences, they will usually be pleased to recommend your services to friends, family members, and business associates. Because they do not often think of it, plant the idea in their minds. This type of promotion is more successful than any type of paid advertising. In fact, when all sources of promotion are considered, referrals bring in more new customers than any other means, resulting in 25.2 percent of new business. (See Figure 11-4.) You will definitely receive many more referrals if you ask for them rather than leave them

WHY PEOPLE SELECT A PARTICULAR AGENCY[1]

➤ A friend referred me 25.2%

➤ Know an agency employee 21.7%

➤ Newspaper ad. 13.3%

➤ Direct mail. 6.9%

➤ Radio 6.6%

➤ Employer does business with agency 6.0%

➤ Yellow pages. 3.7%

➤ Television 1.3%

➤ Travel folder 9%

➤ Other 14.4%

---

[1] Robert T. Reilly, *Travel and Tourism Marketing Techniques* (Wheaton, IL: Merton House Publishing Co., 1980): 47.

FIGURE 11-4

Reasons why people select a particular agency.

to chance. Referrals already bring in such a high percentage of customers. By making it a point to ask every satisfied returning tourist for referrals, we can increase this number significantly. Make it part of your routine!

Discussion Questions

1. What are the two most popular methods of follow-up used in the tourism industry?

2. What are the four advantages of doing your follow-up by telephone?

3. What are five points that you should cover in a follow-up telephone call?

4. Describe how you would conduct follow-up procedures in each of the eight sectors of the tourism industry.

5. Explain the importance of asking for referrals.

CHAPTER 12

The Most Important Sale You Make May Be Your First!

OBJECTIVES

After studying this chapter, you should be able to:

● Identify what the most important sale you will make will be

● Explain how a thorough knowledge of the sales process will help you obtain the job

● Explain which closing technique is most appropriate in most job interviews

● Describe a situation in which each of the ten closing techniques could be used in a job interview

KEY TERMS

information interview   tough sell

In Chapter 1, the importance of sales within the tourism industry was discussed. And it ended with the statement, "The most important sale you make, might be your first!"

THE MOST IMPORTANT SALE YOU MAKE MAY BE YOUR FIRST!

Talking about the importance of sales in Chapter 1, we concluded, "The most important sale you make, might be your first!" The prospect is a potential employer. The product is your services. If your sales approach is successful, you will get the job and have plenty of opportunities to complete other sales. If you are unable to successfully complete this first sale, you will not have another chance to sell until your next job opportunity.

SEARCHING FOR A PROSPECTIVE EMPLOYER

First, you must search for a prospective employer that may have a need for your services. Before you start, you must do a careful evaluation of your abilities, education, and experience. Then you must search for possible employers that may have a need for your services. The objective at this stage is to obtain an interview so that you will have an opportunity to sell your abilities, your services, and indeed yourself to the company or organization. You must determine a strategy for approaching the potential employer in order to create a favorable first impression.

Research the Job Market

Getting the job is much like an outside sale rather than an inside sale. You cannot wait at your desk for the phone to ring. You have to go after this sale (the job)! The starting point is to research the job market. Of course you will scrutinize both the classified advertisements and the career opportunities listed in the business section in the newspapers. Also, you will register with both government and private sector employment services. But, many jobs never get advertised.

Study all eight sectors of the tourism industry. Decide in which sectors and subsectors you have an interest. Make a list of as many possible employers in each sector and sub-sector as possible. Use the yellow pages of the telephone book, trade magazines of the tourism industry, and offices of state, provincial, or national tourism organizations to determine as many potential employers as possible. Once you have established a thorough list, establish your priorities.

Determine Your Long-Range Goal

Determine your long-range goal. What position do you hope to hold 10 years from now? Who occupies such a position now? Schedule an

information interview with this person. The information interview is the opposite of a job interview. You interview the person who has the type of job you ultimately want. You want to find out details of what the job is like to determine if it is really like the job that you envision. You want to determine the qualifications and experience that the person holding the job has. Also, you want to determine the steps that the person you are interviewing took in order to gain his or her present position. Ask for advice regarding the steps you should take to embark on a similar career. Most people like to talk about their careers, but you have to use a diplomatic approach to obtain the interview.

Which Interview to Schedule First?

It might be a good idea not to approach your principal or second preferences first. It is likely that you will make some errors in your first couple of approaches. Even if you do not make a major error, you probably will learn some things that will help to polish your presentation and help you gain more confidence.

Once you have selected a potential employer, you need to research the company or organization. You need to know their background, their *raison d'être* (reason for being), their goals, their plans for the future, and most important, their needs. You want to match your abilities, training, experience, and ambitions to their needs and goals.

Contact the Right Person

Make sure that your application and résumé get to the right person. Find out the correct name and title of the person responsible for hiring. If possible, deliver your application and résumé in person. Make a positive first impression. Before leaving, state, "I would really appreciate an opportunity for an interview so that I can demonstrate how I can contribute to the success of *ABC Company*." Of course, this statement should be modified according to the precise situation and to suit your own personality and word choice.

Why This Company or Organization?

It is a good idea to state why you want to work for this company or organization. But refrain from any tone relating to your need for a job. Instead, stress why you chose this organization over others. It is vital that you design your sales points to how you can serve the company or organization. Can you do something to generate profits, save on costs, bring in more customers, or improve the image of the company or organization?

It may seem strange that you are the person being interviewed and that you are going to qualify the interviewers. Early in the interview process, you want to ask some qualifying questions to ensure that you understand the needs of the company or organization. Asking intelligent questions establishes that you have "done your homework" and are seriously interested in the job.

Ensuring that you fully understand the needs of the company or organization will aid you in answering the questions you are asked in a favorable manner. If you are not sure how to answer a question, probe. Ask questions to clarify the direction you should take in answering the interviewer's question. It also provides you with a little extra time to contemplate your response.

In some situations with more than one interviewer, they have a strategy to determine how the interviewee will respond under stress. One interviewer will ask a question and before the interviewee can completely answer the first question, another interviewer will ask another question. Relieve the pressure. Say, "I will be pleased to answer both of your questions, but I will finish responding to Miss Polley's question and then I will answer your question, Mr. Roberts."

Why the Employer Needs You

Recommend a service that will meet your client's (employer's) needs. *YOU!* Relate your abilities, training, and experience to how they can meet the employer's needs. Provide enough information about yourself to create acceptance.

USING CLOSING TECHNIQUES TO CLOSE THE DEAL (GET THE JOB)

Close the deal! Think of several different methods of closing the deal so that you are ready for a number of different situations. Remember that timing is crucial. Look for a closing signal and proceed toward closing, that is, getting the job.

The Summary Close is probably the most appropriate technique in most cases. Summarize your attributes and show how they can help the organization. (See Figure 12-1.)

If the interviewers have brought up some shortcomings in your training, experience, or background, use the T-Account Close to show how your positive attributes outweigh any negative ones. For example, "You have pointed out some shortcomings in my experience and background. However, if you examine the disadvantages of me as a candidate and compare them with the advantages of hiring me, I think you will find that the advantages outweigh the disadvantages."

THE SUMMARY CLOSE

"Miss Jones, I would like to summarize my attributes which would be an asset to World Wide Vacations.

1. As a graduate of College of the Americas, you know I have been taught by excellent instructors.

2. My status as an honor student establishes me as one of the top students in my class.

3. My knowledge of Spanish and French, in addition to English, will be an asset to World Wide Vacations, which has a diversified clientele and serves destinations in many parts of the world.

4. I am very proud of my top mark in *Tourist Destinations of the World* which means that I have a great deal of product knowledge of the destinations served by World Wide Vacations and that I have the ability and drive to become an expert in product knowledge of the wide variety of tours that you offer.

5. I really, really want to work for World Wide Vacations because of the impeccable reputation that the company has and the multitude of destinations it serves."

FIGURE 12-1

The Summary Close

Because the problem is the disadvantages and the solution is the advantages, I would put the disadvantages on the left side and the advantages on the right side to show how the advantages outweigh the disadvantages. (See Figure 12-2.)

If you have a **tough sell**, perhaps the Minor Points Close could be used. Get the interviewers to accept your individual sales points one at a time until you are able to get them to accept the whole package—*you!*

The Closing to Resistance Close could be used when one or more interviewers have come up with a serious objection to your qualifications or experience for the job. After you have successfully overcome the objection, try to get the person who had the objection to agree that you have countered it, and ask for the sale (I mean the job). The wording must be delicate and tailored to the particular situation, but it could go something like this: "Do you agree, Mrs. Wilson, that my expertise on the new generation of computer software outweighs my lack of experience with your existing system? If so, will you give me a chance to prove how I can use my knowledge to save *XYZ Corporation* time and money?"

The Option Close would be used in a situation where you have another job offer and have a limited time to make a decision. In this case, you would inform the interviewers that you really want to work

---

THE T-ACCOUNT CLOSE

Disadvantages	*Advantages*
You are looking for a person who is bilingual in English and Spanish, and although I know some Spanish, I am not fluent at the present time.	I studied Spanish in high school for four years, during which I maintained an "A" average. I have already enrolled in Advanced Conversational Spanish in an evening program at Central Michigan University.
You are looking for a person with experience in sales, and I have never had a permanent position in sales.	I have had a four-month cooperative work placement in sales with Niagara Falls Sightseeing by Sheridan. I have also had a four-month co-operative work placement in sales with Gray Line of New York City. I earned an "A" in my course "Selling Tourism" at Niagara College. I graduated from the Tourism Program at Niagara College with honors. I believe that World Wide Vacations has the best tours going, and I am confident that I can convince your customers to make a positive decision to buy World Wide tours.

FIGURE 12-2

The T-Account Close

for their organization and that you will be available until the option date. In other words, after that date, you will take the other job.

The Special Deal Close would be used when the interviewers want to hire you but are not willing to meet your salary or other expectations. In this case, you may be willing to negotiate working for less remuneration or other concessions under certain conditions.

The Choice Close in an interview situation would arise from a situation where the interviewers obviously want to hire the interviewee and have mentioned several or more possibilities of employment. If the interviewee would be happy with either of two job possibilities, he or she should clearly state that he or she would be willing to accept either of the two choices. This would help influence the decision-makers to offer one of the preferred choices.

The I Would Recommend Close could be used in a situation where you felt that there were a lot of positive feelings both for the interviewers and the interviewee but there were some problems to be worked out. The interviewee could suggest solutions or a time frame for solving the problems and suggest another meeting to solve the problem.

An interviewee would use the Shortage Close only when he or she was confident that there was a greater demand for his or her service than there were positions available. In this case, it would be important not to appear arrogant but to make it clear that he or she requires a quick decision because of other offers.

The Assumed Sold Close would be used only when you know that the company or organization really needs your services. In order to speed up the process, you might ask a question like, "When would you like me to start?" or "What will my starting salary be?"

One difference between a normal sale and getting the job is that you usually do not find out if you were successful in getting the job until some time after your sales presentation (interview). However, if you have said something during the interview that has brought the interviewers to a buying decision (that is, to hire you), you have indeed closed the sale.

Anticipate objections and be prepared to counter them. If confronted with an unexpected objection, probe (ask questions) about the objection to determine that you understand it precisely, and in the meantime you will have enough time to construct your response. For example, the interviewers may be stressing some skill, knowledge, or experience that you had not included on your résumé, but you are able to convince them that you have what they require; or perhaps the interviewers may have had the opinion that you are not available to work weekends or holidays, and you persuade them that you are able and willing to work any shift; or again, the interviewers may be reacting negatively to your lack of knowledge of Spanish, but you are perfectly fluent in the language. Select the interviewer who is most fluent in Spanish and converse with him or her until you have convinced all the interviewers that you are indeed fluent.

These are just three examples of objections. Of course, the number of objections could be without limit. But, whenever you have overcome the objection, observe closely for a closing signal. This would usually be some acknowledgment that the perceived problem has been removed. It might be a good opportunity to use the Closing to Resistance Close.

Selling-Up

The next step in the sales process is selling-up. Because your objective in this case was to get the job, selling-up probably does not apply in this situation, but in certain cases it might. There might be an opportunity to negotiate a higher salary, or rate of commission, or better terms. You must assess the situation. Is the employer going to have difficulty obtaining someone with your qualifications or are you going to be in competition with a number of other qualified candidates?

Following Up

Following up can increase your chances of being hired. Send a polite letter to each of the interviewers thanking them for the opportunity of the interview. (See Figure 12-3.) Tell each one that it was a pleasure

36 Ramada Road
Grand Island, NE 68801

April 22, 2002

Mrs. J. D. Wright
Gray Line of Yellowstone
P.O. Box 1168
Red Lodge, MT 59068

Dear Mrs. Wright:

I would like to thank you and the other members of the interview committee who made time in their busy schedules to interview me for the position of tour escort last Friday. I was excited about the possibility of working for Gray Line of Yellowstone before I came to Red Lodge, Montana, but after learning more about your exciting tours of Yellowstone, I am fascinated with the possibility of revealing the history, secrets, and charms of Yellowstone to your customers.

The members of your interview committee impressed me as the type of people I would like to work with and learn from. I look forward to hearing your decision soon.

Yours sincerely,

John Henry Hancock

John Henry Hancock

cc: George Clark
     Lynda G. Alias
     Sergio Fernadez
     J. C. Higenbottom

FIGURE 12-3

Sample polite follow-up letter to interviewers.

to meet him or her and that you hope you will have the opportunity of working with him or her. Personalize each letter so that the respondent feels that it is a first copy letter. At the time of the interview, you should have asked the question regarding when you can expect notification of a decision. If you have not received a decision by this date, telephone to check whether a decision has been made.

Providing service, follow-up, and selling repeat business is living up to the high level of quality that you promised to your client (I mean employer) during the interview. These three items will guarantee you a successful career in sales.

If You Are Unsuccessful

As in any sales situation, if you are unsuccessful, determine why! Did you make any fundamental error? Was your research regarding the company or organization incorrect or incomplete? Was your strategy, approach, or timing inappropriate? What changes can you make for future interviews?

Good luck! Go get it! And close that sale! Get the job!

Discussion Questions

1. What might be the most important sale you ever make?
2. Explain how a thorough knowledge of the sales process can help you obtain a job.
3. Which closing technique is most appropriate in most job interviews?
4. Describe a situation in which each of the 10 closing signals might be used to close the deal in a job interview.

Appendix

USEFUL WEB SITES

American Society of Travel Agents	<http://www.astanet.com>
Business Travel Planner	<http://www.northstartravelmedia.com>
The Caribbean Gold Book	<http://www.caribbeantravel.com>
Centers for Disease Control and Prevention	<http://www.cdc.gov/travel>
Cruise Lines International Association	<http://www.cruising.org>
Cruise Travel Magazine	<http://www.cruisetravelmag.com>
Forsyth Travel Library, Inc.	<http://www.forsyth.com>
Hotel and Travel Index	<http://www.northstartravelmedia.com>
Official Hotel Guide	<http://www.northstartravelmedia.com>
Official Meetings Guide	<http://www.northstartravelmedia.com>
Official Meetings Facilities Guide	<http://www.northstartravelmedia.com>
Official Meetings Facilities Guide—International	<http://www.northstartravelmedia.com>
Official Cruise Guide	<http://www.northstartravelmedia.com>
Russell's Guides, Inc.	<http://www.russellsprinting.com>
Star Service, The Critical Guide to Hotels and Cruise Ships	<http://www.starserviceonline.com>
United States Tour Operators Association	<http://www.ustoa.com>
Weissman Travel Reports	<http://www.northstartravelmedia.com>
World Association of Travel Agencies	<http://www.wata.net>

Glossary

A + PS = MS—Attitude plus problem solving equals more sales

closing signal—any indication, verbal or nonverbal, indicating that a prospect is ready to make a buying decision.

all-inclusive—a term used in the tourism business to describe a tour that includes everything in its price including all meals, snacks, liquor, beer, wine, and tobacco.

amenities—features conducive to the attractiveness and value of accommodations in the tourism industry.

assumed sold approach—The salesperson takes the stance that the prospect is going to buy and begins to process the sale bypassing steps 2–6 of the sales process.

Assumed Sold Close—used when the salesperson takes the position that the prospect is going to buy and begins to process the order. For any type of service that has to be booked, the salesperson goes to the reservation computer or telephone and starts the reservation process asking the customer for the required information including the number of people, names, dates, time, and so on. Other versions of the Assumed Sold Close include starting to fill in an order form or counting out the required number of tickets.

benefits—things that people perceive to promote well-being. In tourism these are the things that motivate people to travel.

blind search—looking for information for a customer when you do not know where to start.

bottom line—the line at the end of a financial report that shows the net profit or loss.

break-even—the point at which cost and income are equal and there is neither profit nor loss.

captive audience—as used in this book insinuates that you have a group of tourists assembled and that they are obliged to remain together in the same place for a period of time.

check-in time—in the Accommodations sector, the time at which a hotel or motel room is ready for occupancy; in the Transportation sector, the time at which a passenger must register at a terminal before departure.

207

Choice Close—the salesperson simply asks a question to determine which of two choices the client prefers. If the client responds positively to either choice, consider the sale closed.

client profile—a summary of the needs and desires that a customer has when he or she travels and the information that you need to satisfy that customer.

close—the process of bringing a prospect to the point of making a buying decision.

closing—the process of asking a prospect a question that solicits an answer that gives the salesperson consent to complete the sale.

closing techniques—strategies to be used to bring a customer to a buying decision.

Closing to Resistance Close—used when a customer has a major objection that you have successfully overcome.

club class—for rail transportation is the equivalent of first class by air transportation.

cold calls—calls to a list of phone numbers at which you have no idea whether the respondents have any interest in your product or service.

collision damage waiver (CDW)—a daily fee that relieves the client of his or her liability for the deductible amount, not covered by the insurance, for loss or damage to a rented vehicle. Some companies use the term loss damage waiver (LDW) for the same thing.

commissions—fees paid to an agent or employee for transacting a piece of business usually based on a percentage of the sale.

computer reservations system (CRS)—a computerized booking system used by major carriers in the Transportation sector or organizations in the Accommodations sector. These systems contain timetables, inventory, tariffs, plus a plethora of tourism information.

confidential tariff—a price list of the cost of goods or services to the seller to which a markup must be added to cover the seller's costs and profit. It is more or less the same as a net tariff. Confidential tariff is a publication of the rates or prices for tourism products or services for the use of the salesperson only, and not the customer.

continuum—something consisting of a series of variations in regular order between two extremes.

cost comparison—a detailed list of expenses for two or more vacation packages, or a package compared to doing the same trip independently.

cost price squeeze—a term used to describe a situation when the cost of operations increases but the company cannot increase its prices proportionately because the public would perceive the service to be too expensive and stop using it. In order to maintain relatively stable prices, the company must sell a greater and greater amount of its product to remain viable.

credit card authorization—a number or code given to a vendor by a financial institution to verify that a purchase for a specified price has been approved using a customer's credit card.

cruise-and-stay—a package tour that includes a cruise and a stopover at one of the ports of call.

decision-maker—the person who has the largest say in selecting a product or service.

dependent people—friendly, warm, and thoughtful.

desk copy—the copy of a brochure that is retained by the salesperson. It will usually have important sales features highlighted or underlined and contain handwritten notes of answers to key questions.

detached people—cold, businesslike, and may seem unfriendly. These people are concerned with facts and logic. They resist emotional appeals.

domestic—as used within the airline industry means within the United States of America and/or within Canada.

dominant people—attempt to assert themselves over others and are motivated by self-esteem needs. They want to be looked up to by others. They expect a salesperson to be seasoned and firm.

economic value—a detailed list of inclusions of a vacation package in order to demonstrate its merit for the price paid.

ecotours—tours that feature sustainable, nonconsumptive, environmentally based activities such as bird watching, wildlife viewing, nature hikes, canoeing, and white-water rafting.

fauna—term used to describe animal life, especially the animals characteristic of a region.

favor—term used in Canada for an item given to a customer without charge to enhance the company's image and to serve as a constant reminder of the company's service. It is usually called a novelty in the United States.

flora—term used to describe plant life, especially plants characteristic of a region.

fly-cruise—is a travel package that includes the airfare to and from the port of embarkation plus the cruise itself. It usually includes the transfers between the airport and the cruise ship.

follow-up call—to contact a customer after he or she has returned from a trip or after participating in a tourism experience to determine the customer's level of satisfaction. The purpose is to gain insight regarding both positive and negative aspects of the experience, to begin corrective action if necessary, and to encourage referrals and repeat business.

frequent flier programs—are promotional membership clubs for regular clients of an airline and its hotel, car rental, and other partners, which offer valuable benefits to loyal customers.

greet the customer by name—If you know the prospect's name, employ a pleasant salutation using the client's name.

guest comment cards—usually placed on the table in restaurants or in conspicuous places in a hotel room requesting customers to comment on the quality of the service, facilities, ambience, and overall satisfaction with the guest's visit.

guest mix—a term to describe the type of people (based on demographics like age, family status, income level, occupation, etc.) who usually stay at a hotel or other accommodation facility.

head them off at the pass—a colloquial expression from cowboy culture that means to solve a problem quickly before it becomes an immense predicament.

hot calls—telephone calls to prospects who can benefit from the product or service that you have to offer.

I Would Recommend Close—the perfect response for the customer who asks which choice you would recommend. These customers have more or less made up their minds to buy and just need a little help to decide which one.

icebreaker approach—establishing rapport with the prospect by starting a conversation about some neutral subject of common interest and then gradually steering the conversation toward the item being sold.

inclusion—a term used in the tourism business to describe which items are included in the price of the tour.

inclusive tour—includes a number of tour elements such as airfare, accommodations, and transfers between the airport and accommodations.

independent tour—a preplanned, prepaid set of tourism arrangements, custom designed for a particular customer.

information interview—the opposite of a job interview. You interview the person who has the type of job you ultimately desire. You want to determine the qualifications and experience that the person has who is holding the job. Also you want to determine the steps that the person you are interviewing took in order to gain his or her present position.

introduction approach—starts by the salesperson introducing himself or herself and encouraging the prospect to do the same. This approach establishes rapport and solicits the customer's name to be used from this point on.

Inuit—the aboriginal people of the northern extremities of North America. They are known by many as Eskimos, a misnomer given to them by the Abnaki Indians, meaning raw fish eaters. The Inuit usually resent being called Eskimos.

load factor—the percentage of available seats paid for and occupied on an aircraft or other transportation vehicle.

loose ends—things left undecided or undone. As used in this book, the term refers to arrangements for a future date or business encounter in which the day, time, and place are not clearly specified.

loss damage waiver (LDW)—a daily fee that relieves the client of his or her liability for the deductible amount not covered by insurance for loss or damage to a rented vehicle. Some companies use the term collision damage waiver (CDW) for the same thing.

markup—an amount added to the seller's costs of goods or services to allow for the cost of marketing plus an allowance for a profit.

merchandise approach—If the salesperson observes that the customer is focusing on a particular piece of merchandise, the salesperson will use a compliment about the item as an opener to begin the sales conversation.

Minor Points Close—works well for big sales. People are hesitant to make a buying decision regarding expensive items. In this situation, get the customer to agree with parts of your sales proposal and gradually lead them toward accepting the entire package.

modern approach—to address a prospect by asking, "How may I help you?"

NAQP—an acronym for Not a Qualified Prospect.

needs—essential requirements whether a person is cognizant of them or not.

net rates—the cost of goods or services to the seller or tour operator to which a markup to cover the seller's or tour operator's costs and profit must be added.

net tariff—a price list of the cost of goods or services to the seller to which a markup must be added to cover the seller's costs and profit. It is more or less the same as a confidential tariff.

novelty—term used in the U.S.A. for an item given to a customer without charge to enhance the company's image and to serve as a constant reminder of the company's service. It is usually called a favor in Canada.

occupancy rate—the percentage of rooms sold in a hotel or other accommodation facility.

office copy—the copy of a brochure that is retained until the new edition is received, even if it is an outdated brochure.

option—as used in the tour and transportation businesses, is a reservation or booking that is held for a limited length of time with no obligation for the customer.

Option Close—the technique used by a salesperson in the tourism industry to persuade a customer to allow the salesperson to make a booking or reservation, with the understanding that the customer can change or cancel the reservation within a specified time, with no penalty or obligation.

option date—the date that money, either the deposit or full payment, must be made or otherwise the reservation will be cancelled.

overhead—all the costs of doing business that must be added to the cost of goods or services before determining the selling price.

override commissions—a greater rate of commission for selling more.

per diem—the average cost of a tour per day, derived by dividing the total cost of a tour by the number of nights of the tour.

piece system—a free baggage allowance system used by certain air carriers for specified routes. The number of pieces of free baggage, their size (as determined by adding the dimensions of the width, length, and height) and the maximum weight for each piece are specified.

predisposed to buy—a term used to describe a potential customer who telephones a company or organization with the attitude that he or she will buy, place an order, or make a reservation if he or she receives the information required.

prepaid air tickets—tickets paid for by someone other than the passenger at the destination to which the passenger will be flying.

price-break information—news of a special price that is such a value that it will stimulate the public to respond instantaneously.

principal—the company that provides the goods or services that another company or salesperson is selling.

profit margin—the amount of money added to the cost of providing goods or services to provide the company or seller with earnings.

proof of citizenship—a document proving that one is a citizen of a particular country. This is usually a passport, but for a person born in the country of citizenship, it could be a birth certificate or citizenship card. For a naturalized citizen, it could be his or her naturalization papers or citizenship card.

proof of identity—a document that proves you are who you say you are. It is an official document, usually government issued, with a photo plus a signature.

prospect—a potential buyer, customer, or likely candidate.

psyched-up—a colloquial term frequently used to describe developing a positive, confident mental attitude that enhances performance.

qualified prospect—a person who could benefit from your product or service.

qualify—the process of asking prospects questions to determine if you have a product or service to meet their needs.

qualifying questions—questions that elicit answers to determine whether a prospect could benefit from your product or service.

read between the lines—a term used to combine your knowledge of the person you are listening to and what he or she is not saying in combination with what has been said to obtain a more complete picture of the total situation.

referrals—prospective clients who have been recommended to a particular company, organization, or salesperson by a satisfied customer.

runaround—describes the situation when a customer has to go from one person or department to another, then another, and so on, before receiving the attention he or she requires.

seat sales—a term initiated by the airline industry but now used throughout the transportation industry. It usually involves a limited number of seats (excess inventory) at deep discount prices (often 50 percent or more) off normal prices, for a limited time period. They are usually subject to a number of restrictive conditions.

self-esteem needs—enhance one's sense of personal dignity when satisfied.

sell down—to offer a client a less expensive product or service. In tourism this is usually done by offering a product or service of lower quality; or, a shorter stay, tour, or adventure; or, a destination that is closer.

sell-up (selling-up)—increasing the amount of the sale. This can be done in two ways: (1) by upgrading, which means selling a better-quality tourism product; (2) by selling additional services. For example: A travel agent convinces a client to upgrade to an ocean front room instead of a standard room; a salesperson at a special event sells a weekend pass instead of a single event ticket; a reservationist for an airline or railway sells a tour or hotel accommodations in conjunction with a transportation ticket.

selling additional services—the process of selling complementary services or products that will enhance the original purchase.

Shortage Close—utilizes the suggestion that there may not be space available.

Shortage of space is the strongest closing aid. The salesperson indicates that it might not be possible to obtain the space the customer would like to have. Then the salesperson offers to check on the computer or telephone whether space is available. If there is, an offer to reserve it for the customer is usually all that is required to close the deal.

space-limited—has taken on a new meaning with the introduction of seat sales by the airlines. Not all seats are available at the special seat sale advertised price, but only those seats that are considered excess capacity.

Special Deal Close—used to nudge a prospect into making a buying decision now when otherwise they would be inclined to postpone a buying decision. Of course, this technique is only successful when the offer is really a special deal.

split payment—term used when a customer uses two or more forms of payment for a purchase. For example, a customer might want to make a partial payment by check or cash and put the balance on his or her credit card.

Summary Close—effective when a prospect has agreed with your sales points or responded positively to a series of trial closes. The most meaningful benefits should be emphasized, using the customer's own words when possible.

symphonic alphabet—a word spelling method used by most international air carriers that substitutes an easily identified word for each letter when spelling a name, address, file locator, or any word.

T-Account Close—really a variation of the Summary Close. When a decision obviously has not only benefits but also some disadvantages, divide a sheet of paper in half. List the benefits and advantages on the left side of the paper and the disadvantages on the right side. Customers appreciate the logic and fairness of this method. Help the client with the advantage side and ask them for the disadvantages. Overcome the objections if necessary.

testimonial—statement by a customer affirming satisfaction regarding a product or service.

the sale—has a number of different meanings in different contexts. In this book, it is used as a synonym for buying decision, booking, or reservation.

time-limited—in the tourism business can have two meanings. First, it may mean that a certain price is available only until a certain date. Second, it may mean that a reservation must be made a certain number of days before travel. Often both of these conditions are applicable.

tough sell—any situation in which it is difficult to close the sale because the prospect is reluctant to reveal the qualifying information you require or has objections that are difficult to overcome.

tourism industry—an umbrella term for many industries that collectively provide the products and services desired by people while they are away from home.

traditional approach—to address a prospect by asking, "May I help you?" It is usually not successful.

transborder—as used in the airline business refers to flights between the United States of America and Canada.

transfer—the transportation between an air, sea, or rail terminal and one's accommodations. Transfer can also mean the transportation from one airport to another or between terminals at the same airport.

trial close—a question asked during the early stages of a sales presentation to determine how effective you have been up to that point. Often the trial close is based on a statement that the prospect has made and is asked to confirm you have understood what he or she has been saying. It also reinforces a positive sales point you have made.

unqualified prospects—potential clients who do not have the time, financial resources, or need of the goods or services that you are selling at the present time.

upgrading—a specialized type of selling-up focused on selling a higher-quality product—for example, selling first-class or business class air transportation rather than coach class. In the Accommodations sector, it could be selling an ocean view room or a suite rather than a garden view room.

wants—conscious desires or cravings for a particular thing or experience.

weight system—a free baggage allowance system used by certain air carriers on specified routes. The total number of pounds or kilograms permitted determines the amount of free baggage allowed.

Bibliography

Allen, Robert Y., Robert F. Spohn, and I. Herbert Wilson. *Selling Dynamics*. New York: McGraw-Hill Book Company, 1984.

Brownstone, David M. *Successful Selling Skills for Small Business*. New York: John Wiley & Sons Inc., 1978.

Burke, James F., Ph.D., and Barry F. Resnick, Ed.D. *Marketing and Selling the Travel Product*. Cincinnati, OH: South Western Publishing Co., 1991.

Chaput, Jean-Marc. *Living Is Selling*. Toronto, ON: Ampersand Publishing Services Inc., 1975.

Clabaugh, Maurice G., Jr., and Jessie L. Forbes. *Professional Selling*. St. Paul, MN: West Publishing Company, 1992.

Davidoff, Philip G., and Doris S. Davidoff. *Sales and Marketing for Travel and Tourism*. Englewood Cliffs, NJ: Prentice Hall Career and Technology, 1994.

English, Richard. *Successful Selling*. London, UK: Columbus Press Limited, 1996.

Fisher, Judith E. *Telephone Skills at Work*. Burr Ridge, IL: Irwin Professional Publishing, 1994.

Joselyn, Dr. Robert W., CTC. *Essential Sales Skills: Mastering the Art of Collaborative Selling*. Toronto, ON: Canadian Institute of Travel Counsellors of Ontario, 1998.

Jung, Gerald P. *A Practical Guide to Selling Travel*. Englewood Cliffs, NJ: Prentice Hall, 1993.

MacNeill, Debra J. *Customer Service Excellence*. Chicago, IL: Irwin Professional Publishing, 1994.

McGill, Ann M. *Supervising the Difficult Employee.* Burr Ridge, IL: Irwin Professional Publishing, 1994.

McNamara, Dawn, CTC, DMATP. *Closing More Sales.* Vancouver, BC: Canadian Institute of Travel Counsellors of British Columbia and Yukon.

Metalka, Charles J. *The Dictionary of Tourism, 2nd Ed.* Wheaton, IL: Merton House Travel and Tourism Publishers Inc., 1986.

Noble, Cinnie, C.M., LL.B. *The Disabled Traveller: A Guide for Travel Counsellors.* Toronto, ON: Canadian Institute of Travel Counsellors of Ontario, 1991.

Pimentel, Larry, CTC. *The Magic of Selling.* San Francisco, CA: Seabourn Cruise Line.

The Psychology of Travel Selling—The B.E.S.T. Formula for Sales Success. Vancouver, BC: Canadian Institute of Travel Counsellors of British Columbia and Yukon.

Reilly, Robert T., *Travel and Tourism Marketing Techniques, 2nd Ed.* Albany, New York: Delmar Learning, 1988.

Robinson, Leslie, M.Ed, DMATP, CTC. *Maintaining a Diverse Clientele.* Toronto, ON: Canadian Institute of Travel Counsellors of Ontario, 1997.

———. *Making The Sale.* Toronto, ON: Canadian Institute of Travel Counsellors of Ontario, 1997.

Wright, David. *Professional Travel Counselling.* Etobicoke, ON: Canadian Institute of Travel Counsellors of Ontario, 1995.

Index

Note: Page references in *italics* refer to figures.

A

Acceptance, creating, 77–89
Accommodations sector, *4*, 148–49, *149–150*
Additional services, selling, 147
Adventure and recreation sector, *4*, 150, *151*
Airline references, 65–66
Airports/terminals, 162–64
All-inclusive, 76
Amenities, 5
American Society of Travel Agents (ASTA), 179
Answering questions, 75
Approaching prospect, 17–23
A + PS = MS, 133
Assumed Sold Close, 21, 110–11, 202
Attractions sector, *4*, 150, *151*

B

Baggage allowances, 174–75
Benefits, 84
Blind search, 72
Bottom line, 3
Break-even, 13
Brochures, 62–63
Budget, 171–72
Business travelers, 47–48, 76–77

C

Captive audience, 191
Caribbean Gold Book, 71
Car rentals, 176
Check-in time, 173
Choice Close, 94, 96–97, *97*, 201
Classifications for special services, 50, *51*, 52
CLIA Cruise Manual, 66
Client profile, 38–45, *39–43*
   disabled traveler, *53–54*
Close:
   Assumed Sold, 21, *110–11*, 202
   Choice, 94, 96–97, *97*, 201
   Closing to Resistance, 105–6, *106*, 200
   I Would Recommend, 97–98, 202
   Minor Points, 100–102
   Option, 108–10, 200–201
   Shortage, 106–7, 202
   Special Deal, 107–8, 201
   Summary, 98–100, 199, *200*
   T-Account, *103–4*, 103–5, 199, *201*
   Trial, 92
Closing, 25, 91
   to decision-maker, 112
   techniques for, 94–111, *97*
   ten closing signals, 92–93
   by type of prospect, 112
   when not to, 93

Closing again, 146
Closing To Resistance Close, 105–6, *106*, 200
Club class, 154
Colleagues, 185–86
Collision damage waiver (CDW), 176
Commission, 8, *9*, 10–12
    override, 8
Comparative analysis for tours, *85–87*
Complicated tours, 27, 29
Computer reservations system (CRS), 63–65
Confidential tariff, 62
Continuum, 29
Cost comparison, 89, *89*
Cost price squeeze, 7
Cruise-and-stay, 158
Cruise references, 66–68
Cruise Travel, 68
Customers, 63
Customer service, 162
    ethics in selling tourism, 178–86, *179–180*
    information you must tell your client,
        162–76, *166–167, 170*
    novelties or favors, 186
    preparing customer's package, 176–78, *177*
Customs, 165, *167*, 167–68

D
Dalton, John, 27
Decision-maker, 112
Dependent people, 112
Desk copy, 63
Detached people, 112
Dietary needs, special, 47
*The Disabled Traveller—A Guide for Travel
        Counsellors* (Noble), 48
Disabled travelers, 48–50, *49*
Documentation, 164
Domestic, 11
Dominant people, 112

E
Economic value, 87
Ecotours, 191
Ethics, 178–86, *179–180*
Events and conferences sector, *4*, 150–51

F
Favors, 78, 186
Flight schedules, 176
Follow-up procedures, 188–89
    follow-up sheet, 189–95, *190, 192, 194–195*
    in job search, *203*, 203–4
Follow-up sheet, 189–95, *190, 192, 194–195*
Food and beverage sector, *4*, 151–52
Ford's International Cruise Guide, 67
Foreign currency exchange, 168–69
Frequent flier program, 77

G
The Game (Dalton), 26–27, *28*
Global distribution systems, 63–65
Glossary, 207–14
Gratuities, 172–73
Greeting by name approach, 20
Guest comment cards, 193
Guest mix, 5

H
*Handi-Travel: A Resourcebook for Disabled and
        Elderly Travellers*, 48
Hazards, avoiding, 165, *166*
Head them off at the pass, 191
Health requirements, 164–65
Hearing impairments, 55–56
Hotel and accommodations references,
        70–71
Hotel and Travel Index, 70

I
Icebreaker approach, 21–22
Inclusive tour, 176
Incoming calls, 115–20, *118–119*
Independent tour, 178
Information interview, 198
Interest, arousing, 15–16
International travellers, 69
Introduction approach, 20–21
Inuit, 58
I Would Recommend Close, 97–98, 202

J
Job market, 197

K
Know Before You Go, 167, *167*

L
Load factor, 7
Long-range goal, 197–98
Loose ends, 22
Loss damage waiver (LDW), 176

M
Markup, 11, 62
Master-Key, 72
Merchandise approach, 21
Minor Points Close, 100–102
Mobility impairments, 52, 55
Modern approach, 20
Motor coach reference, 69

N
NAQP, 133
Needs, 38
Net rates, 62, 184
Net tariff, 62
Noble, Cinnie, 48, 52
Novelties, 78, 186

O
OAG Cruise & Ferry Guide, 67
OAG Travel Planners, 70–71
Objections. *See* Overcoming objections
Occupancy rate, 5
Office copy, 63
Official Airline Guide, 65–66
Official Cruise Guide, 67
Official Hotel Guide, 70
Official Steamship Guide, 67
Official Tour Directory, 71
Option, 109
Option Close, 108–10, 200–201
Option date, 108
Option terms, 175
Outgoing calls, 122–27, *125*

Overcoming objections, 132–45, *134–135,*
    137–138, 140–43
Overhead, 62
Override commissions, 8

P
Passenger Air Tariff, 66
Per diem, 155, *156*
Personal experience, 78–81
Piece system, 174
Prepaid air tickets, 11
Principal, 62
Product knowledge, 60
    coping when inadequate, 72–73
    importance of, 61–62
    sources of, 62–72
Profit margin, 62
Proof of citizenship, 26
Proof of identity, 26
Prospect, 14
    approaching, 17–23
    commitment types, 56–58
    qualified, 21
    unqualified, 13
Purchase inclusions/exclusions, 169–70, *170*
Purpose of travel, 29–32, *30–32*

Q
Qualified prospect, 21
Qualifying, 5, 24
    client profile, 38–45, *39–43*
    for complex domestic/foreign independent
        tours, 27, 29
    the game, 26–27, *28*
    identifying special needs/interests, 29–38
    initial questions, 25–26
    mistake to avoid, 58
    travelers with special needs/requests,
        45–56, *49–51, 53–54*
    types of prospects by commitment, 56–58
Qualifying questions, 22
Quality of accommodations, 32–34
Quality of tours, 34

R

Rail references, 68–69

Recommending product/service, 75–77

Referrals, 5

Runaround, 171

Russell's Official National Motor Coach Guide, 69

S

Safety concerns, 81–83, *82–83*

Salary, 8, 10

Salary plus commission, 12–14

The sale, 5

Sales, importance of, 3, 5–14

Sales process:

    Step 1: Arousing interest to travel, 15–16

    Step 2: Approaching the prospect, 17–23

    Step 3: Qualifying, 24–58

    Step 4: Answering client's questions, 75

    Step 5: Recommending product/service to meet client's needs, 75–77

    Step 6: Creating acceptance, 77–89

    Step 7: Closing the sale, 91–113

    Step 8: Overcoming objections, 132–45

    Step 9: Closing again, 146

    Step 10: Selling–up, 147–60

    Step 11: Providing customer service, 162–86

    Step 12: Follow-up procedures, 188–95

    twelve steps in, 14–15

Security concerns, 34–38, *36–38*

Sell down, 139–44

Selling-up, 26, 147, 202–3

    accommodations sector, 148–49

    adventure and recreation sectors, 150

    attractions sector, 150

    events and conferences sector, 150–51

    fifteen ways to help client accept higher-priced product, 159–60

    food and beverage sector, 151–52

    tourism services sector, 153–54

    transportation sector, 154–55

    travel trade sector, 155–56

    twelve more opportunities for, 158–59

Service charges, 172–73

Shortage Close, 106–7, 202

Special Deal Close, 107–8, 201

Special needs/requests, 29–38, 45–56, *49–51, 53–54*

Split payment, 144

Star Service, 71

Star Service, The Critical Guide to Hotels and Cruise Ships, 68

Summary Close, 98–100, 199, *200*

Symphonic alphabet, 127, 129

T

T-Account Close, *103–4*, 103–5, 199, *201*

Telephone selling techniques, 115

    incoming calls, 115–20, *118–119*

    outgoing calls, 122–27, *125*

    voice and language skills, using effectively, 120–22

    word spelling, 127–30, *128*

Testimonial, 78

Thomas Cook European Timetable, 68

Thomas Cook Overseas Timetable, 69

Time-limited, 108

Tips, 172–73

Tough sell, 200

Tourism industry, 2

    eight sectors of, 3, *4*, 44–45, 148–56

    importance of sales in, 3, 5–14

Tourism services sector, *4, 153*, 153–54

Tour references, 71–72

Tours:

    comparative analysis of, *85–87*

    complicated, 27, 29

    ecotours, 191

    inclusive, 176

    quality of, 34

    references for, 71–72

Trade reference manuals, 65

Traditional approach, 20

Transborder, 11

Transfer, 164

Transportation sector, *4*, 154–55

Travel Information Manual, 69

Travel insurance, 175

Travel trade sector, *4*, 155–56, *156–157*

Trial close, 92

U
Unaccompanied minors, 46–47
United States Tour Operators Association
         (USTOA), 180
Unqualified prospect, 13
Upgrading, 147

V
Visual impairments, 55

W
Wants, 38
Web sites, list, 205
Weight system, 174
Word spelling, 127–30, *128*

Y
Young children, 45